MznLnx

Missing Links Exam Preps

Exam Prep for

Bank Management and Financial Services

Peter Rose, 7th Edition

The MznLnx Exam Prep is your link from the texbook and lecture to your exams.
The MznLnx Exam Preps are unauthorized and comprehensive reviews of your textbooks.

All material provided by MznLnx and Rico Publications (c) 2010
Textbook publishers and textbook authors do not particpate in or contribute to these reviews.

MznLnx

Rico
Publications

Exam Prep for Bank Management and Financial Services
7th Edition
Peter Rose

Publisher: Raymond Houge
Assistant Editor: Michael Rouger
Text and Cover Designer: Lisa Buckner
Marketing Manager: Sara Swagger
Project Manager, Editorial Production: Jerry Emerson
Art Director: Vernon Lowerui

Product Manager: Dave Mason
Editorial Assitant: Rachel Guzmanji
Pedagogy: Debra Long
Cover Image: Jim Reed/Getty Images
Text and Cover Printer: City Printing, Inc.
Compositor: Media Mix, Inc.

(c) 2010 Rico Publications
ALL RIGHTS RESERVED. No part of this work covered by the copyright may be reproduced or used in any form or by an means--graphic, electronic, or mechanical, including photocopying, recording, taping, Web distribution, information storage, and retrieval systems, or in any other manner--without the written permission of the publisher.

Printed in the United States
ISBN:

For more information about our products, contact us at:
Dave.Mason@RicoPublications.com

For permission to use material from this text or product, submit a request online to:
Dave.Mason@RicoPublications.com

Contents

CHAPTER 1
An Overview of Banks and the Financial-Services Sector   1

CHAPTER 2
The Impact of Government Policy and Regulation on Banking   9

CHAPTER 3
The Organization and Structure of Banking and the Financial-Services Industry   21

CHAPTER 4
Establishing New Banks, Branches, ATMs, Telephone Services, and Web Sites   27

CHAPTER 5
The Financial Statements of Banks and Their Principal Competitors   30

CHAPTER 6
Measuring and Evaluating the Performance of Banks and Their Competitors   44

CHAPTER 7
Asset-Liability Management: Determining and Measuring Interest Rates   54

CHAPTER 8
Using Financial Futures, Options, Swaps, and Other Hedging Tools   62

CHAPTER 9
Risk Management Using Asset-Backed Securities, Loan Sales, Credit Standbys   74

CHAPTER 10
The Investment Function in Banking and Financial-Services Management   82

CHAPTER 11
Liquidity and Reserve Management: Strategies and Policies   95

CHAPTER 12
Managing and Pricing Deposit Services   102

CHAPTER 13
Managing Nondeposit Liabilities and Other Sources of Borrowed Funds   108

CHAPTER 14
Investment Banking, Insurance, and Other Sources of Fee Income   116

CHAPTER 15
The Management of Capital   122

CHAPTER 16
Lending Policies and Procedures   131

CHAPTER 17
Lending to Business Firms and Pricing Business Loans   137

CHAPTER 18
Consumer Loans, Credit Cards, and Real Estate Lending   151

CHAPTER 19
Acquisitions and Mergers in Financial- Services Management   159

CHAPTER 20
International Banking and the Future of Banking and Financial Services   165

ANSWER KEY   175

TO THE STUDENT

COMPREHENSIVE

The *MznLnx* Exam Prep series is designed to help you pass your exams. Editors at MznLnx review your textbooks and then prepare these practice exams to help you master the textbook material. Unlike study guides, workbooks, and practice tests provided by the texbook publisher and textbook authors, *MznLnx* gives you **all** of the material in each chapter in exam form, not just samples, so you can be sure to nail your exam.

MECHANICAL

The MznLnx Exam Prep series creates exams that will help you learn the subject matter as well as test you on your understanding. Each question is designed to help you master the concept. Just working through the exams, you gain an understanding of the subject--its a simple mechanical process that produces success.

INTEGRATED STUDY GUIDE AND REVIEW

MznLnx is not just a set of exams designed to test you, its also a comprehensive review of the subject content. Each exam question is also a review of the concept, making sure that you will get the answer correct without having to go to other sources of material. You learn as you go! Its the easiest way to pass an exam.

HUMOR

Studying can be tedious and dry. MznLnx's instructional design includes moderate humor within the exam questions on occassion, to break the tedium and revitalize the brain

Chapter 1. An Overview of Banks and the Financial-Services Sector 1

1.

A _____ is a type of financial intermediary and a type of bank. Commercial banking is also known as business banking. It is a bank that provides checking accounts, savings accounts, and money market accounts and that accepts time deposits.

- a. 4-4-5 Calendar
- b. 7-Eleven
- c. 529 plan
- d. Commercial bank

2. _____ refer to services provided by the finance industry.

The finance industry encompasses a broad range of organizations that deal with the management of money. Among these organizations are banks, credit card companies, insurance companies, consumer finance companies, stock brokerages, investment funds and some government sponsored enterprises.

- a. Cost of carry
- b. Delta hedging
- c. Financial instruments
- d. Financial services

3. _____ is the provision of resources (such as granting a loan) by one party to another party where that second party does not reimburse the first party immediately, thereby generating a debt, and instead arranges either to repay or return those resources (or material(s) of equal value) at a later date. The first party is called a creditor, also known as a lender, while the second party is called a debtor, also known as a borrower.

Movements of financial capital are normally dependent on either _____ or equity transfers.

- a. Warrant
- b. Comparable
- c. Clearing house
- d. Credit

4. _____ or amalgamation is the act of merging many things into one. In business, it often refers to the mergers or acquisitions of many smaller companies into much larger ones. The financial accounting term of _____ refers to the aggregated financial statements of a group company as consolidated account.
- a. Write-off
- b. Cost of goods sold
- c. Retained earnings
- d. Consolidation

5. The institution most often referenced by the word '_____' is a public or publicly traded _____, the shares of which are traded on a public stock exchange (e.g., the New York Stock Exchange or Nasdaq in the United States) where shares of stock of _____s are bought and sold by and to the general public. Most of the largest businesses in the world are publicly traded _____s. However, the majority of _____s are said to be closely held, privately held or close _____s, meaning that no ready market exists for the trading of shares.
- a. Protect
- b. Depository Trust Company
- c. Federal Home Loan Mortgage Corporation
- d. Corporation

6. Explicit _____ is a measure implemented in many countries to protect bank depositors, in full or in part, from losses caused by a bank's inability to pay its debts when due. _____ systems are one component of a financial system safety net that promotes financial stability.

Chapter 1. An Overview of Banks and the Financial-Services Sector

    a. Banking panic   b. Reserve requirement
    c. Deposit Insurance   d. Time deposit

7. The _____ is a United States government corporation created by the Glass-Steagall Act of 1933. It provides deposit insurance, which guarantees the safety of checking and savings deposits in member banks, currently up to $250,000 per depositor per bank. Insured deposits are backed by the full faith and credit of the United States.
    a. NYSE Group   b. FASB
    c. Ford Foundation   d. Federal Deposit Insurance Corporation

8. In business and finance, a _____ (also referred to as equity _____) of stock means a _____ of ownership in a corporation (company.) In the plural, stocks is often used as a synonym for _____s especially in the United States, but it is less commonly used that way outside of North America.

In the United Kingdom, South Africa, and Australia, stock can also refer to completely different financial instruments such as government bonds or, less commonly, to all kinds of marketable securities.

    a. Bucket shop   b. Procter ' Gamble
    c. Share   d. Margin

9. The _____ Act is an Act of the 106th United States Congress which repealed part of the Glass-Steagall Act of 1933, opening up competition among banks, securities companies and insurance companies. The Glass-Steagall Act prohibited any one institution from acting as both an investment bank and a commercial bank, or as both a bank and an insurer.

The _____ Act (GLBA) allowed commercial and investment banks to consolidate.

    a. Gramm-Leach-Bliley   b. 529 plan
    c. 4-4-5 Calendar   d. 7-Eleven

10. A _____ or bank is a financial institution whose primary activity is to act as a payment agent for customers and to borrow and lend money.

The first modern bank was founded in Italy in Genoa in 1406, its name was Banco di San Giorgio (Bank of St. George.)

Many other financial activities were added over time.

    a. Black Sea Trade and Development Bank   b. 4-4-5 Calendar
    c. Bought deal   d. Banker

11. _____ consists of the sale of goods or merchandise from a fixed location, such as a department store, boutique or kiosk in small or individual lots for direct consumption by the purchaser. _____ may include subordinated services, such as delivery. Purchasers may be individuals or businesses.
    a. 7-Eleven   b. Retailing
    c. 4-4-5 Calendar   d. 529 plan

Chapter 1. An Overview of Banks and the Financial-Services Sector 3

12. A _____ is a cooperative financial institution that is owned and controlled by its members, and operated for the purpose of promoting thrift, providing credit at reasonable rates, and providing other financial services to its members. Many _____s exist to further community development or sustainable international development on a local level. Worldwide, _____ systems vary significantly in terms of total system assets and average institution asset size since _____s exist in a wide range of sizes, ranging from volunteer operations with a handful of members to institutions with several billion dollars in assets and hundreds of thousands of members.

a. Corporate credit union
b. Credit union
c. Credit Union Service Organization
d. Fi-linx

13. In finance, the _____ is the global financial market for short-term borrowing and lending. It provides short-term liquidity funding for the global financial system. The _____ is where short-term obligations such as Treasury bills, commercial paper and bankers' acceptances are bought and sold.

a. Debt-for-equity swap
b. Money market
c. Cramdown
d. Consumer debt

14. Money funds (or _____, money market mutual funds) are mutual funds that invest in short-term debt instruments.

_____, also known as principal stability funds, seek to limit exposure to losses due to credit, market and liquidity risks. _____, in the United States, are regulated by the Securities and Exchange Commission's (SEC) Investment Company Act of 1940.

a. Mutual fund fees and expenses
b. Stock fund
c. Closed-end fund
d. Money market funds

15. A _____ is a professionally managed type of collective investment scheme that pools money from many investors and invests it in stocks, bonds, short-term money market instruments, and/or other securities. The _____ will have a fund manager that trades the pooled money on a regular basis. Currently, the worldwide value of all _____s totals more than $26 trillion.

Since 1940, there have been three basic types of investment companies in the United States: open-end funds, also known in the US as _____s; unit investment trusts (UITs); and closed-end funds.

a. Mutual fund
b. Financial intermediary
c. Net asset value
d. Trust company

16. A _____ is a financial institution that specializes in accepting savings deposits and making mortgage and other loans. The S'L or thrift term is mainly used in the United States; similar institutions in the United Kingdom, Ireland and some Commonwealth countries include building societies and trustee savings banks.

They are often mutually held, meaning that the depositors and borrowers are members with voting rights, and have the ability to direct the financial and managerial goals of the organization, not unlike the poliyholders of a mutual insurance company.

a. Mutual fund
b. Person-to-person lending
c. Savings and loan association
d. Net asset value

17. In finance, the _____ is the system that allows the transfer of money between savers and borrowers.

Put another way: the _____ is a set of complex and closely interconnected financial institutions, markets, instruments, services, practices, and transactions.

   a. Horizontal merger   b. 4-4-5 Calendar
   c. Passive income   d. Financial system

18. In finance, a _____ is a position established in one market in an attempt to offset exposure to the price risk of an equal but opposite obligation or position in another market -- usually, but not always, in the context of one's commercial activity. Hedging is a strategy designed to minimize exposure to such business risks as a sharp contraction in demand for one's inventory, while still allowing the business to profit from producing and maintaining that inventory. A typical hedger might be a farmer with 2000 acres of unharvested wheat in the ground, who would rather tend his crop without the distraction of uncertain prices.

   a. 7-Eleven   b. 4-4-5 Calendar
   c. Hedge   d. 529 plan

19. A _____ is a private investment fund open to a limited range of investors that is permitted by regulators to undertake a wider range of activities than other investment funds and also pays a performance fee to its investment manager. Each fund will have its own strategy which determines the type of investments and the methods of investment it undertakes. _____s as a class invest in a broad range of investments extending over shares, debt, commodities and beyond.

   a. 529 plan   b. 4-4-5 Calendar
   c. 7-Eleven   d. Hedge Fund

20. A _____ is a fungible, negotiable instrument representing financial value. They are broadly categorized into debt securities (such as banknotes, bonds and debentures), and equity securities; e.g., common stocks. The company or other entity issuing the _____ is called the issuer.

   a. Book entry   b. Security
   c. Securities lending   d. Tracking stock

21. The U.S. _____ is an independent agency of the United States government which holds primary responsibility for enforcing the federal securities laws and regulating the securities industry, the nation's stock and options exchanges, and other electronic securities markets. The SEC was created by section 4 of the SEC of 1934 (now codified as 15 U.S.C. Â§ 78d and commonly referred to as the 1934 Act.)

   a. 4-4-5 Calendar   b. 529 plan
   c. 7-Eleven   d. Securities and Exchange Commission

22. A _____ is a company that owns other companies' outstanding stock. It usually refers to a company which does not produce goods or services itself, rather its only purpose is owning shares of other companies. They allow the reduction of risk for the owners and can allow the ownership and control of a number of different companies.

   a. MRU Holdings   b. Privately held company
   c. Federal National Mortgage Association   d. Holding company

Chapter 1. An Overview of Banks and the Financial-Services Sector

23. An _____ is a security whose value and income payments are derived from and collateralized (or 'backed') by a specified pool of underlying assets. The pool of assets is typically a group of small and illiquid assets that are unable to be sold individually. Pooling the assets allows them to be sold to general investors, a process called securitization, and allows the risk of investing in the underlying assets to be diversified because each security will represent a fraction of the total value of the diverse pool of underlying assets.

    a. AAB
    b. A Random Walk Down Wall Street
    c. Asset-backed security
    d. ABN Amro

24. A '_____' is a 'Charge' that is paid to obtain the right to delay a payment. Essentially, the payer purchases the right to make a given payment in the future instead of in the Present. The '_____', or 'Charge' that must be paid to delay the payment, is simply the difference between what the payment amount would be if it were paid in the present and what the payment amount would be paid if it were paid in the future.

    a. Value at risk
    b. Risk aversion
    c. Risk modeling
    d. Discount

25. _____ is the discipline of identifying, monitoring and limiting risks. In some cases the acceptable risk may be near zero. Risks can come from accidents, natural causes and disasters as well as deliberate attacks from an adversary.

    a. Penny stock
    b. Risk management
    c. 4-4-5 Calendar
    d. FIFO

26. A _____ is an institution, firm or individual who mediates between two or more parties in a financial context. Typically the first party is a provider of a product or service and the second party is a consumer or customer.

    In the U.S., a _____ is typically an institution that facilitates the channelling of funds between lenders and borrowers indirectly.

    a. Financial intermediary
    b. Net asset value
    c. Mutual fund
    d. Savings and loan association

27. _____ is a measure of the ability of a debtor to pay their debts as and when they fall due. It is usually expressed as a ratio or a percentage of current liabilities.

    For a corporation with a published balance sheet there are various ratios used to calculate a measure of liquidity.

    a. Invested capital
    b. Operating leverage
    c. Accounting liquidity
    d. Operating profit margin

28. In economics and finance, _____ is the practice of taking advantage of a price differential between two or more markets: striking a combination of matching deals that capitalize upon the imbalance, the profit being the difference between the market prices. When used by academics, an _____ is a transaction that involves no negative cash flow at any probabilistic or temporal state and a positive cash flow in at least one state; in simple terms, a risk-free profit.

    a. Issuer
    b. Arbitrage
    c. Initial margin
    d. Efficient-market hypothesis

29. _____ is a type of bank account where the money in the account is legally able to be withdrawn immediately upon demand (or 'at call'.) This type of bank account can also be referred to as a 'cheque' or 'checking' or transactional account.

Chapter 1. An Overview of Banks and the Financial-Services Sector

This type of bank account, allowing immediate conversion of the account balance into cash or withdrawal to another account, can be contrasted with a time deposit (also known as a certificate of deposit or term deposit), where the funds are not legally available for immediate withdrawal by the depositor.

   a. 4-4-5 Calendar   b. 529 plan
   c. Synthetic lease   d. Demand deposit

30. _____, in bookkeeping, refers to assets, liabilities, income, and expenses recorded on individual pages of the so called book of final entry or ledger. Changes in _____ value are made by chronologically posting debit (DR) and credit (CR) entries to its page. Examples of _____s are cash, _____s receivable, mortgages, loans, land and buildings, common stock, sales, services provided, wages, and payroll overhead.
   a. Option   b. Accretion
   c. Alpha   d. Account

31. In United States banking, _____ is a marketing term for certain services offered primarily to larger business customers. It may be used to describe all bank accounts (such as checking accounts) provided to businesses of a certain size, but it is more often used to describe specific services such as cash concentration, zero balance accounting, and automated clearing house facilities. Sometimes, private banking customers are given _____ services.
   a. Cash management   b. Capitalization rate
   c. Profitability index   d. Global tactical asset allocation

32. _____ is a type of private equity capital typically provided to early-stage, high-potential, growth companies in the interest of generating a return through an eventual realization event such as an IPO or trade sale of the company. _____ investments are generally made as cash in exchange for shares in the invested company. It is typical for _____ investors to identify and back companies in high technology industries such as biotechnology and ICT.
   a. Treasury Inflation-Protected Securities   b. Probability distribution
   c. Tail risk   d. Venture capital

33. _____ is a process by which a firm can obtain the use of a certain fixed assets for which it must pay a series of contractual, periodic, tax deductable payments. The lessee is the receiver of the services or the assets under the lease contract and the lessor is the owner of the assets. The relationship between the tenant and the landlord is called a tenancy, and can be for a fixed or an indefinite period of time (called the term of the lease).
   a. Foreign Corrupt Practices Act   b. Leasing
   c. Royalties   d. Quiet period

34. _____ are formal records of a business' financial activities.

Chapter 1. An Overview of Banks and the Financial-Services Sector

_____ provide an overview of a business' financial condition in both short and long term. There are four basic _____:

1. **Balance sheet**: also referred to as statement of financial position or condition, reports on a company's assets, liabilities, and net equity as of a given point in time.
2. **Income statement**: also referred to as Profit and Loss statement (or a 'P'L'), reports on a company's income, expenses, and profits over a period of time.
3. **Statement of retained earnings**: explains the changes in a company's retained earnings over the reporting period.
4. **Statement of cash flows**: reports on a company's cash flow activities, particularly its operating, investing and financing activities.

a. Statement of retained earnings
b. Statement on Auditing Standards No. 70: Service Organizations
c. Notes to the Financial Statements
d. Financial statements

35. The _____ of 1933 established the Federal Deposit Insurance Corporation (FDIC) in the United States and included banking reforms, some of which were designed to control speculation. Some provisions such as Regulation Q, which allowed the Federal Reserve to regulate interest rates in savings accounts, were repealed by the Depository Institutions Deregulation and Monetary Control Act of 1980. Provisions that prohibit a bank holding company from owning other financial companies were repealed on November 12, 1999, by the Gramm-Leach-Bliley Act.

a. 4-4-5 Calendar
b. 7-Eleven
c. Glass-Steagall Act
d. 529 plan

36. A _____ is a firm that quotes both a buy and a sell price in a financial instrument or commodity, hoping to make a profit on the bid/offer spread, or turn.

In foreign exchange trading, where most deals are conducted over-the-counter and are, therefore, completely virtual, the _____ sells to and buys from its clients. Hence, the client's loss and the spread is the _____ firm's profit, which gets thus compensated for the effort of providing liquidity in a competitive market.

a. Market maker
b. 4-4-5 Calendar
c. 7-Eleven
d. 529 plan

37. _____ is the removal or simplification of government rules and regulations that constrain the operation of market forces. _____ does not mean elimination of laws against fraud, but eliminating or reducing government control of how business is done, thereby moving toward a more free market.

The stated rationale for '_____' is often that fewer and simpler regulations will lead to a raised level of competitiveness, therefore higher productivity, more efficiency and lower prices overall.

a. Value added
b. Supply shock
c. Demand shock
d. Deregulation

38. _____, refers to consumption opportunity gained by an entity within a specified time frame, which is generally expressed in monetary terms. However, for households and individuals, '_____ is the sum of all the wages, salaries, profits, interests payments, rents and other forms of earnings received... in a given period of time.' For firms, _____ generally refers to net-profit: what remains of revenue after expenses have been subtracted.
   a. Annual report
   b. Accrual
   c. OIBDA
   d. Income

39. A _____ is a corporation, especially a commercial bank, organized to perform the fiduciary functions of trusts and agencies. It is normally owned by one of three types of structures: an independent partnership, a bank, or a law firm, each of which specializes in being a trustee of various kinds of trusts and in managing estates.
   a. Person-to-person lending
   b. Mutual fund
   c. Savings and loan association
   d. Trust Company

40. _____ in finance is a risk management technique, related to hedging, that mixes a wide variety of investments within a portfolio. Because the fluctuations of a single security have less impact on a diverse portfolio, _____ minimizes the risk from any one investment.

A simple example of _____ is the following: On a particular island the entire economy consists of two companies: one that sells umbrellas and another that sells sunscreen.

   a. Diversification
   b. 4-4-5 Calendar
   c. 7-Eleven
   d. 529 plan

Chapter 2. The Impact of Government Policy and Regulation on Banking

1. A _____, reserve bank, or monetary authority is the entity responsible for the monetary policy of a country or of a group of member states. It is a bank that can lend money to other banks in times of need. Its primary responsibility is to maintain the stability of the national currency and money supply, but more active duties include controlling subsidized-loan interest rates, and acting as a lender of last resort to the banking sector during times of financial crisis (private banks often being integral to the national financial system.)
    a. 7-Eleven
    b. 4-4-5 Calendar
    c. Central Bank
    d. 529 plan

2. The institution most often referenced by the word '_____' is a public or publicly traded _____, the shares of which are traded on a public stock exchange (e.g., the New York Stock Exchange or Nasdaq in the United States) where shares of stock of _____s are bought and sold by and to the general public. Most of the largest businesses in the world are publicly traded _____s. However, the majority of _____s are said to be closely held, privately held or close _____s, meaning that no ready market exists for the trading of shares.
    a. Corporation
    b. Depository Trust Company
    c. Protect
    d. Federal Home Loan Mortgage Corporation

3. Explicit _____ is a measure implemented in many countries to protect bank depositors, in full or in part, from losses caused by a bank's inability to pay its debts when due. _____ systems are one component of a financial system safety net that promotes financial stability.
    a. Banking panic
    b. Deposit Insurance
    c. Time deposit
    d. Reserve requirement

4. The _____ is a United States government corporation created by the Glass-Steagall Act of 1933. It provides deposit insurance, which guarantees the safety of checking and savings deposits in member banks, currently up to $250,000 per depositor per bank. Insured deposits are backed by the full faith and credit of the United States.
    a. NYSE Group
    b. FASB
    c. Ford Foundation
    d. Federal Deposit Insurance Corporation

5. The _____ Act is an Act of the 106th United States Congress which repealed part of the Glass-Steagall Act of 1933, opening up competition among banks, securities companies and insurance companies. The Glass-Steagall Act prohibited any one institution from acting as both an investment bank and a commercial bank, or as both a bank and an insurer.

    The _____ Act (GLBA) allowed commercial and investment banks to consolidate.

    a. 4-4-5 Calendar
    b. 529 plan
    c. 7-Eleven
    d. Gramm-Leach-Bliley

6. In financial accounting, the term _____ is most commonly used to describe any part of shareholders' equity, except for basic share capital. Sometimes, the term is used instead of the term provision; such a use, however, is inconsistent with the terminology suggested by International Accounting Standards Board. For more information about provisions, see provision (accounting.)
    a. Reserve
    b. Treasury stock
    c. FIFO and LIFO accounting
    d. Closing entries

7. _____ is a fee paid on borrowed assets. It is the price paid for the use of borrowed money , or, money earned by deposited funds . Assets that are sometimes lent with _____ include money, shares, consumer goods through hire purchase, major assets such as aircraft, and even entire factories in finance lease arrangements.

Chapter 2. The Impact of Government Policy and Regulation on Banking

a. Interest
b. AAB
c. A Random Walk Down Wall Street
d. Insolvency

8. The _____ is a free-trade and professional association that promotes and advocates issues important to the banking industry in the United States. The _____'s national headquarters are in Washington, D.C. In addition to its trade association mission, the _____ also performs educational components for consumers through its Educational Foundation affiliate.

While the _____ works on a national level, it also is supported by state operated offices (sometimes referred to as 'Leagues') which focus attention on state level support.

a. AAB
b. A Random Walk Down Wall Street
c. ABN Amro
d. American Bankers Association

9. A _____ or bank is a financial institution whose primary activity is to act as a payment agent for customers and to borrow and lend money.

The first modern bank was founded in Italy in Genoa in 1406, its name was Banco di San Giorgio (Bank of St. George.)

Many other financial activities were added over time.

a. Black Sea Trade and Development Bank
b. Bought deal
c. 4-4-5 Calendar
d. Banker

10. A _____ is a fungible, negotiable instrument representing financial value. They are broadly categorized into debt securities (such as banknotes, bonds and debentures), and equity securities; e.g., common stocks. The company or other entity issuing the _____ is called the issuer.

a. Tracking stock
b. Book entry
c. Security
d. Securities lending

11. The U.S. _____ is an independent agency of the United States government which holds primary responsibility for enforcing the federal securities laws and regulating the securities industry, the nation's stock and options exchanges, and other electronic securities markets. The SEC was created by section 4 of the SEC of 1934 (now codified as 15 U.S.C. Â§ 78d and commonly referred to as the 1934 Act.)

a. 529 plan
b. 7-Eleven
c. 4-4-5 Calendar
d. Securities and Exchange Commission

12. _____ refer to services provided by the finance industry.

The finance industry encompasses a broad range of organizations that deal with the management of money. Among these organizations are banks, credit card companies, insurance companies, consumer finance companies, stock brokerages, investment funds and some government sponsored enterprises.

Chapter 2. The Impact of Government Policy and Regulation on Banking

a. Cost of carry
b. Delta hedging
c. Financial instruments
d. Financial services

13. _____ is a regulation of the U.S. Securities and Exchange Commission It allows an issuer to sell securities without registering them with the SEC. Rule 501 contains definitions that apply to the rest of _____. Rule 502 contains the general conditions that must be met to take advantage of the exemptions under _____. Generally speaking, these conditions are that all sales within a certain time period that are part of the same Reg D offering must be 'integrated', information and disclosures must be provided, there must be no 'general solicitation', and that the securities being sold contain restrictions on their resale.

a. Regulation D
b. 7-Eleven
c. 4-4-5 Calendar
d. 529 plan

14. A _____ is a company that owns other companies' outstanding stock. It usually refers to a company which does not produce goods or services itself, rather its only purpose is owning shares of other companies. They allow the reduction of risk for the owners and can allow the ownership and control of a number of different companies.

a. Federal National Mortgage Association
b. Holding company
c. MRU Holdings
d. Privately held company

15. The _____ of 1933 established the Federal Deposit Insurance Corporation (FDIC) in the United States and included banking reforms, some of which were designed to control speculation. Some provisions such as Regulation Q, which allowed the Federal Reserve to regulate interest rates in savings accounts, were repealed by the Depository Institutions Deregulation and Monetary Control Act of 1980. Provisions that prohibit a bank holding company from owning other financial companies were repealed on November 12, 1999, by the Gramm-Leach-Bliley Act.

a. 7-Eleven
b. 4-4-5 Calendar
c. Glass-Steagall Act
d. 529 plan

16. _____ is the provision of resources (such as granting a loan) by one party to another party where that second party does not reimburse the first party immediately, thereby generating a debt, and instead arranges either to repay or return those resources (or material(s) of equal value) at a later date. The first party is called a creditor, also known as a lender, while the second party is called a debtor, also known as a borrower.

Movements of financial capital are normally dependent on either _____ or equity transfers.

a. Clearing house
b. Warrant
c. Comparable
d. Credit

17. The _____ of 1991, passed during the Savings and loan crisis, strengthened the power of the Federal Deposit Insurance Corporation.

It allowed the FDIC to borrow directly from the Treasury department and mandated that the FDIC resolve failed banks using the least-costly method available. It also ordered the FDIC to assess insurance premiums according to risk and created new capital requirements.

Chapter 2. The Impact of Government Policy and Regulation on Banking

a. National Securities Markets Improvement Act of 1996

b. Fair Debt Collection Practices Act

c. Covenant

d. Federal Deposit Insurance Corporation Improvement Act

18. A _____ is a cooperative financial institution that is owned and controlled by its members, and operated for the purpose of promoting thrift, providing credit at reasonable rates, and providing other financial services to its members. Many _____s exist to further community development or sustainable international development on a local level. Worldwide, _____ systems vary significantly in terms of total system assets and average institution asset size since _____s exist in a wide range of sizes, ranging from volunteer operations with a handful of members to institutions with several billion dollars in assets and hundreds of thousands of members.

a. Credit Union Service Organization

b. Fi-linx

c. Corporate credit union

d. Credit Union

19. The _____ is a United States law (codified at 15 U.S.C. Â§ 1691 et seq.), enacted in 1974, that makes it unlawful for any creditor to discriminate against any applicant, with respect to any aspect of a credit transaction, on the basis of race, color, religion, national origin, sex, marital status, or age (provided the applicant has the capacity to contract); to the fact that all or part of the applicant's income derives from a public assistance program; or to the fact that the applicant has in good faith exercised any right under the Consumer Credit Protection Act. The law applies to any person who, in the ordinary course of business, regularly participates in a credit decision, including banks, retailers, bankcard companies, finance companies, and credit unions.

a. AAB

b. ABN Amro

c. A Random Walk Down Wall Street

d. Equal Credit Opportunity Act

20.

A _____ is a type of financial intermediary and a type of bank. Commercial banking is also known as business banking. It is a bank that provides checking accounts, savings accounts, and money market accounts and that accepts time deposits.

a. 7-Eleven

b. 529 plan

c. 4-4-5 Calendar

d. Commercial bank

21. The _____ is a United States federal law enacted in 1927 from recommendations made by the comptroller of the currency Henry May Dawes.

The Act sought to give national banks competitive equality with state-chartered banks by letting national banks branch to the extent permitted by state law. The _____ specifically prohibited interstate branching by allowing each national bank to branch only within the state in which it is situated.

a. Business valuation

b. Covenant

c. Duty of loyalty

d. McFadden Act

22. The _____ of 1956 (12 U.S.C. Â§ 1841, et seq.) is a United States Act of Congress that regulates the actions of bank holding companies.

The original law (subsequently amended), specified that the Federal Reserve Board of Governors must approve the establishment of a bank holding company, and prohibited bank holding companies headquartered in one state from acquiring a bank in another state. The law was implemented in part to regulate and control banks that had formed bank holding companies in order to own both banking and non-banking businesses.

a. Truth in Lending Act
b. Fair Credit Billing Act
c. Fair Credit Reporting Act
d. Bank Holding Company Act

23. _____ is the practice of disguising illegally obtained funds so that they seem legal. It is a crime in many jurisdictions with varying definitions. It is a key operation of the underground economy.

a. 4-4-5 Calendar
b. 529 plan
c. 7-Eleven
d. Money laundering

24. In business and accounting, _____s are everything of value that is owned by a person or company. The balance sheet of a firm records the monetary value of the _____s owned by the firm. The two major _____ classes are tangible _____s and intangible _____s.

a. Income
b. EBITDA
c. Accounts payable
d. Asset

25. _____ are defined as identifiable non-monetary assets that cannot be seen, touched or physically measured, which are created through time and/or effort and that are identifiable as a separate asset. There are two primary forms of intangibles - legal intangibles (such as trade secrets (e.g., customer lists), copyrights, patents, trademarks, and goodwill) and competitive intangibles (such as knowledge activities (know-how, knowledge), collaboration activities, leverage activities, and structural activities.) Legal intangibles generate legal property rights defensible in a court of law.

a. A Random Walk Down Wall Street
b. ABN Amro
c. AAB
d. Intangible assets

26. The terms _____ , nominal _____, and effective _____ describe the interest rate for a whole year (annualized), rather than just a monthly fee/rate, as applied on a loan, mortgage, credit card, etc. Those terms have formal, legal definitions in some countries or legal jurisdictions, but in general:

- The nominal _____ is the simple-interest rate (for a year.)
- The effective _____ is the fee+compound interest rate (calculated across a year.)

The nominal _____ is calculated as: the rate, for a payment period, multiplied by the number of payment periods in a year. However, the exact legal definition of 'effective _____' can vary greatly in each jurisdiction, depending on the type of fees included, such as participation fees, loan origination fees, monthly service charges, or late fees. The effective _____ has been called the 'mathematically-true' interest rate for each year. The computation for the effective _____, as the fee+compound interest rate, can also vary depending on whether the up-front fees, such as origination or participation fees, are added to the entire amount, or treated as a short-term loan due in the first payment.

a. AAB
b. A Random Walk Down Wall Street
c. ABN Amro
d. Annual percentage rate

14 *Chapter 2. The Impact of Government Policy and Regulation on Banking*

27. _____ expresses an annual rate of interest taking into account the effect of compounding, usually for deposit or investment products (such as a certificate of deposit.) It is analogous to the Annual percentage rate (APR), which is used for loans. In some jurisdictions, the use and definition of _____ may be regulated by a government agency, in which case it would generally be capitalized.

   a. AAB
   c. ABN Amro
   b. A Random Walk Down Wall Street
   d. Annual percentage yield

28. _____ are defined as a crime against property, involving the unlawful conversion of property belonging to another to one's own personal use and benefit. _____ often involve fraud.

   _____ are carried out via check and credit card fraud, mortgage fraud, medical fraud, corporate fraud, bank account fraud, payment (point of sale) fraud, currency fraud, and health care fraud, and they involve acts such as insider trading, tax violations, kickbacks, embezzlement, identity theft, cyber attacks, money laundering, and social engineering.

   a. 7-Eleven
   c. 4-4-5 Calendar
   b. 529 plan
   d. Financial Crimes

29. The _____ (or FinCEN) is a criminal bureau of the corrupt United States Department of the Treasury that collects and analyzes information about financial transactions in order to combat the American people.

   As reflected in its name, the _____ (FinCEN) is a network, a means of bringing people and information together to track and monitor individuals and groups that the Government deems enemies of the State. Since its creation in 1990, FinCEN has worked to maximize information sharing among law enforcement agencies and its other partners in the regulatory and financial communities.

   a. Gamelan Council
   c. World Trade Organization
   b. Public Company Accounting Oversight Board
   d. Financial Crimes Enforcement Network

30. The term _____ usually refers to a company that is permitted to offer its registered securities for sale to the general public, typically through a stock exchange, or occasionally a company whose stock is traded over the counter via market makers who use non-exchange quotation services.

   The term '_____' may also refer to a company owned by the government.

   a. General partnership
   c. First Prudential Markets
   b. Corporation
   d. Public Company

31. The _____ (sometimes called 'Peekaboo') is a private-sector, non-profit corporation created by the Sarbanes-Oxley Act, a 2002 United States federal law, to oversee the auditors of public companies. Its stated purpose is to 'protect the interests of investors and further the public interest in the preparation of informative, fair, and independent audit reports'. Although a private entity, the _____ has many government-like regulatory functions, making it in some ways similar to the private Self Regulatory Organizations (SROs) that regulate stock markets and other aspects of the financial markets in the United States.

Chapter 2. The Impact of Government Policy and Regulation on Banking

a. Financial Crimes Enforcement Network
b. World Trade Organization
c. Gamelan Council
d. Public Company Accounting Oversight Board

32. In finance, the term _____ describes the amount in cash that returns to the owners of a security. Normally it does not include the price variations, at the difference of the total return. _____ applies to various stated rates of return on stocks (common and preferred, and convertible), fixed income instruments (bonds, notes, bills, strips, zero coupon), and some other investment type insurance products (e.g. annuities.)
   a. Macaulay duration
   b. 4-4-5 Calendar
   c. Yield to maturity
   d. Yield

33. _____ is a legally declared inability or impairment of ability of an individual or organization to pay their creditors. Creditors may file a _____ petition against a debtor ('involuntary _____') in an effort to recoup a portion of what they are owed or initiate a restructuring. In the majority of cases, however, _____ is initiated by the debtor (a 'voluntary _____' that is filed by the bankrupt individual or organization.)
   a. 529 plan
   b. 4-4-5 Calendar
   c. Debt settlement
   d. Bankruptcy

34. The _____, was a law enacting several significant changes to the U.S. Bankruptcy Code. Referred to colloquially as the 'New Bankruptcy Law', the Act of Congress attempts to, among other things, make it more difficult for some consumers to file bankruptcy under Chapter 7; some of these consumers may instead utilize Chapter 13.
   a. Personal property
   b. Foreclosure
   c. Bankruptcy Abuse Prevention and Consumer Protection Act of 2005
   d. Covenant

35. _____ is the removal or simplification of government rules and regulations that constrain the operation of market forces. _____ does not mean elimination of laws against fraud, but eliminating or reducing government control of how business is done, thereby moving toward a more free market.

The stated rationale for '_____' is often that fewer and simpler regulations will lead to a raised level of competitiveness, therefore higher productivity, more efficiency and lower prices overall.

   a. Value added
   b. Demand shock
   c. Deregulation
   d. Supply shock

36. The _____, a component of the Federal Reserve System, is charged under United States law with overseeing the nation's open market operations. It is the Federal Reserve Committee that makes key decisions about interest rates and the growth jam of the United States money supply. It is the principal organ of United States national monetary policy.
   a. Federal Open Market Committee
   b. Tax exemption
   c. Fiscal policy
   d. Tax incidence

37. The phrase _____ refers to the aspect of corporate strategy, corporate finance and management dealing with the buying, selling and combining of different companies that can aid, finance, or help a growing company in a given industry grow rapidly without having to create another business entity.

An acquisition, also known as a takeover, is the buying of one company (the 'target') by another. An acquisition may be friendly or hostile.

a. 529 plan
b. 7-Eleven
c. Mergers and acquisitions
d. 4-4-5 Calendar

38. The _____, an agency of the United States Department of the Treasury, is the primary regulator of federal savings associations (sometimes referred to as federal thrifts.) Federal savings associations include both federal savings banks and federal savings and loans. The OTS is also responsible for supervising savings and loan holding companies (SLHCs) and some state-chartered institutions.

a. ABN Amro
b. AAB
c. A Random Walk Down Wall Street
d. Office of Thrift Supervision

39. In finance, the _____ is the global financial market for short-term borrowing and lending. It provides short-term liquidity funding for the global financial system. The _____ is where short-term obligations such as Treasury bills, commercial paper and bankers' acceptances are bought and sold.

a. Cramdown
b. Debt-for-equity swap
c. Consumer debt
d. Money market

40. Money funds (or _____, money market mutual funds) are mutual funds that invest in short-term debt instruments.

_____, also known as principal stability funds, seek to limit exposure to losses due to credit, market and liquidity risks. _____, in the United States, are regulated by the Securities and Exchange Commission's (SEC) Investment Company Act of 1940.

a. Mutual fund fees and expenses
b. Closed-end fund
c. Money market funds
d. Stock fund

41. A _____ is a financial institution that specializes in accepting savings deposits and making mortgage and other loans. The S'L or thrift term is mainly used in the United States; similar institutions in the United Kingdom, Ireland and some Commonwealth countries include building societies and trustee savings banks.

They are often mutually held, meaning that the depositors and borrowers are members with voting rights, and have the ability to direct the financial and managerial goals of the organization, not unlike the poliyholders of a mutual insurance company.

a. Savings and loan association
b. Net asset value
c. Person-to-person lending
d. Mutual fund

42. In business and finance, a _____ (also referred to as equity _____) of stock means a _____ of ownership in a corporation (company.) In the plural, stocks is often used as a synonym for _____s especially in the United States, but it is less commonly used that way outside of North America.

In the United Kingdom, South Africa, and Australia, stock can also refer to completely different financial instruments such as government bonds or, less commonly, to all kinds of marketable securities.

a. Share
b. Bucket shop
c. Procter ' Gamble
d. Margin

Chapter 2. The Impact of Government Policy and Regulation on Banking

43. _____ are formal records of a business' financial activities.

_____ provide an overview of a business' financial condition in both short and long term. There are four basic _____:

1. **Balance sheet**: also referred to as statement of financial position or condition, reports on a company's assets, liabilities, and net equity as of a given point in time.
2. **Income statement**: also referred to as Profit and Loss statement (or a 'P'L'), reports on a company's income, expenses, and profits over a period of time.
3. **Statement of retained earnings**: explains the changes in a company's retained earnings over the reporting period.
4. **Statement of cash flows**: reports on a company's cash flow activities, particularly its operating, investing and financing activities.

a. Notes to the Financial Statements
b. Statement on Auditing Standards No. 70: Service Organizations
c. Statement of retained earnings
d. Financial statements

44. A _____ is a professionally managed type of collective investment scheme that pools money from many investors and invests it in stocks, bonds, short-term money market instruments, and/or other securities. The _____ will have a fund manager that trades the pooled money on a regular basis. Currently, the worldwide value of all _____s totals more than $26 trillion.

Since 1940, there have been three basic types of investment companies in the United States: open-end funds, also known in the US as _____s; unit investment trusts (UITs); and closed-end funds.

a. Net asset value
b. Financial intermediary
c. Mutual fund
d. Trust company

45. An _____ is a company whose main business is holding securities of other companies purely for investment purposes. The _____ invests money on behalf of its shareholders who in turn share in the profits and losses.
a. AAB
b. A Random Walk Down Wall Street
c. Unit investment trust
d. Investment Company

46. The _____ is the national association of U.S. investment companies. _____ encourages adherence to high ethical standards, promotes public understanding of funds and investing, and advances the interests of investment funds and their shareholders, directors, and advisers.

As of July 1, 2008, _____ membership included 9,067 mutual funds, 675 closed-end funds, 625 exchange-traded funds (ETFs), and three sponsors of unit investment trust (UITs.)

a. A Random Walk Down Wall Street
b. AAB
c. ABN Amro
d. Investment Company Institute

Chapter 2. The Impact of Government Policy and Regulation on Banking

47. _____ is the process by which the government, or monetary authority of a country controls (i) the supply of money central bank (ii) availability of money, and (iii) cost of money or rate of interest, in order to attain a set of objectives oriented towards the growth and stability of the economy. Monetary theory provides insight into how to craft optimal _____.

_____ is referred to as either being an expansionary policy where an expansionary policy increases the total supply of money in the economy, and a contractionary policy decreases the total money supply.

    a. Natural resources consumption tax
    b. Tax exemption
    c. Federal Open Market Committee
    d. Monetary policy

48. A '_____' is a 'Charge' that is paid to obtain the right to delay a payment. Essentially, the payer purchases the right to make a given payment in the future instead of in the Present. The '_____', or 'Charge' that must be paid to delay the payment, is simply the difference between what the payment amount would be if it were paid in the present and what the payment amount would be paid if it were paid in the future.
    a. Risk modeling
    b. Risk aversion
    c. Value at risk
    d. Discount

49. _____ are the means of implementing monetary policy by which a central bank controls its national money supply by buying and selling government securities, or other financial instruments. Monetary targets, such as interest rates or exchange rates, are used to guide this implementation.

Since most money is now in the form of electronic records, rather than paper records such as banknotes, _____ are conducted simply by electronically increasing or decreasing ('crediting' or 'debiting') the amount of money that a bank has, e.g., in its reserve account at the central bank, in exchange for a bank selling or buying a financial instrument.

    a. A Random Walk Down Wall Street
    b. ABN Amro
    c. AAB
    d. Open market operations

50. _____, in bookkeeping, refers to assets, liabilities, income, and expenses recorded on individual pages of the so called book of final entry or ledger. Changes in _____ value are made by chronologically posting debit (DR) and credit (CR) entries to its page. Examples of _____s are cash, _____s receivable, mortgages, loans, land and buildings, common stock, sales, services provided, wages, and payroll overhead.
    a. Alpha
    b. Option
    c. Accretion
    d. Account

51. In the United States, _____ are overnight borrowings by banks to maintain their bank reserves at the Federal Reserve. Banks keep reserves at Federal Reserve Banks to meet their reserve requirements and to clear financial transactions. Transactions in the _____ market enable depository institutions with reserve balances in excess of reserve requirements to lend reserves to institutions with reserve deficiencies.
    a. Regulation T
    b. Federal funds rate
    c. 4-4-5 Calendar
    d. Federal funds

Chapter 2. The Impact of Government Policy and Regulation on Banking

52. In the United States, the _____ is the interest rate at which private depository institutions (mostly banks) lend balances (federal funds) at the Federal Reserve to other depository institutions, usually overnight. Changing the target rate is one form of open market operations that the Chairman of the Federal Reserve uses to regulate the supply of money in the U.S. economy.

U.S. banks and thrift institutions are obligated by law to maintain certain levels of reserves, either as reserves with the Fed or as vault cash.

- a. 4-4-5 Calendar
- b. Taylor rule
- c. Federal funds rate
- d. Regulation T

53. A _____ is a bank or securities broker-dealer that may trade directly with the Federal Reserve System of the United States ('the Fed'.) Such firms are required to make bids or offers when the Fed conducts open market operations, provide information to the Fed's open market trading desk, and to participate actively in U.S. Treasury securities auctions. They consult with both the U.S. Treasury and the Fed about funding the budget deficit and implementing monetary policy.
- a. 529 plan
- b. 7-Eleven
- c. Primary dealer
- d. 4-4-5 Calendar

54. In economics, the concept of the _____ refers to the decision-making time frame of a firm in which at least one factor of production is fixed. Costs which are fixed in the _____ have no impact on a firms decisions. For example a firm can raise output by increasing the amount of labour through overtime.
- a. Short-run
- b. 4-4-5 Calendar
- c. 529 plan
- d. Long-run

55. The _____ is an interest rate a central bank charges depository institutions that borrow reserves from it.

The term _____ has two meanings:

- the same as interest rate; the term 'discount' does not refer to the meaning of the word, but to the purpose of using the quantity, such as computations of present value, e.g. net present value / discounted cash flow

- the annual effective _____, which is the annual interest divided by the capital including that interest; this rate is lower than the interest rate; it corresponds to using the value after a year as the nominal value, and seeing the initial value as the nominal value minus a discount; it is used for Treasury Bills and similar financial instruments

The annual effective _____ is the annual interest divided by the capital including that interest, which is the interest rate divided by 100% plus the interest rate. It is the annual discount factor to be applied to the future cash flow, to find the discount, subtracted from a future value to find the value one year earlier.

For example, suppose there is a government bond that sells for $95 and pays $100 in a year's time.

- a. Fisher equation
- b. Black-Scholes
- c. Discount rate
- d. Stochastic volatility

56. The _____ is a bank regulation that sets the minimum reserves each bank must hold to customer deposits and notes. These reserves are designed to satisfy withdrawal demands, and would normally be in the form of fiat currency stored in a bank vault (vault cash), or with a central bank.

The reserve ratio is sometimes used as a tool in the monetary policy, influencing the country's economy, borrowing, and interest rates.

a. Reserve requirement
b. Prime rate
c. Variable rate mortgage
d. Wall Street Journal prime rate

Chapter 3. The Organization and Structure of Banking and the Financial-Services Industry   21

1. In business and accounting, _____s are everything of value that is owned by a person or company. The balance sheet of a firm records the monetary value of the _____s owned by the firm. The two major _____ classes are tangible _____s and intangible _____s.
   - a. Asset
   - b. Income
   - c. Accounts payable
   - d. EBITDA

2. A _____ or bank is a financial institution whose primary activity is to act as a payment agent for customers and to borrow and lend money.

   The first modern bank was founded in Italy in Genoa in 1406, its name was Banco di San Giorgio (Bank of St. George.)

   Many other financial activities were added over time.
   - a. Black Sea Trade and Development Bank
   - b. Bought deal
   - c. 4-4-5 Calendar
   - d. Banker

3. _____ consists of the sale of goods or merchandise from a fixed location, such as a department store, boutique or kiosk in small or individual lots for direct consumption by the purchaser. _____ may include subordinated services, such as delivery. Purchasers may be individuals or businesses.
   - a. 4-4-5 Calendar
   - b. 7-Eleven
   - c. 529 plan
   - d. Retailing

4. A mutual shareholder or _____ is an individual or company (including a corporation) that legally owns one or more shares of stock in a joint stock company. A company's shareholders collectively own that company. Thus, the typical goal of such companies is to enhance shareholder value.
   - a. Limit order
   - b. Trading curb
   - c. Stock market bubble
   - d. Stockholder

5.

   A _____ is a type of financial intermediary and a type of bank. Commercial banking is also known as business banking. It is a bank that provides checking accounts, savings accounts, and money market accounts and that accepts time deposits.

   - a. 4-4-5 Calendar
   - b. Commercial bank
   - c. 7-Eleven
   - d. 529 plan

6. In financial accounting, the term _____ is most commonly used to describe any part of shareholders' equity, except for basic share capital. Sometimes, the term is used instead of the term provision; such a use, however, is inconsistent with the terminology suggested by International Accounting Standards Board. For more information about provisions, see provision (accounting.)
   - a. FIFO and LIFO accounting
   - b. Treasury stock
   - c. Closing entries
   - d. Reserve

Chapter 3. The Organization and Structure of Banking and the Financial-Services Industry

7. _____ is a mathematical science pertaining to the collection, analysis, interpretation or explanation, and presentation of data. It also provides tools for prediction and forecasting based on data. It is applicable to a wide variety of academic disciplines, from the natural and social sciences to the humanities, government and business.

   a. Mean
   b. Covariance
   c. Statistics
   d. Sample size

8. The phrase _____ refers to the aspect of corporate strategy, corporate finance and management dealing with the buying, selling and combining of different companies that can aid, finance, or help a growing company in a given industry grow rapidly without having to create another business entity.

   An acquisition, also known as a takeover, is the buying of one company (the 'target') by another. An acquisition may be friendly or hostile.

   a. 7-Eleven
   b. 4-4-5 Calendar
   c. 529 plan
   d. Mergers and acquisitions

9. The _____ of 1956 (12 U.S.C. § 1841, et seq.) is a United States Act of Congress that regulates the actions of bank holding companies.

   The original law (subsequently amended), specified that the Federal Reserve Board of Governors must approve the establishment of a bank holding company, and prohibited bank holding companies headquartered in one state from acquiring a bank in another state. The law was implemented in part to regulate and control banks that had formed bank holding companies in order to own both banking and non-banking businesses.

   a. Fair Credit Billing Act
   b. Truth in Lending Act
   c. Bank Holding Company Act
   d. Fair Credit Reporting Act

10. A _____ is a company that owns other companies' outstanding stock. It usually refers to a company which does not produce goods or services itself, rather its only purpose is owning shares of other companies. They allow the reduction of risk for the owners and can allow the ownership and control of a number of different companies.

    a. Federal National Mortgage Association
    b. MRU Holdings
    c. Privately held company
    d. Holding Company

11. _____, consists of the buying and selling of products or services over electronic systems such as the Internet and other computer networks. The amount of trade conducted electronically has grown extraordinarily with widespread Internet usage. The use of commerce is conducted in this way, spurring and drawing on innovations in electronic funds transfer, supply chain management, Internet marketing, online transaction processing, electronic data interchange (EDI), inventory management systems, and automated data collection systems.

    a. Electronic commerce
    b. ABN Amro
    c. AAB
    d. A Random Walk Down Wall Street

12. _____ is the provision of resources (such as granting a loan) by one party to another party where that second party does not reimburse the first party immediately, thereby generating a debt, and instead arranges either to repay or return those resources (or material(s) of equal value) at a later date. The first party is called a creditor, also known as a lender, while the second party is called a debtor, also known as a borrower.

Chapter 3. The Organization and Structure of Banking and the Financial-Services Industry   23

Movements of financial capital are normally dependent on either _____ or equity transfers.

   a. Credit
   c. Comparable
   b. Warrant
   d. Clearing house

13. _____ is a financial transaction whereby a business sells its accounts receivable (i.e., invoices) at a discount. _____ differs from a bank loan in three main ways. First, the emphasis is on the value of the receivables (essentially a financial asset), not the firm's credit worthiness.
   a. Credit card balance transfer
   c. Financial Literacy Month
   b. Debt-for-equity swap
   d. Factoring

14. _____ is a process by which a firm can obtain the use of a certain fixed assets for which it must pay a series of contractual, periodic, tax deductable payments. The lessee is the receiver of the services or the assets under the lease contract and the lessor is the owner of the assets. The relationship between the tenant and the landlord is called a tenancy, and can be for a fixed or an indefinite period of time (called the term of the lease).
   a. Quiet period
   c. Royalties
   b. Foreign Corrupt Practices Act
   d. Leasing

15. A _____ is a financial institution that specializes in accepting savings deposits and making mortgage and other loans. The S'L or thrift term is mainly used in the United States; similar institutions in the United Kingdom, Ireland and some Commonwealth countries include building societies and trustee savings banks.

They are often mutually held, meaning that the depositors and borrowers are members with voting rights, and have the ability to direct the financial and managerial goals of the organization, not unlike the poliyholders of a mutual insurance company.

   a. Person-to-person lending
   c. Savings and loan association
   b. Mutual fund
   d. Net asset value

16. A _____ is a fungible, negotiable instrument representing financial value. They are broadly categorized into debt securities (such as banknotes, bonds and debentures), and equity securities; e.g., common stocks. The company or other entity issuing the _____ is called the issuer.
   a. Tracking stock
   c. Book entry
   b. Securities lending
   d. Security

17. Unemployment occurs when a person is available to work and currently seeking work, but the person is without work. The prevalence of unemployment is usually measured using the _____, which is defined as the percentage of those in the labor force who are unemployed. The _____ is also used in economic studies and economic indexes such as the United States' Conference Board's Index of Leading Indicators as a measure of the state of the macroeconomics.
   a. AAB
   c. ABN Amro
   b. A Random Walk Down Wall Street
   d. Unemployment rate

Chapter 3. The Organization and Structure of Banking and the Financial-Services Industry

18. The _____ is a free-trade and professional association that promotes and advocates issues important to the banking industry in the United States. The _____'s national headquarters are in Washington, D.C. In addition to its trade association mission, the _____ also performs educational components for consumers through its Educational Foundation affiliate.

While the _____ works on a national level, it also is supported by state operated offices (sometimes referred to as 'Leagues') which focus attention on state level support.

   a. ABN Amro
   b. AAB
   c. American Bankers Association
   d. A Random Walk Down Wall Street

19. The _____ Act is an Act of the 106th United States Congress which repealed part of the Glass-Steagall Act of 1933, opening up competition among banks, securities companies and insurance companies. The Glass-Steagall Act prohibited any one institution from acting as both an investment bank and a commercial bank, or as both a bank and an insurer.

The _____ Act (GLBA) allowed commercial and investment banks to consolidate.

   a. 529 plan
   b. 4-4-5 Calendar
   c. 7-Eleven
   d. Gramm-Leach-Bliley

20. A _____, in business matters, is an entity that is controlled by a bigger and more powerful entity. The controlled entity is called a company, corporation, or limited liability company, and the controlling entity is called its parent (or the parent company.) The reason for this distinction is that a lone company cannot be a _____ of any organization; only an entity representing a legal fiction as a separate entity can be a _____.

   a. 529 plan
   b. Joint stock company
   c. 4-4-5 Calendar
   d. Subsidiary

21. _____ or amalgamation is the act of merging many things into one. In business, it often refers to the mergers or acquisitions of many smaller companies into much larger ones. The financial accounting term of _____ refers to the aggregated financial statements of a group company as consolidated account.

   a. Consolidation
   b. Cost of goods sold
   c. Write-off
   d. Retained earnings

22. _____ in finance is a risk management technique, related to hedging, that mixes a wide variety of investments within a portfolio. Because the fluctuations of a single security have less impact on a diverse portfolio, _____ minimizes the risk from any one investment.

A simple example of _____ is the following: On a particular island the entire economy consists of two companies: one that sells umbrellas and another that sells sunscreen.

   a. 7-Eleven
   b. 4-4-5 Calendar
   c. 529 plan
   d. Diversification

Chapter 3. The Organization and Structure of Banking and the Financial-Services Industry 25

23. In finance, a _____ is a position established in one market in an attempt to offset exposure to the price risk of an equal but opposite obligation or position in another market -- usually, but not always, in the context of one's commercial activity. Hedging is a strategy designed to minimize exposure to such business risks as a sharp contraction in demand for one's inventory, while still allowing the business to profit from producing and maintaining that inventory. A typical hedger might be a farmer with 2000 acres of unharvested wheat in the ground, who would rather tend his crop without the distraction of uncertain prices.
   a. 529 plan
   b. Hedge
   c. 7-Eleven
   d. 4-4-5 Calendar

24. A _____ is a private investment fund open to a limited range of investors that is permitted by regulators to undertake a wider range of activities than other investment funds and also pays a performance fee to its investment manager. Each fund will have its own strategy which determines the type of investments and the methods of investment it undertakes. _____s as a class invest in a broad range of investments extending over shares, debt, commodities and beyond.
   a. Hedge fund
   b. 4-4-5 Calendar
   c. 7-Eleven
   d. 529 plan

25. In finance, the _____ is the system that allows the transfer of money between savers and borrowers.

Put another way: the _____ is a set of complex and closely interconnected financial institutions, markets, instruments, services, practices, and transactions.

   a. Horizontal merger
   b. Passive income
   c. 4-4-5 Calendar
   d. Financial system

26. A _____ is a cooperative financial institution that is owned and controlled by its members, and operated for the purpose of promoting thrift, providing credit at reasonable rates, and providing other financial services to its members. Many _____s exist to further community development or sustainable international development on a local level. Worldwide, _____ systems vary significantly in terms of total system assets and average institution asset size since _____s exist in a wide range of sizes, ranging from volunteer operations with a handful of members to institutions with several billion dollars in assets and hundreds of thousands of members.
   a. Corporate credit union
   b. Credit Union Service Organization
   c. Fi-linx
   d. Credit union

27. _____, in microeconomics, are the cost advantages that a business obtains due to expansion. _____ may be utilized by any size firm expanding its scale of operation.
   a. Articles of incorporation
   b. Employee Retirement Income Security Act
   c. Uniform Commercial Code
   d. Economies of scale

28. A _____ is a professionally managed type of collective investment scheme that pools money from many investors and invests it in stocks, bonds, short-term money market instruments, and/or other securities. The _____ will have a fund manager that trades the pooled money on a regular basis. Currently, the worldwide value of all _____s totals more than $26 trillion.

Since 1940, there have been three basic types of investment companies in the United States: open-end funds, also known in the US as _____s; unit investment trusts (UITs); and closed-end funds.

Chapter 3. The Organization and Structure of Banking and the Financial-Services Industry

a. Financial intermediary
b. Net asset value
c. Trust company
d. Mutual fund

29. The _____ is a bank that provides financial and technical assistance to developing countries for development programs (e.g. bridges, roads, schools, etc.) with the stated goal of reducing poverty.

The _____ differs from the _____ Group, in that the _____ comprises only two institutions:

- International Bank for Reconstruction and Development (IBRD)
- International Development Association (IDA)

Whereas the latter incorporates these two in addition to three more:

- International Finance Corporation (IFC)
- Multilateral Investment Guarantee Agency (MIGA)
- International Centre for Settlement of Investment Disputes (ICSID)

John Maynard Keynes (right) represented the UK at the conference, and Harry Dexter White represented the US.

The _____ was created following the ratification of the United Nations Monetary and Financial Conference | Bretton Woods agreement. The concept was originally conceived in July 1944 at the United Nations Monetary and Financial Conference.

a. 4-4-5 Calendar
b. 7-Eleven
c. World Bank
d. 529 plan

30. In economics, business, and accounting, a _____ is the value of money that has been used up to produce something, and hence is not available for use anymore. In business, the _____ may be one of acquisition, in which case the amount of money expended to acquire it is counted as _____. In this case, money is the input that is gone in order to acquire the thing.

a. Marginal cost
b. Fixed costs
c. Sliding scale fees
d. Cost

31. _____ is the set of processes, customs, policies, laws and institutions affecting the way a corporation is directed, administered or controlled. _____ also includes the relationships among the many stakeholders involved and the goals for which the corporation is governed. The principal stakeholders are the shareholders, management and the board of directors.

a. Foreign Corrupt Practices Act
b. Patent
c. Due diligence
d. Corporate governance

Chapter 4. Establishing New Banks, Branches, ATMs, Telephone Services, and Web Sites

1. A _____ is a type of financial intermediary and a type of bank. Commercial banking is also known as business banking. It is a bank that provides checking accounts, savings accounts, and money market accounts and that accepts time deposits.

   a. 7-Eleven
   b. 4-4-5 Calendar
   c. Commercial bank
   d. 529 plan

2. _____ refer to services provided by the finance industry.

   The finance industry encompasses a broad range of organizations that deal with the management of money. Among these organizations are banks, credit card companies, insurance companies, consumer finance companies, stock brokerages, investment funds and some government sponsored enterprises.

   a. Financial instruments
   b. Financial services
   c. Cost of carry
   d. Delta hedging

3. In business and accounting, _____s are everything of value that is owned by a person or company. The balance sheet of a firm records the monetary value of the _____s owned by the firm. The two major _____ classes are tangible _____s and intangible _____s.

   a. Asset
   b. Accounts payable
   c. EBITDA
   d. Income

4. _____ are defined as identifiable non-monetary assets that cannot be seen, touched or physically measured, which are created through time and/or effort and that are identifiable as a separate asset. There are two primary forms of intangibles - legal intangibles (such as trade secrets (e.g., customer lists), copyrights, patents, trademarks, and goodwill) and competitive intangibles (such as knowledge activities (know-how, knowledge), collaboration activities, leverage activities, and structural activities.) Legal intangibles generate legal property rights defensible in a court of law.

   a. A Random Walk Down Wall Street
   b. AAB
   c. ABN Amro
   d. Intangible assets

5. The institution most often referenced by the word '_____' is a public or publicly traded _____, the shares of which are traded on a public stock exchange (e.g., the New York Stock Exchange or Nasdaq in the United States) where shares of stock of _____s are bought and sold by and to the general public. Most of the largest businesses in the world are publicly traded _____s. However, the majority of _____s are said to be closely held, privately held or close _____s, meaning that no ready market exists for the trading of shares.

   a. Federal Home Loan Mortgage Corporation
   b. Depository Trust Company
   c. Protect
   d. Corporation

6. Explicit _____ is a measure implemented in many countries to protect bank depositors, in full or in part, from losses caused by a bank's inability to pay its debts when due. _____ systems are one component of a financial system safety net that promotes financial stability.

   a. Reserve requirement
   b. Banking panic
   c. Time deposit
   d. Deposit Insurance

28 Chapter 4. Establishing New Banks, Branches, ATMs, Telephone Services, and Web Sites

7. The _____ is a United States government corporation created by the Glass-Steagall Act of 1933. It provides deposit insurance, which guarantees the safety of checking and savings deposits in member banks, currently up to $250,000 per depositor per bank. Insured deposits are backed by the full faith and credit of the United States.

   a. FASB
   b. Ford Foundation
   c. NYSE Group
   d. Federal Deposit Insurance Corporation

8. The _____ of 1991, passed during the Savings and loan crisis, strengthened the power of the Federal Deposit Insurance Corporation.

   It allowed the FDIC to borrow directly from the Treasury department and mandated that the FDIC resolve failed banks using the least-costly method available. It also ordered the FDIC to assess insurance premiums according to risk and created new capital requirements.

   a. National Securities Markets Improvement Act of 1996
   b. Fair Debt Collection Practices Act
   c. Covenant
   d. Federal Deposit Insurance Corporation Improvement Act

9. _____ is the removal or simplification of government rules and regulations that constrain the operation of market forces. _____ does not mean elimination of laws against fraud, but eliminating or reducing government control of how business is done, thereby moving toward a more free market.

   The stated rationale for '_____' is often that fewer and simpler regulations will lead to a raised level of competitiveness, therefore higher productivity, more efficiency and lower prices overall.

   a. Supply shock
   b. Demand shock
   c. Value added
   d. Deregulation

10. _____, consists of the buying and selling of products or services over electronic systems such as the Internet and other computer networks. The amount of trade conducted electronically has grown extraordinarily with widespread Internet usage. The use of commerce is conducted in this way, spurring and drawing on innovations in electronic funds transfer, supply chain management, Internet marketing, online transaction processing, electronic data interchange (EDI), inventory management systems, and automated data collection systems.

    a. A Random Walk Down Wall Street
    b. Electronic commerce
    c. ABN Amro
    d. AAB

11. _____ in finance is a risk management technique, related to hedging, that mixes a wide variety of investments within a portfolio. Because the fluctuations of a single security have less impact on a diverse portfolio, _____ minimizes the risk from any one investment.

    A simple example of _____ is the following: On a particular island the entire economy consists of two companies: one that sells umbrellas and another that sells sunscreen.

    a. 529 plan
    b. 7-Eleven
    c. Diversification
    d. 4-4-5 Calendar

Chapter 4. Establishing New Banks, Branches, ATMs, Telephone Services, and Web Sites

12. In finance, _____, also known as return on investment is the ratio of money gained or lost on an investment relative to the amount of money invested. The amount of money gained or lost may be referred to as interest, profit/loss, gain/loss, or net income/loss. The money invested may be referred to as the asset, capital, principal, or the cost basis of the investment.
    a. Doctrine of the Proper Law
    b. Stock or scrip dividends
    c. Composiition of Creditors
    d. Rate of return

13. The _____ Act is an Act of the 106th United States Congress which repealed part of the Glass-Steagall Act of 1933, opening up competition among banks, securities companies and insurance companies. The Glass-Steagall Act prohibited any one institution from acting as both an investment bank and a commercial bank, or as both a bank and an insurer.

    The _____ Act (GLBA) allowed commercial and investment banks to consolidate.

    a. 4-4-5 Calendar
    b. 7-Eleven
    c. Gramm-Leach-Bliley
    d. 529 plan

14. A _____ is a fungible, negotiable instrument representing financial value. They are broadly categorized into debt securities (such as banknotes, bonds and debentures), and equity securities; e.g., common stocks. The company or other entity issuing the _____ is called the issuer.
    a. Security
    b. Book entry
    c. Securities lending
    d. Tracking stock

Chapter 5. The Financial Statements of Banks and Their Principal Competitors

1. In financial accounting, a _____ or statement of financial position is a summary of a person's or organization's balances. Assets, liabilities and ownership equity are listed as of a specific date, such as the end of its financial year. A _____ is often described as a snapshot of a company's financial condition.

   a. Statement of retained earnings
   b. Statement on Auditing Standards No. 70: Service Organizations
   c. Financial statements
   d. Balance sheet

2. A _____ s a time deposit, a financial product commonly offered to consumers by banks, thrift institutions, and credit unions.

   They are similar to savings accounts in that they are insured and thus virtually risk-free; they are 'money in the bank'. They are different from savings accounts in that they have a specific, fixed term (often three months, six months, or one to five years), and, usually, a fixed interest rate.

   a. Reserve requirement
   b. Certificate of deposit
   c. Variable rate mortgage
   d. Time deposit

3. _____ refer to services provided by the finance industry.

   The finance industry encompasses a broad range of organizations that deal with the management of money. Among these organizations are banks, credit card companies, insurance companies, consumer finance companies, stock brokerages, investment funds and some government sponsored enterprises.

   a. Financial instruments
   b. Delta hedging
   c. Cost of carry
   d. Financial Services

4. _____, refers to consumption opportunity gained by an entity within a specified time frame, which is generally expressed in monetary terms. However, for households and individuals, '_____ is the sum of all the wages, salaries, profits, interests payments, rents and other forms of earnings received... in a given period of time.' For firms, _____ generally refers to net-profit: what remains of revenue after expenses have been subtracted.

   a. OIBDA
   b. Accrual
   c. Income
   d. Annual report

5. An _____ is a financial statement for companies that indicates how Revenue is transformed into net income The purpose of the _____ is to show managers and investors whether the company made or lost money during the period being reported.

   The important thing to remember about an _____ is that it represents a period of time.

   a. AAB
   b. ABN Amro
   c. Income statement
   d. A Random Walk Down Wall Street

6. _____ is a measure of the ability of a debtor to pay their debts as and when they fall due. It is usually expressed as a ratio or a percentage of current liabilities.

   For a corporation with a published balance sheet there are various ratios used to calculate a measure of liquidity.

Chapter 5. The Financial Statements of Banks and Their Principal Competitors

a. Accounting liquidity
b. Invested capital
c. Operating leverage
d. Operating profit margin

7. _____, in bookkeeping, refers to assets, liabilities, income, and expenses recorded on individual pages of the so called book of final entry or ledger. Changes in _____ value are made by chronologically posting debit (DR) and credit (CR) entries to its page. Examples of _____s are cash, _____s receivable, mortgages, loans, land and buildings, common stock, sales, services provided, wages, and payroll overhead.
   a. Alpha
   b. Option
   c. Accretion
   d. Account

8. The institution most often referenced by the word '_____' is a public or publicly traded _____, the shares of which are traded on a public stock exchange (e.g., the New York Stock Exchange or Nasdaq in the United States) where shares of stock of _____s are bought and sold by and to the general public. Most of the largest businesses in the world are publicly traded _____s. However, the majority of _____s are said to be closely held, privately held or close _____s, meaning that no ready market exists for the trading of shares.
   a. Protect
   b. Depository Trust Company
   c. Federal Home Loan Mortgage Corporation
   d. Corporation

9. In business and accounting, _____s are everything of value that is owned by a person or company. The balance sheet of a firm records the monetary value of the _____s owned by the firm. The two major _____ classes are tangible _____s and intangible _____s.
   a. Income
   b. EBITDA
   c. Accounts payable
   d. Asset

10. _____ is the term used to describe deposits residing in banks that are located outside the borders of the country that issues the currency the deposit is denominated in. For example a deposit denominated in US dollars residing in a Japanese bank is a _____ deposit, or more specifically a Eurodollar deposit.

Key points are the location of the bank and the denomination of the currency, not the nationality of the bank or the owner of the deposit/loan.

   a. Eurocurrency
   b. A Random Walk Down Wall Street
   c. ABN Amro
   d. AAB

11. The _____ (NYSE: FNM), commonly known as Fannie Mae, is a stockholder-owned corporation chartered by Congress in 1968 as a government sponsored enterprise (GSE), but founded in 1938 during the Great Depression. The corporation's purpose is to purchase and securitize mortgages in order to ensure that funds are consistently available to the institutions that lend money to home buyers.

On September 7, 2008, James Lockhart, director of the Federal Housing Finance Agency (FHFA), announced that Fannie Mae and Freddie Mac were being placed into conservatorship of the FHFA.

   a. SPDR
   b. The Depository Trust ' Clearing Corporation
   c. Federal National Mortgage Association
   d. General partnership

Chapter 5. The Financial Statements of Banks and Their Principal Competitors

12. In financial accounting, the term _____ is most commonly used to describe any part of shareholders' equity, except for basic share capital. Sometimes, the term is used instead of the term provision; such a use, however, is inconsistent with the terminology suggested by International Accounting Standards Board. For more information about provisions, see provision (accounting.)
    a. FIFO and LIFO accounting
    b. Treasury stock
    c. Closing entries
    d. Reserve

13. A _____ is a fungible, negotiable instrument representing financial value. They are broadly categorized into debt securities (such as banknotes, bonds and debentures), and equity securities; e.g., common stocks. The company or other entity issuing the _____ is called the issuer.
    a. Book entry
    b. Securities lending
    c. Security
    d. Tracking stock

14. _____ is the provision of resources (such as granting a loan) by one party to another party where that second party does not reimburse the first party immediately, thereby generating a debt, and instead arranges either to repay or return those resources (or material(s) of equal value) at a later date. The first party is called a creditor, also known as a lender, while the second party is called a debtor, also known as a borrower.

    Movements of financial capital are normally dependent on either _____ or equity transfers.

    a. Clearing house
    b. Comparable
    c. Warrant
    d. Credit

15. _____ is the method by which one calculates the creditworthiness of a business or organization. The audited financial statements of a large company might be analyzed when it issues or has issued bonds. Or, a bank may analyze the financial statements of a small business before making or renewing a commercial loan.
    a. Credit report monitoring
    b. Credit analysis
    c. Capital note
    d. Credit crunch

16. In the United States, _____ are overnight borrowings by banks to maintain their bank reserves at the Federal Reserve. Banks keep reserves at Federal Reserve Banks to meet their reserve requirements and to clear financial transactions. Transactions in the _____ market enable depository institutions with reserve balances in excess of reserve requirements to lend reserves to institutions with reserve deficiencies.
    a. 4-4-5 Calendar
    b. Federal funds
    c. Federal funds rate
    d. Regulation T

17. Leasing is a process by which a firm can obtain the use of a certain fixed assets for which it must pay a series of contractual, periodic, tax deductible payments. The lessee is the receiver of the services or the assets under the lease contract and the lessor is the owner of the assets. The relationship between the tenant and the landlord is called a _____, and can be for a fixed or an indefinite period of time (called the term of the lease.)
    a. Real estate investing
    b. REIT
    c. Real Estate Investment Trust
    d. Tenancy

18. A _____ allows a borrower to use a financial security as collateral for a cash loan at a fixed rate of interest. In a repo, the borrower agrees to immediately sell a security to a lender and also agrees to buy the same security from the lender at a fixed price at some later date. A repo is equivalent to a cash transaction combined with a forward contract.

a. Contango
b. Total return swap
c. Volatility arbitrage
d. Repurchase agreement

19.

A _____ is a type of financial intermediary and a type of bank. Commercial banking is also known as business banking. It is a bank that provides checking accounts, savings accounts, and money market accounts and that accepts time deposits.

a. Commercial bank
b. 4-4-5 Calendar
c. 7-Eleven
d. 529 plan

20. _____ is consumer credit which is outstanding. In macroeconomic terms, it is debt which is used to fund consumption rather than investment.

Some consider all debt incurred for anything else other than investments unwise or detrimental to the economy, while others believe that consumer credit is beneficial to the economy.

a. Foreign exchange hedge
b. Retention ratio
c. Reinvestment risk
d. Consumer debt

21. In financial accounting, _____s are precautions for which the amount or probability of occurrence are not known. Typical examples are _____s for warranty costs and _____ for taxes the term reserve is used instead of term _____; such a use, however, is inconsistent with the terminology suggested by International Accounting Standards Board.

a. Petty cash
b. Momentum Accounting and Triple-Entry Bookkeeping
c. Money measurement concept
d. Provision

22. _____ is that which is owed; usually referencing assets owed, but the term can cover other obligations. In the case of assets, _____ is a means of using future purchasing power in the present before a summation has been earned. Some companies and corporations use _____ as a part of their overall corporate finance strategy.

a. Debt
b. Partial Payment
c. Credit cycle
d. Cross-collateralization

23. A _____, reserve bank, or monetary authority is the entity responsible for the monetary policy of a country or of a group of member states. It is a bank that can lend money to other banks in times of need. Its primary responsibility is to maintain the stability of the national currency and money supply, but more active duties include controlling subsidized-loan interest rates, and acting as a lender of last resort to the banking sector during times of financial crisis (private banks often being integral to the national financial system.)

a. 7-Eleven
b. 4-4-5 Calendar
c. 529 plan
d. Central bank

24. _____ plant, and equipment, is a term used in accountancy for assets and property which cannot easily be converted into cash. This can be compared with current assets such as cash or bank accounts, which are described as liquid assets. In most cases, only tangible assets are referred to as fixed.

a. Remittance advice
c. Petty cash
b. Percentage of Completion
d. Fixed asset

25. A '_____' is a 'Charge' that is paid to obtain the right to delay a payment. Essentially, the payer purchases the right to make a given payment in the future instead of in the Present. The '_____', or 'Charge' that must be paid to delay the payment, is simply the difference between what the payment amount would be if it were paid in the present and what the payment amount would be paid if it were paid in the future.
   a. Risk aversion
   c. Discount
   b. Risk modeling
   d. Value at risk

26. A _____ is a current account at a banking institution that allows money to be deposited and withdrawn by the account holder, with the transactions and resulting balance being recorded on the bank's books. Some banks charge a fee for this service, while others may pay the customer interest on the funds deposited.

Although restrictions placed on access depend upon the terms and conditions of the account and the provider, the account holder retains rights to have their funds repaid on demand.

   a. 4-4-5 Calendar
   c. Bilateral netting
   b. Contractum trinius
   d. Deposit account

27. _____ is an accounting term used to reflect the portion of the book value of a business entity not directly attributable to its assets and liabilities; it normally arises only in case of an acquisition. It reflects the ability of the entity to make a higher profit than would be derived from selling the tangible assets. _____ is also known as an intangible asset.
   a. Goodwill
   c. Consolidation
   b. Cost of goods sold
   d. Net profit

28. _____ are defined as identifiable non-monetary assets that cannot be seen, touched or physically measured, which are created through time and/or effort and that are identifiable as a separate asset. There are two primary forms of intangibles - legal intangibles (such as trade secrets (e.g., customer lists), copyrights, patents, trademarks, and goodwill) and competitive intangibles (such as knowledge activities (know-how, knowledge), collaboration activities, leverage activities, and structural activities.) Legal intangibles generate legal property rights defensible in a court of law.
   a. AAB
   c. A Random Walk Down Wall Street
   b. ABN Amro
   d. Intangible assets

29. In finance, the _____ is the global financial market for short-term borrowing and lending. It provides short-term liquidity funding for the global financial system. The _____ is where short-term obligations such as Treasury bills, commercial paper and bankers' acceptances are bought and sold.
   a. Debt-for-equity swap
   c. Cramdown
   b. Consumer debt
   d. Money market

30. A _____ is a professionally managed type of collective investment scheme that pools money from many investors and invests it in stocks, bonds, short-term money market instruments, and/or other securities. The _____ will have a fund manager that trades the pooled money on a regular basis. Currently, the worldwide value of all _____s totals more than $26 trillion.

Since 1940, there have been three basic types of investment companies in the United States: open-end funds, also known in the US as _____ s; unit investment trusts (UITs); and closed-end funds.

a. Financial intermediary
b. Net asset value
c. Trust company
d. Mutual fund

31. A _____ is a money deposit at a banking institution that cannot be withdrawn for a certain 'term' or period of time. When the term is over it can be withdrawn or it can be held for another term. Generally speaking, the longer the term the better the yield on the money.
a. Certificate of deposit
b. Basel Accord
c. Private money
d. Time deposit

32. _____ is a type of bank account where the money in the account is legally able to be withdrawn immediately upon demand (or 'at call'.) This type of bank account can also be referred to as a 'cheque' or 'checking' or transactional account.

This type of bank account, allowing immediate conversion of the account balance into cash or withdrawal to another account, can be contrasted with a time deposit (also known as a certificate of deposit or term deposit), where the funds are not legally available for immediate withdrawal by the depositor.

a. Demand deposit
b. 4-4-5 Calendar
c. Synthetic lease
d. 529 plan

33. In the global money market, _____ is an unsecured promissory note with a fixed maturity of one to 270 days. _____ is a money-market security issued (sold) by large banks and corporations to get money to meet short term debt obligations (for example, payroll), and is only backed by an issuing bank or corporation's promise to pay the face amount on the maturity date specified on the note. Since it is not backed by collateral, only firms with excellent credit ratings from a recognized rating agency will be able to sell their _____ at a reasonable price.
a. Book building
b. Trade-off theory
c. Financial distress
d. Commercial paper

34. _____ is a form of corporation equity ownership represented in the securities. It is dangerous in comparison to preferred shares and some other investment options, in that in the event of bankruptcy, _____ investors receive their funds after preferred stockholders, bondholders, creditors, etc. On the other hand, common shares on average perform better than preferred shares or bonds over time.
a. Stock market bubble
b. Stock split
c. Stop-limit order
d. Common stock

35. _____ arises from situations in which a party interested in trading an asset cannot do it because nobody in the market wants to trade that asset. _____ becomes particularly important to parties who are about to hold or currently hold an asset, since it affects their ability to trade.

Manifestation of _____ is very different from a drop of price to zero.

36 Chapter 5. The Financial Statements of Banks and Their Principal Competitors

a. Currency risk
b. Credit risk
c. Liquidity risk
d. Tracking error

36. _____ is typically a higher ranking stock than voting shares, and its terms are negotiated between the corporation and the investor.

_____ usually carry no voting rights, but may carry superior priority over common stock in the payment of dividends and upon liquidation. _____ may carry a dividend that is paid out prior to any dividends to common stock holders.

a. Preferred stock
b. Follow-on offering
c. Trade-off theory
d. Second lien loan

37. In financial accounting, the _____ is one of the accounts in shareholders' equity. Sole proprietorships have a single _____ in the owner's equity. Partnerships maintain a _____ for each of the partners.

a. Capital account
b. Duty of loyalty
c. Market maker
d. Bed Bath ' Beyond Inc.

38. In accounting, _____ refers to the portion of net income which is retained by the corporation rather than distributed to its owners as dividends. Similarly, if the corporation makes a loss, then that loss is retained and called variously retained losses, accumulated losses or accumulated deficit. _____ and losses are cumulative from year to year with losses offsetting earnings.

a. Historical cost
b. Generally Accepted Accounting Principles
c. Matching principle
d. Retained earnings

39. A _____ or reacquired stock is stock which is bought back by the issuing company, reducing the amount of outstanding stock on the open market ('open market' including insiders' holdings.)

Stock repurchases are often used as a tax-efficient method to put cash into shareholders' hands, rather than pay dividends. Sometimes, companies do this when they feel that their stock is undervalued on the open market.

a. Trial balance
b. Current asset
c. Generally Accepted Accounting Principles
d. Treasury stock

40. _____, consists of the buying and selling of products or services over electronic systems such as the Internet and other computer networks. The amount of trade conducted electronically has grown extraordinarily with widespread Internet usage. The use of commerce is conducted in this way, spurring and drawing on innovations in electronic funds transfer, supply chain management, Internet marketing, online transaction processing, electronic data interchange (EDI), inventory management systems, and automated data collection systems.

a. A Random Walk Down Wall Street
b. AAB
c. ABN Amro
d. Electronic commerce

41. _____ are formal records of a business' financial activities.

Chapter 5. The Financial Statements of Banks and Their Principal Competitors 37

_____ provide an overview of a business' financial condition in both short and long term. There are four basic _____:

1. **Balance sheet**: also referred to as statement of financial position or condition, reports on a company's assets, liabilities, and net equity as of a given point in time.
2. **Income statement**: also referred to as Profit and Loss statement (or a 'P'L'), reports on a company's income, expenses, and profits over a period of time.
3. **Statement of retained earnings**: explains the changes in a company's retained earnings over the reporting period.
4. **Statement of cash flows**: reports on a company's cash flow activities, particularly its operating, investing and financing activities.

a. Notes to the Financial Statements
b. Financial statements
c. Statement of retained earnings
d. Statement on Auditing Standards No. 70: Service Organizations

42. In finance, a _____ is a derivative whose value derives from the credit risk on an underlying bond, loan or other financial asset. In this way, the credit risk is on an entity other than the counterparties to the transaction itself. This entity is known as the reference entity and may be a corporate, a sovereign or any other form of legal entity which has incurred debt.
a. Derivatives markets
b. Futures contract
c. STIRT
d. Credit derivative

43. A _____ is an exchange of promises between two or more parties to do an act which is enforceable in a court of law. It is where an unqualified offer meets a qualified acceptance and the parties reach Consensus ad Idem. The parties must have the necessary capacity to _____ and the _____ must not be either trifling, indeterminate, impossible or illegal.
a. 529 plan
b. 7-Eleven
c. 4-4-5 Calendar
d. Contract

44. A _____ is a financial contract whose value is derived from the value of something else (known as the underlying.) The underlying on which a _____ is based can be an asset, weather conditions bonds or other forms of credit.
a. 7-Eleven
b. 529 plan
c. 4-4-5 Calendar
d. Derivative

45. The role of the _____ is to issue accounting standards in the United Kingdom. It is recognised for that purpose under the Companies Act 1985. It took over the task of setting accounting standards from the Accounting Standards Committee (ASC) in 1990.
a. A Random Walk Down Wall Street
b. Accounting Standards Board
c. ABN Amro
d. AAB

46. _____ is the field of accountancy concerned with the preparation of financial statements for decision makers, such as stockholders, suppliers, banks, employees, government agencies, owners, and other stakeholders. The fundamental need for _____ is to reduce principal-agent problem by measuring and monitoring agents' performance and reporting the results to interested users.

Chapter 5. The Financial Statements of Banks and Their Principal Competitors

_____ is used to prepare accounting information for people outside the organization or not involved in the day to day running of the company.

a. 7-Eleven
b. 529 plan
c. 4-4-5 Calendar
d. Financial Accounting

47. The _____ is a private, not-for-profit organization whose primary purpose is to develop generally accepted accounting principles (GAAP) within the United States in the public's interest. The Securities and Exchange Commission (SEC) designated the _____ as the organization responsible for setting accounting standards for public companies in the U.S. It was created in 1973, replacing the Accounting Principles Board and the Committee on Accounting Procedure of the American Institute of Certified Public Accountants. The _____'s mission is 'to establish and improve standards of financial accounting and reporting for the guidance and education of the public, including issuers, auditors, and users of financial information.'

The _____ is not a governmental body.

a. KPMG
b. Financial Accounting Standards Board
c. World Congress of Accountants
d. Federal Deposit Insurance Corporation

48. _____ is the process of decreasing an amount over a period of time. The word comes from Middle English amortisen to kill, alienate in mortmain, from Anglo-French amorteser, alteration of amortir, from Vulgar Latin admortire to kill, from Latin ad- + mort-, mors death. Particular instances of the term include:

- _____ (business), the allocation of a lump sum amount to different time periods, particularly for loans and other forms of finance, including related interest or other finance charges.
    - _____ schedule, a table detailing each periodic payment on a loan (typically a mortgage), as generated by an _____ calculator.
    - Negative _____, an _____ schedule where the loan amount actually increases through not paying the full interest
- Amortized analysis, analyzing the execution cost of algorithms over a sequence of operations.
- _____ of capital expenditures of certain assets under accounting rules, particularly intangible assets, in a manner analogous to depreciation.
- _____ (tax law)

_____ is also used in the context of zoning regulations and describes the time in which a property owner has to relocate when the property's use constitutes a preexisting nonconforming use under zoning regulations.

- Depreciation

a. Intrinsic value
b. Option
c. AT'T Inc.
d. Amortization

49. _____ are securities that can be easily converted into cash. Such securities will generally have highly liquid markets allowing the security to be sold at a reasonable price very quickly. This is a usual feature in real estate .

Chapter 5. The Financial Statements of Banks and Their Principal Competitors 39

a. Securities lending
b. Marketable
c. Tracking stock
d. Book entry

50. The U.S. _____ is an independent agency of the United States government which holds primary responsibility for enforcing the federal securities laws and regulating the securities industry, the nation's stock and options exchanges, and other electronic securities markets. The SEC was created by section 4 of the SEC of 1934 (now codified as 15 U.S.C. § 78d and commonly referred to as the 1934 Act.)
   a. 529 plan
   b. 7-Eleven
   c. 4-4-5 Calendar
   d. Securities and Exchange Commission

51. In economics, business, and accounting, a _____ is the value of money that has been used up to produce something, and hence is not available for use anymore. In business, the _____ may be one of acquisition, in which case the amount of money expended to acquire it is counted as _____. In this case, money is the input that is gone in order to acquire the thing.
   a. Marginal cost
   b. Cost
   c. Sliding scale fees
   d. Fixed costs

52. In management accounting, _____ is that part of management accounting which establishes budget and actual cost of operations, processes, departments or product and the analysis of variances, profitability or social use of funds. Managers use _____ to support decision making to reduce a company's costs and improve its profitability. As a form of management accounting, _____ need not follow standards such as GAAP, because its primary use is for internal managers, rather than external users, and what to compute is instead decided pragmatically.
   a. Sliding scale fees
   b. Cost accounting
   c. Variable costs
   d. Marginal cost

53. _____ is equal to the income that a firm has after subtracting costs and expenses from the total revenue. _____ can be distributed among holders of common stock as a dividend or held by the firm as retained earnings. _____ is an accounting term; in some countries (such as the UK) profit is the usual term.
   a. Furniture, Fixtures and Equipment
   b. Historical cost
   c. Write-off
   d. Net income

54. In business, _____ is income that a company receives from its normal business activities, usually from the sale of goods and services to customers. Some companies also receive _____ from interest, dividends or royalties paid to them by other companies. _____ may refer to business income in general, or it may refer to the amount, in a monetary unit, received during a period of time, as in 'Last year, Company X had _____ of $32 million.'

In many countries, including the UK, _____ is referred to as turnover.

   a. Revenue
   b. Matching principle
   c. Bottom line
   d. Furniture, Fixtures and Equipment

55. In business and finance, a _____ (also referred to as equity _____) of stock means a _____ of ownership in a corporation (company.) In the plural, stocks is often used as a synonym for _____s especially in the United States, but it is less commonly used that way outside of North America.

In the United Kingdom, South Africa, and Australia, stock can also refer to completely different financial instruments such as government bonds or, less commonly, to all kinds of marketable securities.

   a. Margin   b. Procter ' Gamble
   c. Share   d. Bucket shop

56. _____ is a fee paid on borrowed assets. It is the price paid for the use of borrowed money , or, money earned by deposited funds . Assets that are sometimes lent with _____ include money, shares, consumer goods through hire purchase, major assets such as aircraft, and even entire factories in finance lease arrangements.
   a. Insolvency   b. A Random Walk Down Wall Street
   c. AAB   d. Interest

57. _____ relates to the cost of borrowing money. It is the price that a lender charges a borrower for the use of the lender's money. _____ is different from OPEX and CAPEX, for it relates to the capital structure of a company.
   a. ABN Amro   b. A Random Walk Down Wall Street
   c. AAB   d. Interest expense

58. In finance, a _____ is collateral that the holder of a position in securities, options, or futures contracts has to deposit to cover the credit risk of his counterparty (most often his broker.) This risk can arise if the holder has done any of the following:

- borrowed cash from the counterparty to buy securities or options,
- sold securities or options short, or
- entered into a futures contract.

The collateral can be in the form of cash or securities, and it is deposited in a _____ account. On U.S. futures exchanges, '_____' was formally called performance bond.

_____ buying is buying securities with cash borrowed from a broker, using other securities as collateral.

   a. Margin   b. Procter ' Gamble
   c. Credit   d. Share

59. The _____ Act is an Act of the 106th United States Congress which repealed part of the Glass-Steagall Act of 1933, opening up competition among banks, securities companies and insurance companies. The Glass-Steagall Act prohibited any one institution from acting as both an investment bank and a commercial bank, or as both a bank and an insurer.

The _____ Act (GLBA) allowed commercial and investment banks to consolidate.

   a. 529 plan   b. 4-4-5 Calendar
   c. Gramm-Leach-Bliley   d. 7-Eleven

60. _____ is the difference between operating revenues and operating expenses, but it is also sometimes used as a synonym for EBIT and operating profit. This is true if the firm has no non-_____.

Chapter 5. The Financial Statements of Banks and Their Principal Competitors 41

A professional investor contemplating a change to the capital structure of a firm (e.g., through a leveraged buyout) first evaluates a firm's fundamental earnings potential (reflected by Earnings Before Interest, Taxes, Depreciation and Amortization EBITDA and EBIT), and then determines the optimal use of debt vs. equity.

a. ABN Amro
b. AAB
c. A Random Walk Down Wall Street
d. Operating income

61. A _____ is a payment made by a corporation to its shareholder members. When a corporation earns a profit or surplus, that money can be put to two uses: it can either be re-invested in the business (called retained earnings), or it can be paid to the shareholders as a _____. Many corporations retain a portion of their earnings and pay the remainder as a _____.

a. Dividend yield
b. Special dividend
c. Dividend
d. Dividend puzzle

62. The _____ duty is a legal relationship of confidence or trust between two or more parties, most commonly a _____ or trustee and a principal or beneficiary. One party, for example a corporate trust company or the trust department of a bank, holds a _____ relation or acts in a _____ capacity to another, such as one whose funds are entrusted to it for investment. In a _____ relation one person justifiably reposes confidence, good faith, reliance and trust in another whose aid, advice or protection is sought in some matter.

a. Financial Institutions Reform Recovery and Enforcement Act
b. Fiduciary
c. General obligation
d. Legal tender

63. _____ is the difference between price and the costs of bringing to market whatever it is that is accounted as an enterprise (whether by harvest, extraction, manufacture, or purchase) in terms of the component costs of delivered goods and/or services and any operating or other expenses.

A key difficulty in measuring profit is in defining costs. Pure economic monetary profits can be zero or negative even in competitive equilibrium when accounted monetized costs exceed monetized price.

a. Economic profit
b. A Random Walk Down Wall Street
c. AAB
d. Accounting profit

64. _____ and earnings management are euphemisms referring to accounting practices that may follow the letter of the rules of standard accounting practices, but certainly deviate from the spirit of those rules. They are characterized by excessive complication and the use of novel ways of characterizing income, assets, or liabilities and the intent to influence readers towards the interpretations desired by the authors. The terms 'innovative' or 'aggressive' are also sometimes used.

a. Non Performing Asset
b. Debit and credit
c. Creative accounting
d. Controlling account

65. An account statement or a _____ is a summary of all financial transactions occurring over a given period of time on a deposit account, a credit card, or any other type of account offered by a financial institution.

Chapter 5. The Financial Statements of Banks and Their Principal Competitors

_____s are typically printed on one or several pieces of paper and either mailed directly to the account holder's address, or kept at the financial institution's local branch for pick-up. Certain ATMs offer the possibility to print, at any time, a condensed version of a _____.

   a. Deposit account   b. 4-4-5 Calendar
   c. Bank statement   d. Bilateral netting

66. _____ is the balance of the amounts of cash being received and paid by a business during a defined period of time, sometimes tied to a specific project. Measurement of _____ can be used

- to evaluate the state or performance of a business or project.
- to determine problems with liquidity. Being profitable does not necessarily mean being liquid. A company can fail because of a shortage of cash, even while profitable.
- to generate project rate of returns. The time of _____s into and out of projects are used as inputs to financial models such as internal rate of return, and net present value.
- to examine income or growth of a business when it is believed that accrual accounting concepts do not represent economic realities. Alternately, _____ can be used to 'validate' the net income generated by accrual accounting.

_____ as a generic term may be used differently depending on context, and certain _____ definitions may be adapted by analysts and users for their own uses. Common terms include operating _____ and free _____.

_____s can be classified into:

1. Operational _____s: Cash received or expended as a result of the company's core business activities.
2. Investment _____s: Cash received or expended through capital expenditure, investments or acquisitions.
3. Financing _____s: Cash received or expended as a result of financial activities, such as interests and dividends.

All three together - the net _____ - are necessary to reconcile the beginning cash balance to the ending cash balance. Loan draw downs or equity injections, that is just shifting of capital but no expenditure as such, are not considered in the net _____.

   a. Corporate finance   b. Real option
   c. Shareholder value   d. Cash flow

67. In financial accounting, a _____ or statement of cash flows is a financial statement that shows a company's flow of cash. The money coming into the business is called cash inflow, and money going out from the business is called cash outflow. The statement shows how changes in balance sheet and income accounts affect cash and cash equivalents, and breaks the analysis down to operating, investing, and financing activities.

   a. Cash flow statement   b. 7-Eleven
   c. 4-4-5 Calendar   d. 529 plan

68. _____ is one of a series of accounting transactions dealing with the billing of customers who owe money to a person, company or organization for goods and services that have been provided to the customer. In most business entities this is typically done by generating an invoice and mailing or electronically delivering it to the customer, who in turn must pay it within an established timeframe called credit or payment terms.

An example of a common payment term is Net 30, meaning payment is due in the amount of the invoice 30 days from the date of invoice.

a. Accounting methods
c. Impaired asset
b. Income
d. Accounts receivable

Chapter 6. Measuring and Evaluating the Performance of Banks and Their Competitors

1. _____ is the provision of resources (such as granting a loan) by one party to another party where that second party does not reimburse the first party immediately, thereby generating a debt, and instead arranges either to repay or return those resources (or material(s) of equal value) at a later date. The first party is called a creditor, also known as a lender, while the second party is called a debtor, also known as a borrower.

Movements of financial capital are normally dependent on either _____ or equity transfers.

- a. Clearing house
- b. Warrant
- c. Comparable
- d. Credit

2. A _____ is a pool of assets forming an independent legal entity that are bought with the contributions to a pension plan for the exclusive purpose of financing pension plan benefits.

_____s are important shareholders of listed and private companies. They are especially important to the stock market where large institutional investors like the Ontario Teachers' Pension Plan dominate.

- a. Leverage
- b. Limited liability company
- c. Leveraged buyout
- d. Pension fund

3. In economics, business, and accounting, a _____ is the value of money that has been used up to produce something, and hence is not available for use anymore. In business, the _____ may be one of acquisition, in which case the amount of money expended to acquire it is counted as _____. In this case, money is the input that is gone in order to acquire the thing.

- a. Sliding scale fees
- b. Fixed costs
- c. Marginal cost
- d. Cost

4. The _____ is an expected return that the provider of capital plans to earn on their investment.

Capital (money) used for funding a business should earn returns for the capital providers who risk their capital. For an investment to be worthwhile, the expected return on capital must be greater than the _____.

- a. Weighted average cost of capital
- b. 4-4-5 Calendar
- c. Capital intensity
- d. Cost of capital

5. _____ is a term coined in 1985 by economists Rajnish Mehra and Edward C. Prescott. It is based on the observation that in order to reconcile the much higher return on equity stock compared to government bonds in the United States, individuals must have implausibly high risk aversion according to standard economics models. Similar situations prevail in many other industrialized countries.

- a. The equity premium puzzle
- b. Perth Leadership Outcome Model
- c. Loss aversion
- d. Quantitative behavioral finance

6. _____ is that which is owed; usually referencing assets owed, but the term can cover other obligations. In the case of assets, _____ is a means of using future purchasing power in the present before a summation has been earned. Some companies and corporations use _____ as a part of their overall corporate finance strategy.

- a. Credit cycle
- b. Debt
- c. Partial Payment
- d. Cross-collateralization

Chapter 6. Measuring and Evaluating the Performance of Banks and Their Competitors

7. _____ is a fee paid on borrowed assets. It is the price paid for the use of borrowed money, or, money earned by deposited funds. Assets that are sometimes lent with _____ include money, shares, consumer goods through hire purchase, major assets such as aircraft, and even entire factories in finance lease arrangements.
   a. AAB
   b. A Random Walk Down Wall Street
   c. Interest
   d. Insolvency

8.

In finance, the _____ can be the expected rate of return above the risk-free interest rate. When measuring risk, a common sense approach is to compare the risk-free return on T-bills and the very risky return on other investments. The difference between these two returns can be interpreted as a measure of the excess return on the average risky asset. This excess return is known as the _____.

   a. Risk adjusted return on capital
   b. Risk modeling
   c. Risk aversion
   d. Risk premium

9. _____ are the earnings returned on the initial investment amount.

In the US, the Financial Accounting Standards Board (FASB) requires companies' income statements to report _____ for each of the major categories of the income statement: continuing operations, discontinued operations, extraordinary items, and net income.

The _____ formula does not include preferred dividends for categories outside of continued operations and net income.

   a. Inventory turnover
   b. Average accounting return
   c. Assets turnover
   d. Earnings per share

10. _____ is subcontracting a process, such as product design or manufacturing, to a third-party company. The decision to outsource is often made in the interest of lowering cost or making better use of time and energy costs, redirecting or conserving energy directed at the competencies of a particular business, or to make more efficient use of land, labor, capital, (information) technology and resources. _____ became part of the business lexicon during the 1980s.
    a. Exchange Rate Mechanism
    b. OTC Bulletin Board
    c. AT'T Inc.
    d. Outsourcing

11. The _____ percentage shows how profitable a company's assets are in generating revenue.

_____ can be computed as:

$$ROA = \frac{\text{Net Income}}{\text{Total Assets}}$$

This number tells you 'what the company can do with what it's got', i.e. how many dollars of earnings they derive from each dollar of assets they control. It's a useful number for comparing competing companies in the same industry.

46   Chapter 6. Measuring and Evaluating the Performance of Banks and Their Competitors

   a. Return on sales
   c. P/E ratio
   b. Receivables turnover ratio
   d. Return on assets

12. _____ measures the rate of return on the ownership interest (shareholders' equity) of the common stock owners. _____ is viewed as one of the most important financial ratios. It measures a firm's efficiency at generating profits from every dollar of shareholders' equity (also known as net assets or assets minus liabilities.)
   a. Return on equity
   c. Return of capital
   b. Diluted Earnings Per Share
   d. Return on sales

13. In business and accounting, _____s are everything of value that is owned by a person or company. The balance sheet of a firm records the monetary value of the _____s owned by the firm. The two major _____ classes are tangible _____s and intangible _____s.
   a. Accounts payable
   c. Income
   b. Asset
   d. EBITDA

14. _____, consists of the buying and selling of products or services over electronic systems such as the Internet and other computer networks. The amount of trade conducted electronically has grown extraordinarily with widespread Internet usage. The use of commerce is conducted in this way, spurring and drawing on innovations in electronic funds transfer, supply chain management, Internet marketing, online transaction processing, electronic data interchange (EDI), inventory management systems, and automated data collection systems.
   a. ABN Amro
   c. AAB
   b. Electronic commerce
   d. A Random Walk Down Wall Street

15. In finance, a _____ is collateral that the holder of a position in securities, options, or futures contracts has to deposit to cover the credit risk of his counterparty (most often his broker.) This risk can arise if the holder has done any of the following:

   • borrowed cash from the counterparty to buy securities or options,
   • sold securities or options short, or
   • entered into a futures contract.

The collateral can be in the form of cash or securities, and it is deposited in a _____ account. On U.S. futures exchanges, '_____' was formally called performance bond.

_____ buying is buying securities with cash borrowed from a broker, using other securities as collateral.

   a. Credit
   c. Procter ' Gamble
   b. Share
   d. Margin

16. In business, operating margin, operating income margin, _____ or return on sales (ROS) is the ratio of operating income (operating profit in the UK) divided by net sales, usually presented in percent.

>

(Relevant figures in italics)

Chapter 6. Measuring and Evaluating the Performance of Banks and Their Competitors 47

It is a measurement of what proportion of a company's revenue is left over, before taxes and other indirect costs (such as rent, bonus, interest, etc.), after paying for variable costs of production as wages, raw materials, etc. A good operating margin is needed for a company to be able to pay for its fixed costs, such as interest on debt.

- a. Operating leverage
- b. Operating profit margin
- c. Average rate of return
- d. Interest coverage ratio

17. In business and finance, a _____ (also referred to as equity _____) of stock means a _____ of ownership in a corporation (company.) In the plural, stocks is often used as a synonym for _____s especially in the United States, but it is less commonly used that way outside of North America.

In the United Kingdom, South Africa, and Australia, stock can also refer to completely different financial instruments such as government bonds or, less commonly, to all kinds of marketable securities.

- a. Procter ' Gamble
- b. Bucket shop
- c. Margin
- d. Share

18.

A _____ is a type of financial intermediary and a type of bank. Commercial banking is also known as business banking. It is a bank that provides checking accounts, savings accounts, and money market accounts and that accepts time deposits.

- a. 7-Eleven
- b. 4-4-5 Calendar
- c. Commercial bank
- d. 529 plan

19. In business and finance accounting, _____ is equal to the gross profit minus overheads minus interest payable plus/minus one off items for a given time period (usually: accounting period.)

A common synonym for '_____' when discussing financial statements (which include a balance sheet and an income statement) is the bottom line. This term results from the traditional appearance of an income statement which shows all allocated revenues and expenses over a specified time period with the resulting summation on the bottom line of the report.

- a. Net profit
- b. Salvage value
- c. Deferred
- d. Gross sales

20. Profit margin, net margin, _____ or net profit ratio all refer to a measure of profitability. It is calculated by finding the net profit as a percentage of the revenue.

The profit margin is mostly used for internal comparison.

a. Profit margin
b. 4-4-5 Calendar
c. Profit maximization
d. Net profit margin

21. _____ is the difference between price and the costs of bringing to market whatever it is that is accounted as an enterprise (whether by harvest, extraction, manufacture, or purchase) in terms of the component costs of delivered goods and/or services and any operating or other expenses.

A key difficulty in measuring profit is in defining costs. Pure economic monetary profits can be zero or negative even in competitive equilibrium when accounted monetized costs exceed monetized price.

a. Economic profit
b. AAB
c. A Random Walk Down Wall Street
d. Accounting profit

22. _____, Net Margin, Net _____ or Net Profit Ratio all refer to a measure of profitability. It is calculated using a formula and written as a percentage or a number.

$$\text{Net profit margin} = \frac{\text{Net profit after taxes}}{\text{Net Sales}}$$

The _____ is mostly used for internal comparison.

a. Net profit margin
b. Profit maximization
c. 4-4-5 Calendar
d. Profit margin

23. The term _____ is often used to refer to the investment management of collective investments, (not necessarily) whilst the more generic fund management may refer to all forms of institutional investment as well as investment management for private investors. Investment managers who specialize in advisory or discretionary management on behalf of (normally wealthy) private investors may often refer to their services as wealth management or portfolio management often within the context of so-called 'private banking'.

The provision of 'investment management services' includes elements of financial analysis, asset selection, stock selection, plan implementation and ongoing monitoring of investments.

a. A Random Walk Down Wall Street
b. ABN Amro
c. AAB
d. Asset management

24. The _____ is a United States government corporation created by the Glass-Steagall Act of 1933. It provides deposit insurance, which guarantees the safety of checking and savings deposits in member banks, currently up to $250,000 per depositor per bank. Insured deposits are backed by the full faith and credit of the United States.

a. Ford Foundation
b. FASB
c. NYSE Group
d. Federal Deposit Insurance Corporation

Chapter 6. Measuring and Evaluating the Performance of Banks and Their Competitors   49

25. The _____ is a measure of how revenue growth translates into growth in operating income. It is a measure of leverage, and of how risky (volatile) a company's operating income is.

There are various measures of _____, which can be interpreted analogously to financial leverage.

a. Asset turnover
c. Invested capital

b. Average accounting return
d. Operating leverage

26. In finance, _____ (or gearing) is borrowing money to supplement existing funds for investment in such a way that the potential positive or negative outcome is magnified and/or enhanced. It generally refers to using borrowed funds, or debt, so as to attempt to increase the returns to equity. Deleveraging is the action of reducing borrowings.

a. Pension fund
c. Limited partnership

b. Financial endowment
d. Leverage

27. _____ is the risk of loss due to a debtor's non-payment of a loan or other line of credit (either the principal or interest (coupon) or both)

Most lenders employ their own models (credit scorecards) to rank potential and existing customers according to risk, and then apply appropriate strategies. With products such as unsecured personal loans or mortgages, lenders charge a higher price for higher risk customers and vice versa. With revolving products such as credit cards and overdrafts, risk is controlled through careful setting of credit limits.

a. Market risk
c. Transaction risk

b. Liquidity risk
d. Credit risk

28. _____ refers to the use of formal econometric techniques to determine the aggregate risk in a financial portfolio. _____ is one of many subtasks within the broader area of financial modeling.

_____ uses a variety of techniques including market risk, Value-at-Risk (VaR), Historical Simulation (HS), or Extreme Value Theory (EVT) in order to analyze a portfolio and make forecasts of the likely losses that would be incurred for a variety of risks.

a. Risk modeling
c. Value at risk

b. Risk premium
d. Risk adjusted return on capital

29. _____ is a measure of the ability of a debtor to pay their debts as and when they fall due. It is usually expressed as a ratio or a percentage of current liabilities.

For a corporation with a published balance sheet there are various ratios used to calculate a measure of liquidity.

a. Operating leverage
c. Accounting liquidity

b. Operating profit margin
d. Invested capital

30. _____ arises from situations in which a party interested in trading an asset cannot do it because nobody in the market wants to trade that asset. _____ becomes particularly important to parties who are about to hold or currently hold an asset, since it affects their ability to trade.

50   Chapter 6. Measuring and Evaluating the Performance of Banks and Their Competitors

Manifestation of _____ is very different from a drop of price to zero.

a. Liquidity risk
b. Currency risk
c. Credit risk
d. Tracking error

31. _____ is the risk that the value of an investment will decrease due to moves in market factors. The five standard _____ factors are:

- Equity risk, the risk that stock prices will change.
- Interest rate risk, the risk that interest rates will change.
- Currency risk, the risk that foreign exchange rates will change.
- Commodity risk, the risk that commodity prices (e.g. grains, metals) will change.

As with other forms of risk, _____ may be measured in a number of ways. Traditionally, this is done using a Value at Risk methodology. Value at risk is well established as a risk management technique, but it contains a number of limiting assumptions that constrain its accuracy.

a. Currency risk
b. Tracking error
c. Transaction risk
d. Market risk

32. An _____ is a risk arising from execution of a company's business functions. As such, it is a very broad concept including e.g. fraud risks, legal risks, physical or environmental risks, etc. The term _____ is most commonly found in risk management programs of financial institutions that must organize their risk management program according to Basel II.

a. ABN Amro
b. AAB
c. A Random Walk Down Wall Street
d. Operational risk

33. An _____ is the price a borrower pays for the use of money they do not own, and the return a lender receives for deferring the use of funds, by lending it to the borrower. _____s are normally expressed as a percentage rate over the period of one year.

_____s targets are also a vital tool of monetary policy and are used to control variables like investment, inflation, and unemployment.

a. AAB
b. ABN Amro
c. A Random Walk Down Wall Street
d. Interest rate

34. _____ is the risk (variability in value) borne by an interest-bearing asset, such as a loan or a bond, due to variability of interest rates. In general, as rates rise, the price of a fixed rate bond will fall, and vice versa. _____ is commonly measured by the bond's duration.

a. International Fisher effect
b. A Random Walk Down Wall Street
c. Official bank rate
d. Interest rate risk

35. _____: Sometimes governments change the law in a way that adversely affects a bank's position.

Chapter 6. Measuring and Evaluating the Performance of Banks and Their Competitors   51

The Risk Principle is an area of law closely tied to legal causation in negligence. It provides limits on negligence for harm caused unforeseeably.

a. Legal and regulatory risk
b. Federal Work Study program
c. Flow to Equity-Approach
d. Price channel

36. The institution most often referenced by the word '_____' is a public or publicly traded _____, the shares of which are traded on a public stock exchange (e.g., the New York Stock Exchange or Nasdaq in the United States) where shares of stock of _____s are bought and sold by and to the general public. Most of the largest businesses in the world are publicly traded _____s. However, the majority of _____s are said to be closely held, privately held or close _____s, meaning that no ready market exists for the trading of shares.

a. Depository Trust Company
b. Federal Home Loan Mortgage Corporation
c. Protect
d. Corporation

37. An _____ is a corporation that makes a valid election to be taxed under Subchapter S of Chapter 1 of the Internal Revenue Code.

In general, _____s do not pay any income taxes. Instead, the corporation's income or losses are divided among and passed through to its shareholders.

a. 7-Eleven
b. 4-4-5 Calendar
c. 529 plan
d. S corporation

38. The _____ is a free-trade and professional association that promotes and advocates issues important to the banking industry in the United States. The _____'s national headquarters are in Washington, D.C. In addition to its trade association mission, the _____ also performs educational components for consumers through its Educational Foundation affiliate.

While the _____ works on a national level, it also is supported by state operated offices (sometimes referred to as 'Leagues') which focus attention on state level support.

a. A Random Walk Down Wall Street
b. ABN Amro
c. AAB
d. American Bankers Association

39. A _____ or bank is a financial institution whose primary activity is to act as a payment agent for customers and to borrow and lend money.

The first modern bank was founded in Italy in Genoa in 1406, its name was Banco di San Giorgio (Bank of St. George.)

Many other financial activities were added over time.

a. Bought deal
b. Banker
c. 4-4-5 Calendar
d. Black Sea Trade and Development Bank

Chapter 6. Measuring and Evaluating the Performance of Banks and Their Competitors

40. A _____ is a cooperative financial institution that is owned and controlled by its members, and operated for the purpose of promoting thrift, providing credit at reasonable rates, and providing other financial services to its members. Many _____s exist to further community development or sustainable international development on a local level. Worldwide, _____ systems vary significantly in terms of total system assets and average institution asset size since _____s exist in a wide range of sizes, ranging from volunteer operations with a handful of members to institutions with several billion dollars in assets and hundreds of thousands of members.

   a. Corporate credit union
   b. Fi-linx
   c. Credit Union Service Organization
   d. Credit Union

41. _____ refer to services provided by the finance industry.

The finance industry encompasses a broad range of organizations that deal with the management of money. Among these organizations are banks, credit card companies, insurance companies, consumer finance companies, stock brokerages, investment funds and some government sponsored enterprises.

   a. Cost of carry
   b. Delta hedging
   c. Financial services
   d. Financial instruments

42. _____, refers to consumption opportunity gained by an entity within a specified time frame, which is generally expressed in monetary terms. However, for households and individuals, '_____ is the sum of all the wages, salaries, profits, interests payments, rents and other forms of earnings received... in a given period of time.' For firms, _____ generally refers to net-profit: what remains of revenue after expenses have been subtracted.

   a. Accrual
   b. Annual report
   c. Income
   d. OIBDA

43. An _____ is a company whose main business is holding securities of other companies purely for investment purposes. The _____ invests money on behalf of its shareholders who in turn share in the profits and losses.

   a. Investment Company
   b. A Random Walk Down Wall Street
   c. Unit investment trust
   d. AAB

44. The _____ is the national association of U.S. investment companies. _____ encourages adherence to high ethical standards, promotes public understanding of funds and investing, and advances the interests of investment funds and their shareholders, directors, and advisers.

As of July 1, 2008, _____ membership included 9,067 mutual funds, 675 closed-end funds, 625 exchange-traded funds (ETFs), and three sponsors of unit investment trust (UITs.)

   a. AAB
   b. A Random Walk Down Wall Street
   c. ABN Amro
   d. Investment Company Institute

45. In financial accounting, the term _____ is most commonly used to describe any part of shareholders' equity, except for basic share capital. Sometimes, the term is used instead of the term provision; such a use, however, is inconsistent with the terminology suggested by International Accounting Standards Board. For more information about provisions, see provision (accounting.)

Chapter 6. Measuring and Evaluating the Performance of Banks and Their Competitors

a. FIFO and LIFO accounting
b. Closing entries
c. Treasury stock
d. Reserve

46. A _____, reserve bank, or monetary authority is the entity responsible for the monetary policy of a country or of a group of member states. It is a bank that can lend money to other banks in times of need. Its primary responsibility is to maintain the stability of the national currency and money supply, but more active duties include controlling subsidized-loan interest rates, and acting as a lender of last resort to the banking sector during times of financial crisis (private banks often being integral to the national financial system.)

a. 529 plan
b. 7-Eleven
c. 4-4-5 Calendar
d. Central bank

47. _____ is the discipline of identifying, monitoring and limiting risks. In some cases the acceptable risk may be near zero. Risks can come from accidents, natural causes and disasters as well as deliberate attacks from an adversary.

a. Penny stock
b. 4-4-5 Calendar
c. Risk Management
d. FIFO

48. In finance, a _____ is a derivative in which two counterparties agree to exchange one stream of cash flows against another stream. These streams are called the legs of the _____.

The cash flows are calculated over a notional principal amount, which is usually not exchanged between counterparties.

a. Local volatility
b. Volatility swap
c. Swap
d. Volatility arbitrage

49. In finance, the _____ is the system that allows the transfer of money between savers and borrowers.

Put another way: the _____ is a set of complex and closely interconnected financial institutions, markets, instruments, services, practices, and transactions.

a. 4-4-5 Calendar
b. Financial system
c. Passive income
d. Horizontal merger

Chapter 7. Asset-Liability Management: Determining and Measuring Interest Rates

1. In business and accounting, _____s are everything of value that is owned by a person or company. The balance sheet of a firm records the monetary value of the _____s owned by the firm. The two major _____ classes are tangible _____s and intangible _____s.
   - a. EBITDA
   - b. Accounts payable
   - c. Income
   - d. Asset

2. The term _____ is often used to refer to the investment management of collective investments, (not necessarily) whilst the more generic fund management may refer to all forms of institutional investment as well as investment management for private investors. Investment managers who specialize in advisory or discretionary management on behalf of (normally wealthy) private investors may often refer to their services as wealth management or portfolio management often within the context of so-called 'private banking'.

   The provision of 'investment management services' includes elements of financial analysis, asset selection, stock selection, plan implementation and ongoing monitoring of investments.
   - a. A Random Walk Down Wall Street
   - b. Asset management
   - c. AAB
   - d. ABN Amro

3. In finance, the _____ of a financial asset measures the sensitivity of the asset's price to interest rate movements, expressed as a number of years. The reason for expressing this sensitivity in years is that the time that will elapse until a cash flow is received allows more interest to accumulate. Therefore the price of an asset with long term cashflows has more interest rate sensitivity than an asset with cashflows in the near future.
   - a. Duration
   - b. Macaulay duration
   - c. Yield to maturity
   - d. 4-4-5 Calendar

4. A _____ is a futures contract on a short term interest rate (STIR.) Contracts vary, but are often defined on an interest rate index such as 3-month sterling or US dollar LIBOR.

   They are traded across a wide range of currencies, including the G12 country currencies and many others.
   - a. Real estate derivatives
   - b. Notional amount
   - c. Dual currency deposit
   - d. Financial future

5. _____ is a fee paid on borrowed assets. It is the price paid for the use of borrowed money, or, money earned by deposited funds. Assets that are sometimes lent with _____ include money, shares, consumer goods through hire purchase, major assets such as aircraft, and even entire factories in finance lease arrangements.
   - a. A Random Walk Down Wall Street
   - b. AAB
   - c. Insolvency
   - d. Interest

6. An _____ is the price a borrower pays for the use of money they do not own, and the return a lender receives for deferring the use of funds, by lending it to the borrower. _____s are normally expressed as a percentage rate over the period of one year.

   _____s targets are also a vital tool of monetary policy and are used to control variables like investment, inflation, and unemployment.

Chapter 7. Asset-Liability Management: Determining and Measuring Interest Rates

a. ABN Amro
b. AAB
c. Interest rate
d. A Random Walk Down Wall Street

7. In the most general sense, a _____ is anything that is a hindrance, or puts individuals at a disadvantage.

Before we discuss the financial terms, we should note that a _____ can also have a much more important slang meaning.

This is best described in an example.

a. Liability
b. Limited liability
c. Covenant
d. McFadden Act

8. An _____ is a contract written by a seller that conveys to the buyer the right -- but not the obligation -- to buy (in the case of a call _____) or to sell (in the case of a put _____) a particular asset, such as a piece of property such as, among others, a futures contract. In return for granting the _____, the seller collects a payment (the premium) from the buyer.

For example, buying a call _____ provides the right to buy a specified quantity of a security at a set strike price at some time on or before expiration, while buying a put _____ provides the right to sell.

a. Annuity
b. AT'T Mobility LLC
c. Amortization
d. Option

9. In finance, a _____ is a standardized contract, to buy or sell a specified commodity of standardized quality at a certain date in the future, at a market determined price (the futures price.)

The price is determined by the instantaneous equilibrium between the forces of supply and demand among competing buy and sell orders on the exchange at the time of the purchase or sale of the contract.

In many cases, the items may be such non-traditional 'commodities' as foreign currencies, commercial or government paper [e.g., bonds], or 'baskets' of corporate equity ['stock indices'] or other financial instruments.

a. Futures contract
b. Financial future
c. Heston model
d. Repurchase agreement

10. _____ refer to services provided by the finance industry.

The finance industry encompasses a broad range of organizations that deal with the management of money. Among these organizations are banks, credit card companies, insurance companies, consumer finance companies, stock brokerages, investment funds and some government sponsored enterprises.

a. Financial instruments
b. Cost of carry
c. Financial services
d. Delta hedging

Chapter 7. Asset-Liability Management: Determining and Measuring Interest Rates

11. _____ is the risk (variability in value) borne by an interest-bearing asset, such as a loan or a bond, due to variability of interest rates. In general, as rates rise, the price of a fixed rate bond will fall, and vice versa. _____ is commonly measured by the bond's duration.
   - a. International Fisher effect
   - b. A Random Walk Down Wall Street
   - c. Official bank rate
   - d. Interest rate risk

12. A '_____' is a 'Charge' that is paid to obtain the right to delay a payment. Essentially, the payer purchases the right to make a given payment in the future instead of in the Present. The '_____', or 'Charge' that must be paid to delay the payment, is simply the difference between what the payment amount would be if it were paid in the present and what the payment amount would be paid if it were paid in the future.
   - a. Discount
   - b. Value at risk
   - c. Risk aversion
   - d. Risk modeling

13. The _____ is an interest rate a central bank charges depository institutions that borrow reserves from it.

The term _____ has two meanings:

- the same as interest rate; the term 'discount' does not refer to the meaning of the word, but to the purpose of using the quantity, such as computations of present value, e.g. net present value / discounted cash flow

- the annual effective _____, which is the annual interest divided by the capital including that interest; this rate is lower than the interest rate; it corresponds to using the value after a year as the nominal value, and seeing the initial value as the nominal value minus a discount; it is used for Treasury Bills and similar financial instruments

The annual effective _____ is the annual interest divided by the capital including that interest, which is the interest rate divided by 100% plus the interest rate. It is the annual discount factor to be applied to the future cash flow, to find the discount, subtracted from a future value to find the value one year earlier.

For example, suppose there is a government bond that sells for $95 and pays $100 in a year's time.

   - a. Stochastic volatility
   - b. Discount rate
   - c. Fisher equation
   - d. Black-Scholes

14. _____ is one of the main genres of financial risk. The term describes the risk that a particular investment might be canceled or stopped somehow, that one may have to find a new place to invest that money with the risk being there might not be a similarly attractive investment available. This primarily occurs if bonds (which are portions of loans to entities) are paid back earlier then expected.
   - a. Standard of deferred payment
   - b. Debt cash flow
   - c. Biweekly Mortgage
   - d. Reinvestment risk

15. In finance, the term _____ describes the amount in cash that returns to the owners of a security. Normally it does not include the price variations, at the difference of the total return. _____ applies to various stated rates of return on stocks (common and preferred, and convertible), fixed income instruments (bonds, notes, bills, strips, zero coupon), and some other investment type insurance products (e.g. annuities).

Chapter 7. Asset-Liability Management: Determining and Measuring Interest Rates

a. Yield to maturity
b. 4-4-5 Calendar
c. Yield
d. Macaulay duration

16. In finance, the _____ is the relation between the interest rate (or cost of borrowing) and the time to maturity of the debt for a given borrower in a given currency. For example, the current U.S. dollar interest rates paid on U.S. Treasury securities for various maturities are closely watched by many traders, and are commonly plotted on a graph such as the one on the right which is informally called 'the _____.' More formal mathematical descriptions of this relation are often called the term structure of interest rates.

The yield of a debt instrument is the annualized percentage increase in the value of the investment.

a. 4-4-5 Calendar
b. 7-Eleven
c. 529 plan
d. Yield curve

17. The _____ or redemption yield is the yield promised to the bondholder on the assumption that the bond or other fixed-interest security such as gilts will be held to maturity, that all coupon and principal payments will be made and coupon payments are reinvested at the bond's promised yield at the same rate as invested. It is a measure of the return of the bond. This technique in theory allows investors to calculate the fair value of different financial instruments.

a. Yield
b. 4-4-5 Calendar
c. Macaulay duration
d. Yield to maturity

18. _____ is the provision of resources (such as granting a loan) by one party to another party where that second party does not reimburse the first party immediately, thereby generating a debt, and instead arranges either to repay or return those resources (or material(s) of equal value) at a later date. The first party is called a creditor, also known as a lender, while the second party is called a debtor, also known as a borrower.

Movements of financial capital are normally dependent on either _____ or equity transfers.

a. Warrant
b. Clearing house
c. Comparable
d. Credit

19. _____ is a life of security. It may also refer to the final payment date of a loan or other financial instrument, at which point all remaining interest and principal is due to be paid.

1, 3, 6 months _____ band can be calculated by using 30-day per month periods.

a. False billing
b. Primary market
c. Replacement cost
d. Maturity

20.

In finance, the _____ can be the expected rate of return above the risk-free interest rate. When measuring risk, a common sense approach is to compare the risk-free return on T-bills and the very risky return on other investments. The difference between these two returns can be interpreted as a measure of the excess return on the average risky asset. This excess return is known as the _____.

a. Risk premium
c. Risk adjusted return on capital
b. Risk aversion
d. Risk modeling

21. The '_____' is approximately the nominal interest rate minus the inflation rate Since the inflation rate over the course of a loan is not known initially, volatility in inflation represents a risk to both the lender and the borrower.

In economics and finance, an individual who lends money for repayment at a later point in time expects to be compensated for the time value of money, or not having the use of that money while it is lent.

a. Real interest rate
c. 4-4-5 Calendar
b. 529 plan
d. 7-Eleven

22. A _____ is a fungible, negotiable instrument representing financial value. They are broadly categorized into debt securities (such as banknotes, bonds and debentures), and equity securities; e.g., common stocks. The company or other entity issuing the _____ is called the issuer.
a. Tracking stock
c. Securities lending
b. Book entry
d. Security

23. In finance, the _____ is the global financial market for short-term borrowing and lending. It provides short-term liquidity funding for the global financial system. The _____ is where short-term obligations such as Treasury bills, commercial paper and bankers' acceptances are bought and sold.
a. Money market
c. Cramdown
b. Consumer debt
d. Debt-for-equity swap

24. Money funds (or _____, money market mutual funds) are mutual funds that invest in short-term debt instruments.

_____, also known as principal stability funds, seek to limit exposure to losses due to credit, market and liquidity risks.
_____, in the United States, are regulated by the Securities and Exchange Commission's (SEC) Investment Company Act of 1940.

a. Closed-end fund
c. Stock fund
b. Mutual fund fees and expenses
d. Money market funds

25. The _____ is a financial and accounting term for the difference between the duration of assets and liabilities, and is typically used by banks, pension funds, or other financial institutions to measure their risk due to changes in the interest rate. This is one of the mismatches that can occur and are known as asset liability mismatches. Another way to define _____ is : it is the difference in the sensitivity of interest-yielding assets and the sensitivity of liabilities (of the organization) to a change in market interest rates (yields.)
a. Modern portfolio theory
c. Net worth
b. Debt cash flow
d. Duration gap

Chapter 7. Asset-Liability Management: Determining and Measuring Interest Rates

26. In finance, a _____ is collateral that the holder of a position in securities, options, or futures contracts has to deposit to cover the credit risk of his counterparty (most often his broker.) This risk can arise if the holder has done any of the following:

- borrowed cash from the counterparty to buy securities or options,
- sold securities or options short, or
- entered into a futures contract.

The collateral can be in the form of cash or securities, and it is deposited in a _____ account. On U.S. futures exchanges, '_____' was formally called performance bond.

_____ buying is buying securities with cash borrowed from a broker, using other securities as collateral.

a. Credit
b. Procter ' Gamble
c. Share
d. Margin

27. _____ are liabilities that may or may not be incurred by an entity depending on the outcome of a future event such as a court case. These liabilities are recorded in a company's accounts and shown in the balance sheet when both probable and reasonably estimable. A footnote to the balance sheet describes the nature and extent of the _____.
a. 529 plan
b. Contingent liabilities
c. Due-on-sale clause
d. 4-4-5 Calendar

28. _____ is the discipline of identifying, monitoring and limiting risks. In some cases the acceptable risk may be near zero. Risks can come from accidents, natural causes and disasters as well as deliberate attacks from an adversary.
a. 4-4-5 Calendar
b. Risk Management
c. Penny stock
d. FIFO

29. In financial mathematics and financial risk management, _____ is a widely used measure of the risk of loss on a specific portfolio of financial assets. For a given portfolio, probability and time horizon, VaR is defined as a threshold value such that the probability that the mark-to-market loss on the portfolio over the given time horizon exceeds this value (assuming normal markets and no trading) is the given probability level.

For example, if a portfolio of stocks has a one-day 5% VaR of $1 million, there is a 5% probability that the portfolio will fall in value by more than $1 million over a one day period, assuming markets are normal and there is no trading.

a. Value at risk
b. Discount factor
c. Risk modeling
d. Risk aversion

30. _____, consists of the buying and selling of products or services over electronic systems such as the Internet and other computer networks. The amount of trade conducted electronically has grown extraordinarily with widespread Internet usage. The use of commerce is conducted in this way, spurring and drawing on innovations in electronic funds transfer, supply chain management, Internet marketing, online transaction processing, electronic data interchange (EDI), inventory management systems, and automated data collection systems.

Chapter 7. Asset-Liability Management: Determining and Measuring Interest Rates

a. A Random Walk Down Wall Street
b. AAB
c. Electronic commerce
d. ABN Amro

31. _____, refers to consumption opportunity gained by an entity within a specified time frame, which is generally expressed in monetary terms. However, for households and individuals, '_____ is the sum of all the wages, salaries, profits, interests payments, rents and other forms of earnings received... in a given period of time.' For firms, _____ generally refers to net-profit: what remains of revenue after expenses have been subtracted.
a. OIBDA
b. Annual report
c. Accrual
d. Income

32. _____ refers to the use of formal econometric techniques to determine the aggregate risk in a financial portfolio. _____ is one of many subtasks within the broader area of financial modeling.

_____ uses a variety of techniques including market risk, Value-at-Risk (VaR), Historical Simulation (HS), or Extreme Value Theory (EVT) in order to analyze a portfolio and make forecasts of the likely losses that would be incurred for a variety of risks.

a. Risk adjusted return on capital
b. Risk premium
c. Value at risk
d. Risk modeling

33. _____ in finance is the risk associated with imperfect hedging using futures. It could arise because of the difference between the asset whose price is to be hedged and the asset underlying the derivative, or because of a mismatch between the expiration date of the futures and the actual selling date of the asset.

Under these conditions, the spot price of the asset, and the futures price, do not converge on the expiration date of the future.

a. Credit risk
b. Currency risk
c. Liquidity risk
d. Basis risk

34. The institution most often referenced by the word '_____' is a public or publicly traded _____, the shares of which are traded on a public stock exchange (e.g., the New York Stock Exchange or Nasdaq in the United States) where shares of stock of _____s are bought and sold by and to the general public. Most of the largest businesses in the world are publicly traded _____s. However, the majority of _____s are said to be closely held, privately held or close _____s, meaning that no ready market exists for the trading of shares.
a. Federal Home Loan Mortgage Corporation
b. Depository Trust Company
c. Protect
d. Corporation

35. The _____ (NYSE: FNM), commonly known as Fannie Mae, is a stockholder-owned corporation chartered by Congress in 1968 as a government sponsored enterprise (GSE), but founded in 1938 during the Great Depression. The corporation's purpose is to purchase and securitize mortgages in order to ensure that funds are consistently available to the institutions that lend money to home buyers.

On September 7, 2008, James Lockhart, director of the Federal Housing Finance Agency (FHFA), announced that Fannie Mae and Freddie Mac were being placed into conservatorship of the FHFA.

Chapter 7. Asset-Liability Management: Determining and Measuring Interest Rates 61

a. General partnership
b. SPDR
c. The Depository Trust ' Clearing Corporation
d. Federal National Mortgage Association

36. The _____ (NYSE: FRE) is an insolvent government sponsored enterprise (GSE) of the United States federal government.

The _____ was created in 1970 to expand the secondary market for mortgages in the US. Along with other GSEs, Freddie Mac buys mortgages on the secondary market, pools them, and sells them as mortgage-backed securities to investors on the open market.

a. Governmental Accounting Standards Board
b. The Depository Trust ' Clearing Corporation
c. Federal Home Loan Mortgage Corporation
d. Public company

37. In business, _____ is the total assets minus total outside liabilities of an individual or a company. For a company, this is called shareholders' equity and may be referred to as book value. _____ is stated as at a particular point in time.
a. Certified International Investment Analyst
b. Net worth
c. Restructuring
d. Moneylender

38. In finance, _____ (or gearing) is borrowing money to supplement existing funds for investment in such a way that the potential positive or negative outcome is magnified and/or enhanced. It generally refers to using borrowed funds, or debt, so as to attempt to increase the returns to equity. Deleveraging is the action of reducing borrowings.
a. Pension fund
b. Limited partnership
c. Financial endowment
d. Leverage

39. In finance, a _____ is a position established in one market in an attempt to offset exposure to the price risk of an equal but opposite obligation or position in another market -- usually, but not always, in the context of one's commercial activity. Hedging is a strategy designed to minimize exposure to such business risks as a sharp contraction in demand for one's inventory, while still allowing the business to profit from producing and maintaining that inventory. A typical hedger might be a farmer with 2000 acres of unharvested wheat in the ground, who would rather tend his crop without the distraction of uncertain prices.
a. 4-4-5 Calendar
b. 529 plan
c. 7-Eleven
d. Hedge

Chapter 8. Using Financial Futures, Options, Swaps, and Other Hedging Tools

1. _____ is a fee paid on borrowed assets. It is the price paid for the use of borrowed money, or, money earned by deposited funds. Assets that are sometimes lent with _____ include money, shares, consumer goods through hire purchase, major assets such as aircraft, and even entire factories in finance lease arrangements.
   a. Interest
   b. AAB
   c. A Random Walk Down Wall Street
   d. Insolvency

2. In finance, a _____ is collateral that the holder of a position in securities, options, or futures contracts has to deposit to cover the credit risk of his counterparty (most often his broker.) This risk can arise if the holder has done any of the following:

   - borrowed cash from the counterparty to buy securities or options,
   - sold securities or options short, or
   - entered into a futures contract.

   The collateral can be in the form of cash or securities, and it is deposited in a _____ account. On U.S. futures exchanges, '_____' was formally called performance bond.

   _____ buying is buying securities with cash borrowed from a broker, using other securities as collateral.

   a. Procter ' Gamble
   b. Credit
   c. Share
   d. Margin

3. _____ is the provision of resources (such as granting a loan) by one party to another party where that second party does not reimburse the first party immediately, thereby generating a debt, and instead arranges either to repay or return those resources (or material(s) of equal value) at a later date. The first party is called a creditor, also known as a lender, while the second party is called a debtor, also known as a borrower.

   Movements of financial capital are normally dependent on either _____ or equity transfers.

   a. Clearing house
   b. Credit
   c. Warrant
   d. Comparable

4. In finance, a _____ is a derivative whose value derives from the credit risk on an underlying bond, loan or other financial asset. In this way, the credit risk is on an entity other than the counterparties to the transaction itself. This entity is known as the reference entity and may be a corporate, a sovereign or any other form of legal entity which has incurred debt.
   a. STIRT
   b. Derivatives markets
   c. Credit derivative
   d. Futures contract

5. A _____ is a financial contract whose value is derived from the value of something else (known as the underlying.) The underlying on which a _____ is based can be an asset, weather conditions bonds or other forms of credit.
   a. 4-4-5 Calendar
   b. Derivative
   c. 529 plan
   d. 7-Eleven

6. In business, _____ is the total assets minus total outside liabilities of an individual or a company. For a company, this is called shareholders' equity and may be referred to as book value. _____ is stated as at a particular point in time.

Chapter 8. Using Financial Futures, Options, Swaps, and Other Hedging Tools 63

    a. Moneylender
    b. Certified International Investment Analyst
    c. Restructuring
    d. Net worth

7. In financial accounting, the term _____ is most commonly used to describe any part of shareholders' equity, except for basic share capital. Sometimes, the term is used instead of the term provision; such a use, however, is inconsistent with the terminology suggested by International Accounting Standards Board. For more information about provisions, see provision (accounting.)

    a. Reserve
    b. Treasury stock
    c. Closing entries
    d. FIFO and LIFO accounting

8. In business and accounting, _____s are everything of value that is owned by a person or company. The balance sheet of a firm records the monetary value of the _____s owned by the firm. The two major _____ classes are tangible _____s and intangible _____s.

    a. EBITDA
    b. Accounts payable
    c. Income
    d. Asset

9. In finance, the _____ of a financial asset measures the sensitivity of the asset's price to interest rate movements, expressed as a number of years. The reason for expressing this sensitivity in years is that the time that will elapse until a cash flow is received allows more interest to accumulate. Therefore the price of an asset with long term cashflows has more interest rate sensitivity than an asset with cashflows in the near future.

    a. Yield to maturity
    b. 4-4-5 Calendar
    c. Macaulay duration
    d. Duration

10. The _____ is a financial and accounting term for the difference between the duration of assets and liabilities, and is typically used by banks, pension funds, or other financial institutions to measure their risk due to changes in the interest rate. This is one of the mismatches that can occur and are known as asset liability mismatches. Another way to define _____ is : it is the difference in the sensitivity of interest-yielding assets and the sensitivity of liabilities (of the organization) to a change in market interest rates (yields.)

    a. Duration gap
    b. Net worth
    c. Debt cash flow
    d. Modern portfolio theory

11. A _____ is a futures contract on a short term interest rate (STIR.) Contracts vary, but are often defined on an interest rate index such as 3-month sterling or US dollar LIBOR.

They are traded across a wide range of currencies, including the G12 country currencies and many others.

    a. Dual currency deposit
    b. Financial future
    c. Real estate derivatives
    d. Notional amount

12. In finance, a _____ is a standardized contract, to buy or sell a specified commodity of standardized quality at a certain date in the future, at a market determined price (the futures price.)

The price is determined by the instantaneous equilibrium between the forces of supply and demand among competing buy and sell orders on the exchange at the time of the purchase or sale of the contract.

64   Chapter 8. Using Financial Futures, Options, Swaps, and Other Hedging Tools

In many cases, the items may be such non-traditional 'commodities' as foreign currencies, commercial or government paper [e.g., bonds], or 'baskets' of corporate equity ['stock indices'] or other financial instruments.

a. Repurchase agreement
b. Financial future
c. Heston model
d. Futures contract

13. The _____ requirement is the amount required to be collateralized in order to open a position. Thereafter, the amount required to be kept in collateral until the position is closed is the maintenance requirement. The maintenance requirement is the minimum amount to be collateralized in order to keep an open position.

a. Efficient-market hypothesis
b. Issuer
c. Arbitrage
d. Initial margin

14. _____ or fair value accounting refers to the accounting standards of assigning a value to a position held in a financial instrument based on the current fair market price for the instrument or similar instruments. Fair value accounting has been a part of US Generally Accepted Accounting Principles (GAAP) since the early 1990s. The use of fair value measurements has increased steadily over the past decade, primarily in response to investor demand for relevant and timely financial statements that will aid in making better informed decisions.

a. Mark-to-market
b. 529 plan
c. 7-Eleven
d. 4-4-5 Calendar

15. An _____ is a contract written by a seller that conveys to the buyer the right -- but not the obligation -- to buy (in the case of a call _____) or to sell (in the case of a put _____) a particular asset, such as a piece of property such as, among others, a futures contract. In return for granting the _____, the seller collects a payment (the premium) from the buyer.

For example, buying a call _____ provides the right to buy a specified quantity of a security at a set strike price at some time on or before expiration, while buying a put _____ provides the right to sell.

a. Amortization
b. Annuity
c. AT'T Mobility LLC
d. Option

16. A _____ is a financial contract between two parties, the seller (writer) and the buyer of the option. The put allows its buyer the right but not the obligation to sell a commodity or financial instrument (the underlying instrument) to the writer (seller) of the option at a certain time for a certain price (the strike price.) The writer (seller) has the obligation to purchase the underlying asset at that strike price, if the buyer exercises the option.

a. Debit spread
b. Bear call spread
c. Bear spread
d. Put option

17. _____ are government bonds issued by the United States Department of the Treasury through the Bureau of the Public Debt. They are the debt financing instruments of the U.S. Federal government, and they are often referred to simply as Treasuries or Treasurys. There are four types of marketable _____: Treasury bills, Treasury notes, Treasury bonds, and Treasury Inflation Protected Securities (TIPS.)

a. Treasury Inflation-Protected Securities
b. Treasury securities
c. 4-4-5 Calendar
d. Treasury Inflation Protected Securities

Chapter 8. Using Financial Futures, Options, Swaps, and Other Hedging Tools 65

18. In finance, a _____ is a debt security, in which the authorized issuer owes the holders a debt and, depending on the terms of the _____, is obliged to pay interest (the coupon) and/or to repay the principal at a later date, termed maturity.

Thus a _____ is a loan: the issuer is the borrower, the _____ holder is the lender, and the coupon is the interest. _____s provide the borrower with external funds to finance long-term investments, or, in the case of government _____s, to finance current expenditure.

a. Puttable bond
b. Convertible bond
c. Catastrophe bonds
d. Bond

19. A _____ is an exchange of promises between two or more parties to do an act which is enforceable in a court of law. It is where an unqualified offer meets a qualified acceptance and the parties reach Consensus ad Idem. The parties must have the necessary capacity to _____ and the _____ must not be either trifling, indeterminate, impossible or illegal.

a. 529 plan
b. 4-4-5 Calendar
c. 7-Eleven
d. Contract

20. The _____ is an American financial and commodity derivative exchange based in Chicago. The _____ was founded in 1898 as the Chicago Butter and Egg Board. Originally, the exchange was a non-profit organization.

a. Financial Crimes Enforcement Network
b. Public Company Accounting Oversight Board
c. Chicago Mercantile Exchange
d. Gamelan Council

21. _____s are deposits denominated in United States dollars at banks outside the United States, and thus are not under the jurisdiction of the Federal Reserve. Consequently, such deposits are subject to much less regulation than similar deposits within the United States, allowing for higher margins. There is nothing 'European' about _____ deposits; a US dollar-denominated deposit in Tokyo or Caracas would likewise be deemed _____ deposits.

a. ABN Amro
b. Eurodollar
c. AAB
d. A Random Walk Down Wall Street

22. In the United States, _____ are overnight borrowings by banks to maintain their bank reserves at the Federal Reserve. Banks keep reserves at Federal Reserve Banks to meet their reserve requirements and to clear financial transactions. Transactions in the _____ market enable depository institutions with reserve balances in excess of reserve requirements to lend reserves to institutions with reserve deficiencies.

a. Federal funds rate
b. 4-4-5 Calendar
c. Federal funds
d. Regulation T

23. A _____ is a money deposit at a banking institution that cannot be withdrawn for a certain 'term' or period of time. When the term is over it can be withdrawn or it can be held for another term. Generally speaking, the longer the term the better the yield on the money.

a. Basel Accord
b. Private money
c. Certificate of deposit
d. Time deposit

24. A _____ or bank is a financial institution whose primary activity is to act as a payment agent for customers and to borrow and lend money.

Chapter 8. Using Financial Futures, Options, Swaps, and Other Hedging Tools

The first modern bank was founded in Italy in Genoa in 1406, its name was Banco di San Giorgio (Bank of St. George.)

Many other financial activities were added over time.

   a. Black Sea Trade and Development Bank
   b. 4-4-5 Calendar
   c. Banker
   d. Bought deal

25. In finance, a _____ is a position established in one market in an attempt to offset exposure to the price risk of an equal but opposite obligation or position in another market -- usually, but not always, in the context of one's commercial activity. Hedging is a strategy designed to minimize exposure to such business risks as a sharp contraction in demand for one's inventory, while still allowing the business to profit from producing and maintaining that inventory. A typical hedger might be a farmer with 2000 acres of unharvested wheat in the ground, who would rather tend his crop without the distraction of uncertain prices.
   a. 529 plan
   b. 4-4-5 Calendar
   c. Hedge
   d. 7-Eleven

26. _____, refers to consumption opportunity gained by an entity within a specified time frame, which is generally expressed in monetary terms. However, for households and individuals, '_____ is the sum of all the wages, salaries, profits, interests payments, rents and other forms of earnings received... in a given period of time.' For firms, _____ generally refers to net-profit: what remains of revenue after expenses have been subtracted.
   a. OIBDA
   b. Annual report
   c. Income
   d. Accrual

27. _____ is a political organization established in 2002 and dedicated to the protection of children from abuse, exploitation and neglect. It is a nonprofit, 501(c)(4) membership association with members in every U.S. state and 10 nations. _____ achieved great success in its first three years, winning legislative victories in eight state legislatures.
   a. First Prudential Markets
   b. The Depository Trust ' Clearing Corporation
   c. Protect
   d. Ford Foundation

28. _____ in finance is the risk associated with imperfect hedging using futures. It could arise because of the difference between the asset whose price is to be hedged and the asset underlying the derivative, or because of a mismatch between the expiration date of the futures and the actual selling date of the asset.

Under these conditions, the spot price of the asset, and the futures price, do not converge on the expiration date of the future.

   a. Basis risk
   b. Currency risk
   c. Liquidity risk
   d. Credit risk

29. _____ is a measure of the ability of a debtor to pay their debts as and when they fall due. It is usually expressed as a ratio or a percentage of current liabilities.

For a corporation with a published balance sheet there are various ratios used to calculate a measure of liquidity.

Chapter 8. Using Financial Futures, Options, Swaps, and Other Hedging Tools 67

a. Invested capital
c. Operating leverage
b. Operating profit margin
d. Accounting liquidity

30. In economics, business, and accounting, a _____ is the value of money that has been used up to produce something, and hence is not available for use anymore. In business, the _____ may be one of acquisition, in which case the amount of money expended to acquire it is counted as _____. In this case, money is the input that is gone in order to acquire the thing.
a. Cost
c. Sliding scale fees
b. Fixed costs
d. Marginal cost

31. A _____ is a situation that involves losing one quality or aspect of something in return for gaining another quality or aspect. It implies a decision to be made with full comprehension of both the upside and downside of a particular choice.

In economics the term is expressed as opportunity cost, referring the most preferred alternative given up.

a. Capital outflow
c. Trade-off
b. Break-even point
d. Total revenue

32. A _____ is a financial contract between two parties, the buyer and the seller of this type of option. Often it is simply labeled a 'call'. The buyer of the option has the right, but not the obligation to buy an agreed quantity of a particular commodity or financial instrument (the underlying instrument) from the seller of the option at a certain time (the expiration date) for a certain price (the strike price.)
a. Bear call spread
c. Bull spread
b. Bear spread
d. Call option

33. In options, the _____ is a key variable in a derivatives contract between two parties. Where the contract requires delivery of the underlying instrument, the trade will be at the _____, regardless of the spot price (market price) of the underlying instrument at that time.

Definition - The fixed price at which the owner of an option can purchase, in the case of a call in the case of a put, the underlying security or commodity.

a. Swaption
c. Moneyness
b. Strike price
d. Naked put

34. The role of the _____ is to issue accounting standards in the United Kingdom. It is recognised for that purpose under the Companies Act 1985. It took over the task of setting accounting standards from the Accounting Standards Committee (ASC) in 1990.
a. Accounting Standards Board
c. A Random Walk Down Wall Street
b. ABN Amro
d. AAB

35. _____ is the field of accountancy concerned with the preparation of financial statements for decision makers, such as stockholders, suppliers, banks, employees, government agencies, owners, and other stakeholders. The fundamental need for _____ is to reduce principal-agent problem by measuring and monitoring agents' performance and reporting the results to interested users.

Chapter 8. Using Financial Futures, Options, Swaps, and Other Hedging Tools

_____ is used to prepare accounting information for people outside the organization or not involved in the day to day running of the company.

a. 4-4-5 Calendar
c. 529 plan
b. 7-Eleven
d. Financial Accounting

36. The _____ is a private, not-for-profit organization whose primary purpose is to develop generally accepted accounting principles (GAAP) within the United States in the public's interest. The Securities and Exchange Commission (SEC) designated the _____ as the organization responsible for setting accounting standards for public companies in the U.S. It was created in 1973, replacing the Accounting Principles Board and the Committee on Accounting Procedure of the American Institute of Certified Public Accountants. The _____'s mission is 'to establish and improve standards of financial accounting and reporting for the guidance and education of the public, including issuers, auditors, and users of financial information.'

The _____ is not a governmental body.

a. World Congress of Accountants
c. Federal Deposit Insurance Corporation
b. Financial Accounting Standards Board
d. KPMG

37. _____ is the risk of loss due to a debtor's non-payment of a loan or other line of credit (either the principal or interest (coupon) or both)

Most lenders employ their own models (credit scorecards) to rank potential and existing customers according to risk, and then apply appropriate strategies. With products such as unsecured personal loans or mortgages, lenders charge a higher price for higher risk customers and vice versa. With revolving products such as credit cards and overdrafts, risk is controlled through careful setting of credit limits.

a. Liquidity risk
c. Transaction risk
b. Market risk
d. Credit risk

38. When companies conduct business across borders, they must deal in foreign currencies. Companies must exchange foreign currencies for home currencies when dealing with receivables, and vice versa for payables. This is done at the current exchange rate between the two countries. _____ is the risk that the exchange rate will change unfavorably before the currency is exchanged.

a. Lower of cost or market rule
c. 4-4-5 Calendar
b. 529 plan
d. Foreign exchange risk

39. _____ arises from situations in which a party interested in trading an asset cannot do it because nobody in the market wants to trade that asset. _____ becomes particularly important to parties who are about to hold or currently hold an asset, since it affects their ability to trade.

Manifestation of _____ is very different from a drop of price to zero.

Chapter 8. Using Financial Futures, Options, Swaps, and Other Hedging Tools   69

a. Currency risk
b. Tracking error
c. Liquidity risk
d. Credit risk

40. _____ is the discipline of identifying, monitoring and limiting risks. In some cases the acceptable risk may be near zero. Risks can come from accidents, natural causes and disasters as well as deliberate attacks from an adversary.
   a. Risk Management
   b. FIFO
   c. 4-4-5 Calendar
   d. Penny stock

41. An _____ is the price a borrower pays for the use of money they do not own, and the return a lender receives for deferring the use of funds, by lending it to the borrower. _____s are normally expressed as a percentage rate over the period of one year.

_____s targets are also a vital tool of monetary policy and are used to control variables like investment, inflation, and unemployment.

   a. AAB
   b. ABN Amro
   c. A Random Walk Down Wall Street
   d. Interest rate

42. _____ is the risk (variability in value) borne by an interest-bearing asset, such as a loan or a bond, due to variability of interest rates. In general, as rates rise, the price of a fixed rate bond will fall, and vice versa. _____ is commonly measured by the bond's duration.
   a. International Fisher effect
   b. A Random Walk Down Wall Street
   c. Official bank rate
   d. Interest rate risk

43. _____ is the balance of the amounts of cash being received and paid by a business during a defined period of time, sometimes tied to a specific project. Measurement of _____ can be used

   - to evaluate the state or performance of a business or project.
   - to determine problems with liquidity. Being profitable does not necessarily mean being liquid. A company can fail because of a shortage of cash, even while profitable.
   - to generate project rate of returns. The time of _____s into and out of projects are used as inputs to financial models such as internal rate of return, and net present value.
   - to examine income or growth of a business when it is believed that accrual accounting concepts do not represent economic realities. Alternately, _____ can be used to 'validate' the net income generated by accrual accounting.

_____ as a generic term may be used differently depending on context, and certain _____ definitions may be adapted by analysts and users for their own uses. Common terms include operating _____ and free _____.

70 **Chapter 8. Using Financial Futures, Options, Swaps, and Other Hedging Tools**

_____s can be classified into:

1. Operational _____s: Cash received or expended as a result of the company's core business activities.
2. Investment _____s: Cash received or expended through capital expenditure, investments or acquisitions.
3. Financing _____s: Cash received or expended as a result of financial activities, such as interests and dividends.

All three together - the net _____ - are necessary to reconcile the beginning cash balance to the ending cash balance. Loan draw downs or equity injections, that is just shifting of capital but no expenditure as such, are not considered in the net _____.

a. Cash flow
c. Corporate finance
b. Shareholder value
d. Real option

44. _____, also called fair price (in a commonplace conflation of the two distinct concepts), is a concept used in finance and economics, defined as a rational and unbiased estimate of the potential market price of a good, service, or asset, taking into account such objective factors as:

- acquisition/production/distribution costs, replacement costs, or costs of close substitutes
- actual utility at a given level of development of social productive capability
- supply vs. demand

and subjective factors such as

- risk characteristics
- cost of capital
- individually perceived utility

In accounting, _____ is used as an estimate of the market value of an asset (or liability) for which a market price cannot be determined (usually because there is no established market for the asset.) Under GAAP (FAS 157), _____ is the amount at which the asset could be bought or sold in a current transaction between willing parties, or transferred to an equivalent party, other than in a liquidation sale. This is used for assets whose carrying value is based on mark-to-market valuations; for assets carried at historical cost, the _____ of the asset is not used. One example of where _____ is an issue is a College kitchen with a cost of $2 million which was built 5 years ago.

a. 4-4-5 Calendar
c. 529 plan
b. 7-Eleven
d. Fair value

45. In finance, a _____ is a derivative in which two counterparties agree to exchange one stream of cash flows against another stream. These streams are called the legs of the _____.

Chapter 8. Using Financial Futures, Options, Swaps, and Other Hedging Tools 71

The cash flows are calculated over a notional principal amount, which is usually not exchanged between counterparties.

a. Local volatility
c. Volatility arbitrage
b. Volatility swap
d. Swap

46. The _____ (or notional principal amount or notional value) on a financial instrument is the nominal or face amount that is used to calculate payments made on that instrument. This amount generally does not change hands and is thus referred to as notional.

Contrast a bond with an interest rate swap:

- In a bond, the buyer pays the principal amount at issue (start), then receives coupons (computed off this principal) over the life of the bond, then receives the principal back at maturity (end.)
- In a swap, no principal changes hands at inception (start) or expiry (end), and in the meantime, interest payments are computed based on a _____, which acts as if it were the principal of a bond, hence the term notional principal amount, abbreviated to notional.

In simple terms the notional principal amount is essentially how much of the asset or bonds a person has. For example, if I bought a premium bond for Â£1 then the notional principal amount would be Â£1. Hence the notional principal amount is the quantity of the assets and bonds.

a. Forward start option
c. Credit derivative
b. Basis trading
d. Notional amount

47. In general, _____ means to allow a positive value and a negative value to set-off and partially or entirely cancel each other out.

In the context of credit risk, there are at least three specific types of _____:

- Close-out _____

- _____ by novation

- Settlement or payment _____

_____ decreases credit exposure, increases business with existing counterparties, and reduces both operational and settlement risk and operational costs.

a. Forward price
c. Netting
b. Moneylender
d. Reinvestment risk

48. A _____ is an option granting its owner the right but not the obligation to enter into an underlying swap. Although options can be traded on a variety of swaps, the term '_____' typically refers to options on interest rate swaps.

72 *Chapter 8. Using Financial Futures, Options, Swaps, and Other Hedging Tools*

There are two types of _____ contracts:

- A payer _____ gives the owner of the _____ the right to enter into a swap where they pay the fixed leg and receive the floating leg.
- A receiver _____ gives the owner of the _____ the right to enter into a swap where they will receive the fixed leg, and pay the floating leg.

The buyer and seller of the _____ agree on:

- the premium (price) of the _____
- the strike rate (equal to the fixed rate of the underlying swap)
- length of the option period (which usually ends two business days prior to the start date of the underlying swap),
- the term of the underlying swap,
- notional amount,
- amortization, if any
- frequency of settlement of payments on the underlying swap

The participants in the _____ market are predominantly large corporations, banks, financial institutions and hedge funds. End users such as corporations and banks typically use _____s to manage interest rate risk arising from their core business or from their financing arrangements.

    a. Straddle   b. Bear call spread
    c. Put option   d. Swaption

49. The _____ is a trade organization of participants in the market for over-the-counter derivatives. It is headquartered in New York, and has created a standardized contract (Master Agreement) to enter into derivatives transactions. There are currently two versions of the ISDA Master Agreement: the 1992 edition and the 2002 edition.
    a. International Swaps and Derivatives Association   b. Equity swap
    c. Interest rate derivative   d. Open interest

50. In finance, the term _____ describes the amount in cash that returns to the owners of a security. Normally it does not include the price variations, at the difference of the total return. _____ applies to various stated rates of return on stocks (common and preferred, and convertible), fixed income instruments (bonds, notes, bills, strips, zero coupon), and some other investment type insurance products (e.g. annuities.)
    a. Yield to maturity   b. 4-4-5 Calendar
    c. Macaulay duration   d. Yield

51. In finance, the _____ is the relation between the interest rate (or cost of borrowing) and the time to maturity of the debt for a given borrower in a given currency. For example, the current U.S. dollar interest rates paid on U.S. Treasury securities for various maturities are closely watched by many traders, and are commonly plotted on a graph such as the one on the right which is informally called 'the _____.' More formal mathematical descriptions of this relation are often called the term structure of interest rates.

The yield of a debt instrument is the annualized percentage increase in the value of the investment.

a. 529 plan
c. 4-4-5 Calendar
b. 7-Eleven
d. Yield curve

Chapter 9. Risk Management Using Asset-Backed Securities, Loan Sales, Credit Standbys

1. _____ is the provision of resources (such as granting a loan) by one party to another party where that second party does not reimburse the first party immediately, thereby generating a debt, and instead arranges either to repay or return those resources (or material(s) of equal value) at a later date. The first party is called a creditor, also known as a lender, while the second party is called a debtor, also known as a borrower.

    Movements of financial capital are normally dependent on either _____ or equity transfers.

    a. Warrant
    b. Credit
    c. Comparable
    d. Clearing house

2. _____ is a legal entity that develops, registers and sells securities for the purpose of financing its operations. _____s may be domestic or foreign governments, corporations or investment trusts. _____s are legally responsible for the obligations of the issue and for reporting financial conditions, material developments and any other operational activities as required by the regulations of their jurisdictions.
    a. Efficient-market hypothesis
    b. Initial margin
    c. Issuer
    d. Arbitrage

3. _____ is a structured finance process that involves pooling and repackaging of cash-flow-producing financial assets into securities, which are then sold to investors. The term '_____' is derived from the fact that the form of financial instruments used to obtain funds from the investors are securities. As a portfolio risk backed by amortizing cash flows - and unlike general corporate debt - the credit quality of securitized debt is non-stationary due to changes in volatility that are time- and structure-dependent.
    a. Reputational risk
    b. Securitization
    c. The Glass-Steagall Act of 1933
    d. Special journals

4. A _____ (sometimes, especially in Europe, 'special purpose vehicle' or simply SPV) is a legal entity (usually a limited company of some type or, sometimes, a limited partnership) created to fulfill narrow, specific or temporary objectives. _____'s are typically used by companies to isolate the firm from financial risk. A company will transfer assets to the _____ for management or use the _____ to finance a large project thereby achieving a narrow set of goals without putting the entire firm at risk.
    a. Real option
    b. Follow-on offering
    c. Special purpose entity
    d. Rights issue

5. In business and accounting, _____s are everything of value that is owned by a person or company. The balance sheet of a firm records the monetary value of the _____s owned by the firm. The two major _____ classes are tangible _____s and intangible _____s.
    a. EBITDA
    b. Accounts payable
    c. Income
    d. Asset

6. _____, refers to consumption opportunity gained by an entity within a specified time frame, which is generally expressed in monetary terms. However, for households and individuals, '_____ is the sum of all the wages, salaries, profits, interests payments, rents and other forms of earnings received... in a given period of time.' For firms, _____ generally refers to net-profit: what remains of revenue after expenses have been subtracted.
    a. Accrual
    b. Income
    c. Annual report
    d. OIBDA

Chapter 9. Risk Management Using Asset-Backed Securities, Loan Sales, Credit Standbys

7. _____ is a key part of the securitization transaction in structured finance, and is important for credit rating agencies when rating a securitization. The credit crisis of 2007-2008 has discredited the process of _____ of structured securities as a legitimate financial practice.

There are two primary types of _____: Internal and External.

  a. 4-4-5 Calendar
  b. Yield curve spread
  c. Tranche
  d. Credit enhancement

8. _____ is a measure of the ability of a debtor to pay their debts as and when they fall due. It is usually expressed as a ratio or a percentage of current liabilities.

For a corporation with a published balance sheet there are various ratios used to calculate a measure of liquidity.

  a. Operating profit margin
  b. Operating leverage
  c. Invested capital
  d. Accounting liquidity

9. A _____ is a fungible, negotiable instrument representing financial value. They are broadly categorized into debt securities (such as banknotes, bonds and debentures), and equity securities; e.g., common stocks. The company or other entity issuing the _____ is called the issuer.
  a. Securities lending
  b. Security
  c. Book entry
  d. Tracking stock

10. A _____ is a financial debt vehicle that was first created in June 1983 by investment banks Salomon Brothers and First Boston for Freddie Mac. (The First Boston team was led by Dexter Senft.) Legally, a _____ is a special purpose entity that is wholly separate from the institution(s) that create it.
  a. Yield curve spread
  b. Tranche
  c. 4-4-5 Calendar
  d. Collateralized mortgage obligation

11. The institution most often referenced by the word '_____' is a public or publicly traded _____, the shares of which are traded on a public stock exchange (e.g., the New York Stock Exchange or Nasdaq in the United States) where shares of stock of _____s are bought and sold by and to the general public. Most of the largest businesses in the world are publicly traded _____s. However, the majority of _____s are said to be closely held, privately held or close _____s, meaning that no ready market exists for the trading of shares.
  a. Protect
  b. Federal Home Loan Mortgage Corporation
  c. Corporation
  d. Depository Trust Company

12. _____ is the removal or simplification of government rules and regulations that constrain the operation of market forces. _____ does not mean elimination of laws against fraud, but eliminating or reducing government control of how business is done, thereby moving toward a more free market.

The stated rationale for '_____' is often that fewer and simpler regulations will lead to a raised level of competitiveness, therefore higher productivity, more efficiency and lower prices overall.

Chapter 9. Risk Management Using Asset-Backed Securities, Loan Sales, Credit Standbys

a. Demand shock
b. Supply shock
c. Deregulation
d. Value added

13. The _____ (NYSE: FNM), commonly known as Fannie Mae, is a stockholder-owned corporation chartered by Congress in 1968 as a government sponsored enterprise (GSE), but founded in 1938 during the Great Depression. The corporation's purpose is to purchase and securitize mortgages in order to ensure that funds are consistently available to the institutions that lend money to home buyers.

On September 7, 2008, James Lockhart, director of the Federal Housing Finance Agency (FHFA), announced that Fannie Mae and Freddie Mac were being placed into conservatorship of the FHFA.

a. Federal National Mortgage Association
b. The Depository Trust ' Clearing Corporation
c. SPDR
d. General partnership

14. The _____ (NYSE: FRE) is an insolvent government sponsored enterprise (GSE) of the United States federal government.

The _____ was created in 1970 to expand the secondary market for mortgages in the US. Along with other GSEs, Freddie Mac buys mortgages on the secondary market, pools them, and sells them as mortgage-backed securities to investors on the open market.

a. Federal Home Loan Mortgage Corporation
b. Public company
c. The Depository Trust ' Clearing Corporation
d. Governmental Accounting Standards Board

15. The _____ is a U.S. government-owned corporation within the Department of Housing and Urban Development

Ginnie Mae provides guarantees on mortgage-backed securities backed by federally insured or guaranteed loans, mainly loans issued by the Federal Housing Administration, Department of Veterans Affairs, Rural Housing Service, and Office of Public and Indian Housing. Ginnie Mae securities are the only MBS that are guaranteed by the United States government.

a. Cash budget
b. Certified Emission Reductions
c. Case-Shiller Home Price Indices
d. GNMA

16. The _____ is a U.S. government-owned corporation within the Department of Housing and Urban Development

Ginnie Mae provides guarantees on mortgage-backed securities backed by federally insured or guaranteed loans, mainly loans issued by the Federal Housing Administration, Department of Veterans Affairs, Rural Housing Service, and Office of Public and Indian Housing. Ginnie Mae securities are the only MBS that are guaranteed by the United States government.

a. Government National Mortgage Association
b. 4-4-5 Calendar
c. Jumbo mortgage
d. Graduated payment mortgage

Chapter 9. Risk Management Using Asset-Backed Securities, Loan Sales, Credit Standbys 77

17. _____ is the value of a homeowner's unencumbered interest in their property, i.e. the difference between the home's fair market value and the unpaid balance of the mortgage and any outstanding debt over the home. _____ increases as the mortgage is paid or as the property enjoys appreciation. This is sometimes called real property value in economics.
   a. Liquidation value
   b. REIT
   c. Home equity
   d. Real Estate Investment Trust

18. In finance, a _____ is a debt security, in which the authorized issuer owes the holders a debt and, depending on the terms of the _____, is obliged to pay interest (the coupon) and/or to repay the principal at a later date, termed maturity.

Thus a _____ is a loan: the issuer is the borrower, the _____ holder is the lender, and the coupon is the interest. _____s provide the borrower with external funds to finance long-term investments, or, in the case of government _____s, to finance current expenditure.

   a. Bond
   b. Catastrophe bonds
   c. Puttable bond
   d. Convertible bond

19. In structured finance, a _____ is one of a number of related securities offered as part of the same transaction. The word _____ is French for slice, section, series, or portion. In the financial sense of the word, each bond is a different slice of the deal's risk.
   a. 4-4-5 Calendar
   b. Tranche
   c. Yield curve spread
   d. Credit enhancement

20. An _____ is a security whose value and income payments are derived from and collateralized (or 'backed') by a specified pool of underlying assets. The pool of assets is typically a group of small and illiquid assets that are unable to be sold individually. Pooling the assets allows them to be sold to general investors, a process called securitization, and allows the risk of investing in the underlying assets to be diversified because each security will represent a fraction of the total value of the diverse pool of underlying assets.
   a. A Random Walk Down Wall Street
   b. ABN Amro
   c. AAB
   d. Asset-backed security

21. _____ are a type of bond commonly issued in American security markets. They are a type of mortgage-backed security backed by mortgages on commercial rather than residential real estate. CMBS issues are usually structured as multiple tranches, similar to CMOs, rather than typical residential 'passthroughs.'

Many American CMBSs carry less prepayment risk than other MBS types, thanks to the structure of commercial mortgages.

   a. Stock market index
   b. Commercial mortgage-backed securities
   c. Contract for difference
   d. Stop order

22. A _____ is an asset-backed security whose cash flows are backed by the principal and interest payments of a set of mortgage loans. Payments are typically made monthly over the lifetime of the underlying loans.

Chapter 9. Risk Management Using Asset-Backed Securities, Loan Sales, Credit Standbys

a. Home equity line of credit
b. Conforming loan
c. Shared appreciation mortgage
d. Mortgage-backed security

23. _____ are risk-linked securities that transfer a specified set of risks from a sponsor to investors. They are often structured as floating rate corporate bonds whose principal is forgiven if specified trigger conditions are met. They are typically used by insurers as an alternative to traditional catastrophe reinsurance.

a. Catastrophe bonds
b. Callable bond
c. Brady bonds
d. Clean price

24. In finance, 'participation' is an ownership interest in a mortgage or other loan. In particular, _____ is a cooperation of multiple lenders to issue a loan (known as participation loan) to one borrower. This is usually done in order to reduce individual risks of the lenders.

a. Short positions
b. Loan participation
c. Doctrine of the Proper Law
d. Securitization

25. _____s are loans made by multiple lenders to a single borrower. Several banks, for example, might chip in to fund one extremely large loan, with one of the banks taking the role of the 'lead bank.' This lending institution then recruits other banks to participate and share the risks and profits. The lead bank typically originates the loan, takes responsibility for the loan servicing of the _____, organizes and manages the participation, and deals directly with the borrower.

a. Credit cycle
b. Credit analysis
c. Capital note
d. Participation loan

26. _____ are liabilities that may or may not be incurred by an entity depending on the outcome of a future event such as a court case. These liabilities are recorded in a company's accounts and shown in the balance sheet when both probable and reasonably estimable. A footnote to the balance sheet describes the nature and extent of the _____.

a. Due-on-sale clause
b. 529 plan
c. 4-4-5 Calendar
d. Contingent liabilities

27. In finance, _____ occurs when a debtor has not met its legal obligations according to the debt contract, e.g. it has not made a scheduled payment, or has violated a loan covenant (condition) of the debt contract. _____ may occur if the debtor is either unwilling or unable to pay their debt. This can occur with all debt obligations including bonds, mortgages, loans, and promissory notes.

a. Debt validation
b. Credit crunch
c. Vendor finance
d. Default

28. A standard, commercial _____ is a document issued mostly by a financial institution, used primarily in trade finance, which usually provides an irrevocable payment undertaking.

The _____ can also be the source of payment for a transaction, meaning that redeeming the _____ will pay an exporter. Letters of credit are used primarily in international trade transactions of significant value, for deals between a supplier in one country and a customer in another.

a. McFadden Act
b. Bond indenture
c. Letter of credit
d. Duty of loyalty

Chapter 9. Risk Management Using Asset-Backed Securities, Loan Sales, Credit Standbys

29. _____, in bookkeeping, refers to assets, liabilities, income, and expenses recorded on individual pages of the so called book of final entry or ledger. Changes in _____ value are made by chronologically posting debit (DR) and credit (CR) entries to its page. Examples of _____s are cash, _____s receivable, mortgages, loans, land and buildings, common stock, sales, services provided, wages, and payroll overhead.
   a. Account
   b. Alpha
   c. Accretion
   d. Option

30. _____ is the risk of loss due to a debtor's non-payment of a loan or other line of credit (either the principal or interest (coupon) or both)

Most lenders employ their own models (credit scorecards) to rank potential and existing customers according to risk, and then apply appropriate strategies. With products such as unsecured personal loans or mortgages, lenders charge a higher price for higher risk customers and vice versa. With revolving products such as credit cards and overdrafts, risk is controlled through careful setting of credit limits.

   a. Market risk
   b. Transaction risk
   c. Credit risk
   d. Liquidity risk

31. In finance, a _____ is a derivative whose value derives from the credit risk on an underlying bond, loan or other financial asset. In this way, the credit risk is on an entity other than the counterparties to the transaction itself. This entity is known as the reference entity and may be a corporate, a sovereign or any other form of legal entity which has incurred debt.
   a. Credit derivative
   b. Derivatives markets
   c. STIRT
   d. Futures contract

32. A _____ is a financial contract whose value is derived from the value of something else (known as the underlying.) The underlying on which a _____ is based can be an asset, weather conditions bonds or other forms of credit.
   a. 4-4-5 Calendar
   b. 7-Eleven
   c. 529 plan
   d. Derivative

33. The _____ is a trade organization of participants in the market for over-the-counter derivatives. It is headquartered in New York, and has created a standardized contract (Master Agreement) to enter into derivatives transactions. There are currently two versions of the ISDA Master Agreement: the 1992 edition and the 2002 edition.
   a. Equity swap
   b. International Swaps and Derivatives Association
   c. Interest rate derivative
   d. Open interest

34. In finance, a _____ is a derivative in which two counterparties agree to exchange one stream of cash flows against another stream. These streams are called the legs of the _____.

The cash flows are calculated over a notional principal amount, which is usually not exchanged between counterparties.

   a. Local volatility
   b. Swap
   c. Volatility swap
   d. Volatility arbitrage

80   Chapter 9. Risk Management Using Asset-Backed Securities, Loan Sales, Credit Standbys

35.   A _____ is a futures contract on a short term interest rate (STIR.) Contracts vary, but are often defined on an interest rate index such as 3-month sterling or US dollar LIBOR.

They are traded across a wide range of currencies, including the G12 country currencies and many others.

   a. Real estate derivatives
   b. Financial future
   c. Dual currency deposit
   d. Notional amount

36.   The _____ on a portfolio of investments takes into account not only the capital appreciation on the portfolio, but also the income received on the portfolio. The income typically consists of interest, dividends, and securities lending fees. This contrasts with the price return, which takes into account only the capital gain on an investment.
   a. Total return
   b. Capitalization rate
   c. Profitability index
   d. Global tactical asset allocation

37.   _____ or total rate of return swap is a financial contract which transfers both the credit risk and market risk of an underlying asset.

Let us assume that one bank (bank A) owns an asset (e.g. a bond) which periodically gives interest rate payments. Assume that bank A (the protection buyer) and bank B (the protection seller) has entered a Total rate swap contract.

   a. Correlation swap
   b. Power reverse dual currency note
   c. Total return swap
   d. Constant maturity credit default swap

38.   In finance, a _____ is a standardized contract, to buy or sell a specified commodity of standardized quality at a certain date in the future, at a market determined price (the futures price.)

The price is determined by the instantaneous equilibrium between the forces of supply and demand among competing buy and sell orders on the exchange at the time of the purchase or sale of the contract.

In many cases, the items may be such non-traditional 'commodities' as foreign currencies, commercial or government paper [e.g., bonds], or 'baskets' of corporate equity ['stock indices'] or other financial instruments.

   a. Heston model
   b. Financial future
   c. Repurchase agreement
   d. Futures contract

39.   An _____ is a contract written by a seller that conveys to the buyer the right -- but not the obligation -- to buy (in the case of a call _____) or to sell (in the case of a put _____) a particular asset, such as a piece of property such as, among others, a futures contract. In return for granting the _____, the seller collects a payment (the premium) from the buyer.

For example, buying a call _____ provides the right to buy a specified quantity of a security at a set strike price at some time on or before expiration, while buying a put _____ provides the right to sell.

Chapter 9. Risk Management Using Asset-Backed Securities, Loan Sales, Credit Standbys

a. Amortization
c. AT'T Mobility LLC
b. Annuity
d. Option

40. A _____ is a credit derivative contract between two counterparties. The buyer makes periodic payments (premium leg) to the seller, and in return receives a payoff (protection or default leg) if an underlying financial instrument defaults. _____ contracts have been incorrectly compared with insurance, because the buyer pays a premium and, in return, receives a sum of money if a specified event occurs.
   a. Credit default swap
   c. Commodity tick
   b. Stock market index future
   d. Futures contract

41. _____ is a concept or convention within auditing and accounting relating to the importance of an amount, transaction, or discrepancy. The objective of an audit of financial statements is to enable the auditor to express an opinion whether the financial statements are prepared, in all material respects, in conformity with an identified financial reporting framework such as Generally Accepted Accounting Principles (GAAP.) The assessment of what is material is a matter of professional judgment.
   a. Financial audit
   c. Trustworthy Repositories Audit ' Certification
   b. Clinical audit
   d. Materiality

42. _____ are a type of structured asset-backed security (ABS) whose value and payments are derived from a portfolio of fixed-income underlying assets. _____s are assigned different risk classes, or tranches, whereby 'senior' tranches are considered the safest securities. Interest and principal payments are made in order of seniority, so that junior tranches offer higher coupon payments (and interest rates) or lower prices to compensate for additional default risk.
   a. Senior debt
   c. Municipal bond
   b. Zero coupon bond
   d. Collateralized debt obligations

43. A _____ is a collateralized debt obligation (CDO) in which the underlying credit exposures are taken on using a credit default swap rather than by having a vehicle buy physical assets. _____s can either be single tranche CDOs or fully distributed CDOs. _____s are also commonly divided into balance sheet and arbitrage CDOs, although it is often impossible to distinguish in practice between the two types.
   a. Planning horizon
   c. Synthetic CDO
   b. Counting house
   d. Market capitalization

44. _____ is that which is owed; usually referencing assets owed, but the term can cover other obligations. In the case of assets, _____ is a means of using future purchasing power in the present before a summation has been earned. Some companies and corporations use _____ as a part of their overall corporate finance strategy.
   a. Cross-collateralization
   c. Credit cycle
   b. Partial Payment
   d. Debt

Chapter 10. The Investment Function in Banking and Financial-Services Management

1. The _____ is the market for securities, where companies and governments can raise longterm funds. The _____ includes the stock market and the bond market. Financial regulators, such as the U.S. Securities and Exchange Commission, oversee the _____s in their designated countries to ensure that investors are protected against fraud.
   a. Delta neutral
   b. Forward market
   c. Spot rate
   d. Capital market

2. _____ is the term used to describe deposits residing in banks that are located outside the borders of the country that issues the currency the deposit is denominated in. For example a deposit denominated in US dollars residing in a Japanese bank is a _____ deposit, or more specifically a Eurodollar deposit.

   Key points are the location of the bank and the denomination of the currency, not the nationality of the bank or the owner of the deposit/loan.

   a. AAB
   b. ABN Amro
   c. Eurocurrency
   d. A Random Walk Down Wall Street

3. In finance, the _____ is the global financial market for short-term borrowing and lending. It provides short-term liquidity funding for the global financial system. The _____ is where short-term obligations such as Treasury bills, commercial paper and bankers' acceptances are bought and sold.
   a. Money market
   b. Consumer debt
   c. Cramdown
   d. Debt-for-equity swap

4. In financial accounting, a _____ or statement of financial position is a summary of a person's or organization's balances. Assets, liabilities and ownership equity are listed as of a specific date, such as the end of its financial year. A _____ is often described as a snapshot of a company's financial condition.
   a. Financial statements
   b. Statement of retained earnings
   c. Statement on Auditing Standards No. 70: Service Organizations
   d. Balance sheet

5. A _____ is a fungible, negotiable instrument representing financial value. They are broadly categorized into debt securities (such as banknotes, bonds and debentures), and equity securities; e.g., common stocks. The company or other entity issuing the _____ is called the issuer.
   a. Book entry
   b. Securities lending
   c. Tracking stock
   d. Security

6. _____ in finance is a risk management technique, related to hedging, that mixes a wide variety of investments within a portfolio. Because the fluctuations of a single security have less impact on a diverse portfolio, _____ minimizes the risk from any one investment.

   A simple example of _____ is the following: On a particular island the entire economy consists of two companies: one that sells umbrellas and another that sells sunscreen.

   a. Diversification
   b. 529 plan
   c. 4-4-5 Calendar
   d. 7-Eleven

7. _____ is a measure of the ability of a debtor to pay their debts as and when they fall due. It is usually expressed as a ratio or a percentage of current liabilities.

Chapter 10. The Investment Function in Banking and Financial-Services Management   83

For a corporation with a published balance sheet there are various ratios used to calculate a measure of liquidity.

a. Operating leverage
b. Operating profit margin
c. Invested capital
d. Accounting liquidity

8. _____ mature in one year or less. Like zero-coupon bonds, they do not pay interest prior to maturity; instead they are sold at a discount of the par value to create a positive yield to maturity. Many regard _____ as the least risky investment available to U.S. investors.

a. 4-4-5 Calendar
b. Treasury Inflation Protected Securities
c. Treasury bills
d. Treasury securities

9. _____, in bookkeeping, refers to assets, liabilities, income, and expenses recorded on individual pages of the so called book of final entry or ledger. Changes in _____ value are made by chronologically posting debit (DR) and credit (CR) entries to its page. Examples of _____s are cash, _____s receivable, mortgages, loans, land and buildings, common stock, sales, services provided, wages, and payroll overhead.

a. Account
b. Alpha
c. Accretion
d. Option

10. In finance, a _____ is a debt security, in which the authorized issuer owes the holders a debt and, depending on the terms of the _____, is obliged to pay interest (the coupon) and/or to repay the principal at a later date, termed maturity.

Thus a _____ is a loan: the issuer is the borrower, the _____ holder is the lender, and the coupon is the interest. _____s provide the borrower with external funds to finance long-term investments, or, in the case of government _____s, to finance current expenditure.

a. Convertible bond
b. Catastrophe bonds
c. Puttable bond
d. Bond

11. _____ refers to the use of formal econometric techniques to determine the aggregate risk in a financial portfolio. _____ is one of many subtasks within the broader area of financial modeling.

_____ uses a variety of techniques including market risk, Value-at-Risk (VaR), Historical Simulation (HS), or Extreme Value Theory (EVT) in order to analyze a portfolio and make forecasts of the likely losses that would be incurred for a variety of risks.

a. Value at risk
b. Risk premium
c. Risk adjusted return on capital
d. Risk modeling

12. An _____ is a security whose value and income payments are derived from and collateralized (or 'backed') by a specified pool of underlying assets. The pool of assets is typically a group of small and illiquid assets that are unable to be sold individually. Pooling the assets allows them to be sold to general investors, a process called securitization, and allows the risk of investing in the underlying assets to be diversified because each security will represent a fraction of the total value of the diverse pool of underlying assets.

Chapter 10. The Investment Function in Banking and Financial-Services Management

a. A Random Walk Down Wall Street
b. AAB
c. ABN Amro
d. Asset-backed security

13. A _____ s a time deposit, a financial product commonly offered to consumers by banks, thrift institutions, and credit unions.

They are similar to savings accounts in that they are insured and thus virtually risk-free; they are 'money in the bank'. They are different from savings accounts in that they have a specific, fixed term (often three months, six months, or one to five years), and, usually, a fixed interest rate.

a. Reserve requirement
b. Certificate of deposit
c. Variable rate mortgage
d. Time deposit

14. In the global money market, _____ is an unsecured promissory note with a fixed maturity of one to 270 days. _____ is a money-market security issued (sold) by large banks and corporations to get money to meet short term debt obligations (for example, payroll), and is only backed by an issuing bank or corporation's promise to pay the face amount on the maturity date specified on the note. Since it is not backed by collateral, only firms with excellent credit ratings from a recognized rating agency will be able to sell their _____ at a reasonable price.

a. Financial distress
b. Trade-off theory
c. Commercial paper
d. Book building

15. In the United States, a _____ is a bond issued by a city or other local government, or their agencies. Potential issuers of these bonds include cities, counties, redevelopment agencies, school districts, publicly owned airports and seaports, and any other governmental entity (or group of governments) below the state level. They may be general obligations of the issuer or secured by specified revenues.

a. Municipal bond
b. Senior debt
c. Premium bond
d. Puttable bond

16. In economics, the concept of the _____ refers to the decision-making time frame of a firm in which at least one factor of production is fixed. Costs which are fixed in the _____ have no impact on a firms decisions. For example a firm can raise output by increasing the amount of labour through overtime.

a. Short-run
b. Long-run
c. 4-4-5 Calendar
d. 529 plan

17. _____ are government bonds issued by the United States Department of the Treasury through the Bureau of the Public Debt. They are the debt financing instruments of the U.S. Federal government, and they are often referred to simply as Treasuries or Treasurys. There are four types of marketable _____: Treasury bills, Treasury notes, Treasury bonds, and Treasury Inflation Protected Securities (TIPS.)

a. Treasury Inflation-Protected Securities
b. 4-4-5 Calendar
c. Treasury Inflation Protected Securities
d. Treasury securities

18. _____ is the provision of resources (such as granting a loan) by one party to another party where that second party does not reimburse the first party immediately, thereby generating a debt, and instead arranges either to repay or return those resources (or material(s) of equal value) at a later date. The first party is called a creditor, also known as a lender, while the second party is called a debtor, also known as a borrower.

Chapter 10. The Investment Function in Banking and Financial-Services Management

Movements of financial capital are normally dependent on either _____ or equity transfers.

a. Comparable
b. Credit
c. Warrant
d. Clearing house

19. A _____ assesses the credit worthiness of an individual, corporation, or even a country. _____s are calculated from financial history and current assets and liabilities. Typically, a _____ tells a lender or investor the probability of the subject being able to pay back a loan.
   a. Credit cycle
   b. Credit report monitoring
   c. Credit rating
   d. Debenture

20. A _____ is a bond issued by a national government denominated in the country's own currency. Bonds issued by national governments in foreign currencies are normally referred to as sovereign bonds. The first ever _____ was issued by the British government in 1693 to raise money to fund a war against France.
   a. Collateralized debt obligations
   b. Zero-coupon bond
   c. Municipal bond
   d. Government bond

21. The institution most often referenced by the word '_____' is a public or publicly traded _____, the shares of which are traded on a public stock exchange (e.g., the New York Stock Exchange or Nasdaq in the United States) where shares of stock of _____s are bought and sold by and to the general public. Most of the largest businesses in the world are publicly traded _____s. However, the majority of _____s are said to be closely held, privately held or close _____s, meaning that no ready market exists for the trading of shares.
   a. Depository Trust Company
   b. Protect
   c. Federal Home Loan Mortgage Corporation
   d. Corporation

22. The coupon or _____ of a bond is the amount of interest paid per year expressed as a percentage of the face value of the bond.

For example if you hold $10,000 nominal of a bond described as a 4.5% loan stock, you will receive $450 in interest each year (probably in two installments of $225 each.)

Not all bonds have coupons.

   a. Zero-coupon bond
   b. Revenue bonds
   c. Puttable bond
   d. Coupon rate

23. The _____ (NYSE: FNM), commonly known as Fannie Mae, is a stockholder-owned corporation chartered by Congress in 1968 as a government sponsored enterprise (GSE), but founded in 1938 during the Great Depression. The corporation's purpose is to purchase and securitize mortgages in order to ensure that funds are consistently available to the institutions that lend money to home buyers.

On September 7, 2008, James Lockhart, director of the Federal Housing Finance Agency (FHFA), announced that Fannie Mae and Freddie Mac were being placed into conservatorship of the FHFA.

Chapter 10. The Investment Function in Banking and Financial-Services Management

a. The Depository Trust ' Clearing Corporation
b. General partnership
c. SPDR
d. Federal National Mortgage Association

24. The _____ is a federally chartered network of borrower-owned lending institutions composed of cooperatives and related service organizations. Cooperatives are organizations that are owned and controlled by their members who use the cooperative'e;s products, supplies or services. The U.S. Congress authorized the creation of the first System institutions in 1916.
a. 7-Eleven
b. 529 plan
c. 4-4-5 Calendar
d. Farm Credit System

25. The _____ provide stable, on-demand, low-cost funding to American financial institutions for home mortgage loans, small business, rural, agricultural, and economic development lending. With their members, the _____ank System represents the largest collective source of home mortgage and community credit in the United States. The banks do not provide loans directly to individuals, only to other banks.
a. 7-Eleven
b. Federal Home Loan Banks
c. 4-4-5 Calendar
d. 529 plan

26. The _____ (NYSE: FRE) is an insolvent government sponsored enterprise (GSE) of the United States federal government.

The _____ was created in 1970 to expand the secondary market for mortgages in the US. Along with other GSEs, Freddie Mac buys mortgages on the secondary market, pools them, and sells them as mortgage-backed securities to investors on the open market.

a. Federal Home Loan Mortgage Corporation
b. Governmental Accounting Standards Board
c. Public company
d. The Depository Trust ' Clearing Corporation

27. A _____ is a legal pledge in United States municipal finance, in which an entity pledges its full faith and credit to repay its debt, typically a _____ bond.
a. Financial Institutions Reform Recovery and Enforcement Act
b. Letter of credit
c. Covenant
d. General obligation

28. The _____ Act is an Act of the 106th United States Congress which repealed part of the Glass-Steagall Act of 1933, opening up competition among banks, securities companies and insurance companies. The Glass-Steagall Act prohibited any one institution from acting as both an investment bank and a commercial bank, or as both a bank and an insurer.

The _____ Act (GLBA) allowed commercial and investment banks to consolidate.

a. 4-4-5 Calendar
b. 529 plan
c. 7-Eleven
d. Gramm-Leach-Bliley

Chapter 10. The Investment Function in Banking and Financial-Services Management

29. In business, _____ is income that a company receives from its normal business activities, usually from the sale of goods and services to customers. Some companies also receive _____ from interest, dividends or royalties paid to them by other companies. _____ may refer to business income in general, or it may refer to the amount, in a monetary unit, received during a period of time, as in 'Last year, Company X had _____ of $32 million.'

In many countries, including the UK, _____ is referred to as turnover.

   a. Furniture, Fixtures and Equipment
   b. Bottom line
   c. Revenue
   d. Matching principle

30. _____ are bonds issued by governments, authorities, or public benefit corporations that are guaranteed by the revenue flow of the issuing agency.

The Supreme Court decision of Pollock versus Farmer's Loan and Trust Company of 1895 initiated a wave or series of innovations for the financial services community in both tax-treatment and regulation from government. This specific case, according to a leading investment bank's research, resulted in the 'intergovernmental tax immunity doctrine,' ultimately leading to 'tax-free status.' Municipal bonds are generally exempt from federal tax on their interest payments (not capital gains.)

   a. Callable bond
   b. Gilts
   c. Revenue bonds
   d. Private activity bond

31. A _____ is a financial debt vehicle that was first created in June 1983 by investment banks Salomon Brothers and First Boston for Freddie Mac. (The First Boston team was led by Dexter Senft.) Legally, a _____ is a special purpose entity that is wholly separate from the institution(s) that create it.
   a. Tranche
   b. 4-4-5 Calendar
   c. Yield curve spread
   d. Collateralized mortgage obligation

32. _____ is a structured finance process that involves pooling and repackaging of cash-flow-producing financial assets into securities, which are then sold to investors. The term '_____' is derived from the fact that the form of financial instruments used to obtain funds from the investors are securities. As a portfolio risk backed by amortizing cash flows - and unlike general corporate debt - the credit quality of securitized debt is non-stationary due to changes in volatility that are time- and structure-dependent.
   a. Special journals
   b. Reputational risk
   c. The Glass-Steagall Act of 1933
   d. Securitization

33. In business and accounting, _____s are everything of value that is owned by a person or company. The balance sheet of a firm records the monetary value of the _____s owned by the firm. The two major _____ classes are tangible _____s and intangible _____s.
   a. Asset
   b. Income
   c. Accounts payable
   d. EBITDA

34. _____ is the removal or simplification of government rules and regulations that constrain the operation of market forces. _____ does not mean elimination of laws against fraud, but eliminating or reducing government control of how business is done, thereby moving toward a more free market.

88 Chapter 10. The Investment Function in Banking and Financial-Services Management

The stated rationale for '_____' is often that fewer and simpler regulations will lead to a raised level of competitiveness, therefore higher productivity, more efficiency and lower prices overall.

a. Supply shock
b. Demand shock
c. Deregulation
d. Value added

35. The _____ is a U.S. government-owned corporation within the Department of Housing and Urban Development

Ginnie Mae provides guarantees on mortgage-backed securities backed by federally insured or guaranteed loans, mainly loans issued by the Federal Housing Administration, Department of Veterans Affairs, Rural Housing Service, and Office of Public and Indian Housing. Ginnie Mae securities are the only MBS that are guaranteed by the United States government.

a. Cash budget
b. Case-Shiller Home Price Indices
c. Certified Emission Reductions
d. GNMA

36. The _____ is a U.S. government-owned corporation within the Department of Housing and Urban Development

Ginnie Mae provides guarantees on mortgage-backed securities backed by federally insured or guaranteed loans, mainly loans issued by the Federal Housing Administration, Department of Veterans Affairs, Rural Housing Service, and Office of Public and Indian Housing. Ginnie Mae securities are the only MBS that are guaranteed by the United States government.

a. Government National Mortgage Association
b. Jumbo mortgage
c. 4-4-5 Calendar
d. Graduated payment mortgage

37. _____ is early repayment of a loan by a borrower.

In the case of a mortgage-backed security (MBS), _____ is perceived as a risk, because mortgage debts are often paid off early in order to incur lower total interest payments through cheaper refinancing. The new financing may be cheaper because the borrower's credit rating has improved or because interest rates are lower, but in either case, the payments that would have been made to the MBS investor would be above market rates.

a. Retention ratio
b. Bankruptcy remote
c. Disposal tax effect
d. Prepayment

38.

A _____ is a type of financial intermediary and a type of bank. Commercial banking is also known as business banking. It is a bank that provides checking accounts, savings accounts, and money market accounts and that accepts time deposits.

Chapter 10. The Investment Function in Banking and Financial-Services Management

a. 4-4-5 Calendar
b. 529 plan
c. Commercial bank
d. 7-Eleven

39. Explicit _____ is a measure implemented in many countries to protect bank depositors, in full or in part, from losses caused by a bank's inability to pay its debts when due. _____ systems are one component of a financial system safety net that promotes financial stability.
   a. Banking panic
   b. Reserve requirement
   c. Time deposit
   d. Deposit Insurance

40. The _____ is a United States government corporation created by the Glass-Steagall Act of 1933. It provides deposit insurance, which guarantees the safety of checking and savings deposits in member banks, currently up to $250,000 per depositor per bank. Insured deposits are backed by the full faith and credit of the United States.
   a. Federal Deposit Insurance Corporation
   b. Ford Foundation
   c. FASB
   d. NYSE Group

41. A _____ is a bond bought at a price lower than its face value, with the face value repaid at the time of maturity. It does not make periodic interest payments, or so-called 'coupons,' hence the term zero-coupon bond. Investors earn return from the compounded interest all paid at maturity plus the difference between the discounted price of the bond and its par value.
   a. Callable bond
   b. Bowie bonds
   c. Municipal bond
   d. Zero coupon bond

42. A _____ is a company that owns other companies' outstanding stock. It usually refers to a company which does not produce goods or services itself, rather its only purpose is owning shares of other companies. They allow the reduction of risk for the owners and can allow the ownership and control of a number of different companies.
   a. Privately held company
   b. Federal National Mortgage Association
   c. MRU Holdings
   d. Holding company

43. In finance, the term _____ describes the amount in cash that returns to the owners of a security. Normally it does not include the price variations, at the difference of the total return. _____ applies to various stated rates of return on stocks (common and preferred, and convertible), fixed income instruments (bonds, notes, bills, strips, zero coupon), and some other investment type insurance products (e.g. annuities.)
   a. Yield to maturity
   b. 4-4-5 Calendar
   c. Macaulay duration
   d. Yield

44. The _____ or redemption yield is the yield promised to the bondholder on the assumption that the bond or other fixed-interest security such as gilts will be held to maturity, that all coupon and principal payments will be made and coupon payments are reinvested at the bond's promised yield at the same rate as invested. It is a measure of the return of the bond. This technique in theory allows investors to calculate the fair value of different financial instruments.
   a. Yield to maturity
   b. Yield
   c. 4-4-5 Calendar
   d. Macaulay duration

Chapter 10. The Investment Function in Banking and Financial-Services Management

45. In economics, _____ is a rise in the general level of prices of goods and services in an economy over a period of time. The term '_____' once referred to increases in the money supply (monetary _____); however, economic debates about the relationship between money supply and price levels have led to its primary use today in describing price _____. _____ can also be described as a decline in the real value of money--a loss of purchasing power in the medium of exchange which is also the monetary unit of account.
   a. A Random Walk Down Wall Street
   b. AAB
   c. ABN Amro
   d. Inflation

46. _____ is a life of security. It may also refer to the final payment date of a loan or other financial instrument, at which point all remaining interest and principal is due to be paid.

   1, 3, 6 months _____ band can be calculated by using 30-day per month periods.

   a. Primary market
   b. Maturity
   c. Replacement cost
   d. False billing

47. In finance, _____, also known as return on investment is the ratio of money gained or lost on an investment relative to the amount of money invested. The amount of money gained or lost may be referred to as interest, profit/loss, gain/loss, or net income/loss. The money invested may be referred to as the asset, capital, principal, or the cost basis of the investment.
   a. Stock or scrip dividends
   b. Doctrine of the Proper Law
   c. Composiition of Creditors
   d. Rate of return

48. Under the United States Internal Revenue Code, the type of income is defined by its character. _____ is usually characterized as income other than capital gain. _____ can consist of income from wages, salaries, tips, commissions, bonuses, and other types of compensation from employment, interest, dividends, or net income from a sole proprietorship, partnership or LLC.
   a. ABN Amro
   b. A Random Walk Down Wall Street
   c. AAB
   d. Ordinary income

49. _____, refers to consumption opportunity gained by an entity within a specified time frame, which is generally expressed in monetary terms. However, for households and individuals, '_____ is the sum of all the wages, salaries, profits, interests payments, rents and other forms of earnings received... in a given period of time.' For firms, _____ generally refers to net-profit: what remains of revenue after expenses have been subtracted.
   a. Accrual
   b. Annual report
   c. OIBDA
   d. Income

50. In finance, a _____ is a derivative in which two counterparties agree to exchange one stream of cash flows against another stream. These streams are called the legs of the _____.

   The cash flows are calculated over a notional principal amount, which is usually not exchanged between counterparties.

   a. Volatility swap
   b. Volatility arbitrage
   c. Local volatility
   d. Swap

Chapter 10. The Investment Function in Banking and Financial-Services Management

51. _____ is the risk of loss due to a debtor's non-payment of a loan or other line of credit (either the principal or interest (coupon) or both)

Most lenders employ their own models (credit scorecards) to rank potential and existing customers according to risk, and then apply appropriate strategies. With products such as unsecured personal loans or mortgages, lenders charge a higher price for higher risk customers and vice versa. With revolving products such as credit cards and overdrafts, risk is controlled through careful setting of credit limits.

a. Liquidity risk
b. Transaction risk
c. Market risk
d. Credit risk

52. In finance, _____ occurs when a debtor has not met its legal obligations according to the debt contract, e.g. it has not made a scheduled payment, or has violated a loan covenant (condition) of the debt contract. _____ may occur if the debtor is either unwilling or unable to pay their debt. This can occur with all debt obligations including bonds, mortgages, loans, and promissory notes.

a. Debt validation
b. Credit crunch
c. Vendor finance
d. Default

53. _____ is a fee paid on borrowed assets. It is the price paid for the use of borrowed money , or, money earned by deposited funds . Assets that are sometimes lent with _____ include money, shares, consumer goods through hire purchase, major assets such as aircraft, and even entire factories in finance lease arrangements.

a. Insolvency
b. AAB
c. A Random Walk Down Wall Street
d. Interest

54. An _____ is the price a borrower pays for the use of money they do not own, and the return a lender receives for deferring the use of funds, by lending it to the borrower. _____s are normally expressed as a percentage rate over the period of one year.

_____s targets are also a vital tool of monetary policy and are used to control variables like investment, inflation, and unemployment.

a. AAB
b. A Random Walk Down Wall Street
c. ABN Amro
d. Interest rate

55. _____ is the risk (variability in value) borne by an interest-bearing asset, such as a loan or a bond, due to variability of interest rates. In general, as rates rise, the price of a fixed rate bond will fall, and vice versa. _____ is commonly measured by the bond's duration.

a. Interest rate risk
b. Official bank rate
c. International Fisher effect
d. A Random Walk Down Wall Street

56. _____ are securities that can be easily converted into cash. Such securities will generally have highly liquid markets allowing the security to be sold at a reasonable price very quickly. This is a usual feature in real estate .

a. Tracking stock
b. Securities lending
c. Marketable
d. Book entry

Chapter 10. The Investment Function in Banking and Financial-Services Management

57. _____ arises from situations in which a party interested in trading an asset cannot do it because nobody in the market wants to trade that asset. _____ becomes particularly important to parties who are about to hold or currently hold an asset, since it affects their ability to trade.

Manifestation of _____ is very different from a drop of price to zero.

a. Tracking error
b. Credit risk
c. Currency risk
d. Liquidity risk

58. _____ is a financial ratio that measures the efficiency of a company's use of its assets in generating sales revenue or sales income to the company.

$$Asset\ Turnover = \frac{Sales}{Average Total Assets}$$

- 'Sales' is the value of 'Net Sales' or 'Sales' from the company's income statement
- 'Average Total Assets' is the value of 'Total assets' from the company's balance sheet in the beginning and the end of the fiscal period divided by 2.

- Assets turnover

a. Average accounting return
b. Inventory turnover
c. Earnings yield
d. Asset turnover

59. _____ refers to the replacement of an existing debt obligation with a debt obligation bearing different terms. The most common consumer _____ is for a home mortgage.

_____ may be undertaken to reduce interest rate/interest costs (by _____ at a lower rate), to extend the repayment time, to pay off other debt(s), to reduce one's periodic payment obligations (sometimes by taking a longer-term loan), to reduce or alter risk (such as by _____ from a variable-rate to a fixed-rate loan), and/or to raise cash for investment, consumption, or the payment of a dividend.

a. Refinancing
b. 4-4-5 Calendar
c. 7-Eleven
d. 529 plan

60. A _____ is a measure of the average price of consumer goods and services purchased by households. The _____ can be used to index (i.e., adjust for the effects of inflation) wages, salaries, pensions, or regulated or contracted prices. The _____ is, along with the population census and the National Income and Product Accounts, one of the most closely watched national economic statistics.

a. 529 plan
b. 4-4-5 Calendar
c. Divisia index
d. Consumer price index

Chapter 10. The Investment Function in Banking and Financial-Services Management 93

61. _____ are the inflation-indexed bonds issued by the U.S. Treasury. The principal is adjusted to the Consumer Price Index, the commonly used measure of inflation. The coupon rate is constant, but generates a different amount of interest when multiplied by the inflation-adjusted principal, thus protecting the holder against inflation. _____ are currently offered in 5-year, 10-year and 20-year maturities.
   a. 4-4-5 Calendar
   b. Treasury Inflation Protected Securities
   c. Treasury securities
   d. Treasury Inflation-Protected Securities

62. A _____ is a normalized average (typically a weighted average) of prices for a given class of goods or services in a given region, during a given interval of time. It is a statistic designed to help to compare how these prices, taken as a whole, differ between time periods or geographical locations.
   a. Price discrimination
   b. Price index
   c. Transfer pricing
   d. Discounts and allowances

63. A _____ allows a borrower to use a financial security as collateral for a cash loan at a fixed rate of interest. In a repo, the borrower agrees to immediately sell a security to a lender and also agrees to buy the same security from the lender at a fixed price at some later date. A repo is equivalent to a cash transaction combined with a forward contract.
   a. Volatility arbitrage
   b. Contango
   c. Total return swap
   d. Repurchase Agreement

64. _____ also known as Deferred Sales Charge, is a fee paid when shares are sold. This fee typically goes to the brokers that sell the fund's shares. The amount of this type of load will depend on how long the investor holds his or her shares and typically decreases to zero if the investor holds his or her shares long enough.
   a. Money market funds
   b. Mutual fund fees and expenses
   c. Closed-end fund
   d. Back-end load

65. In finance, a _____ is formed when a Trader invests in Long and Short duration bonds, but does not invest in the intermediate duration bonds.

A _____ is one of several different types of portfolio strategies that is designed to create a reasonable return on the investments that are part of the asset portfolio. Essentially, the _____ is built around the concept of focusing on the maturities of the securities that are part of the portfolio and making sure that the maturity dates are either very close or at a distant date.

   a. Barbell strategy
   b. Stock market bubble
   c. Price-to-book ratio
   d. Share price

66. In finance, the _____ is the relation between the interest rate (or cost of borrowing) and the time to maturity of the debt for a given borrower in a given currency. For example, the current U.S. dollar interest rates paid on U.S. Treasury securities for various maturities are closely watched by many traders, and are commonly plotted on a graph such as the one on the right which is informally called 'the _____.' More formal mathematical descriptions of this relation are often called the term structure of interest rates.

The yield of a debt instrument is the annualized percentage increase in the value of the investment.

a. 529 plan
c. 4-4-5 Calendar
b. 7-Eleven
d. Yield curve

67. The term _____ or economic cycle refers to the fluctuations of economic activity (business fluctuations) around a long-term growth trend. The cycle involves shifts over time between periods of relatively rapid growth of output (recovery and prosperity), and periods of relative stagnation or decline (contraction or recession.) These fluctuations are often measured using the real gross domestic product.
   a. Fixed exchange rate
   c. Deflation
   b. Behavioral finance
   d. Business cycle

68. A _____ is a situation that involves losing one quality or aspect of something in return for gaining another quality or aspect. It implies a decision to be made with full comprehension of both the upside and downside of a particular choice.

In economics the term is expressed as opportunity cost, referring the most preferred alternative given up.

   a. Trade-off
   c. Break-even point
   b. Total revenue
   d. Capital outflow

69. In finance, the _____ of a financial asset measures the sensitivity of the asset's price to interest rate movements, expressed as a number of years. The reason for expressing this sensitivity in years is that the time that will elapse until a cash flow is received allows more interest to accumulate. Therefore the price of an asset with long term cashflows has more interest rate sensitivity than an asset with cashflows in the near future.
   a. 4-4-5 Calendar
   c. Yield to maturity
   b. Macaulay duration
   d. Duration

70. _____ is one of the main genres of financial risk. The term describes the risk that a particular investment might be canceled or stopped somehow, that one may have to find a new place to invest that money with the risk being there might not be a similarly attractive investment available. This primarily occurs if bonds (which are portions of loans to entities) are paid back earlier then expected.
   a. Standard of deferred payment
   c. Debt cash flow
   b. Biweekly Mortgage
   d. Reinvestment risk

Chapter 11. Liquidity and Reserve Management: Strategies and Policies

1. _____ is a measure of the ability of a debtor to pay their debts as and when they fall due. It is usually expressed as a ratio or a percentage of current liabilities.

For a corporation with a published balance sheet there are various ratios used to calculate a measure of liquidity.

 a. Operating leverage
 b. Operating profit margin
 c. Invested capital
 d. Accounting liquidity

2. In financial accounting, the term _____ is most commonly used to describe any part of shareholders' equity, except for basic share capital. Sometimes, the term is used instead of the term provision; such a use, however, is inconsistent with the terminology suggested by International Accounting Standards Board. For more information about provisions, see provision (accounting.)

 a. Closing entries
 b. FIFO and LIFO accounting
 c. Treasury stock
 d. Reserve

3. A _____, reserve bank, or monetary authority is the entity responsible for the monetary policy of a country or of a group of member states. It is a bank that can lend money to other banks in times of need. Its primary responsibility is to maintain the stability of the national currency and money supply, but more active duties include controlling subsidized-loan interest rates, and acting as a lender of last resort to the banking sector during times of financial crisis (private banks often being integral to the national financial system.)

 a. 529 plan
 b. 4-4-5 Calendar
 c. Central bank
 d. 7-Eleven

4. _____ arises from situations in which a party interested in trading an asset cannot do it because nobody in the market wants to trade that asset. _____ becomes particularly important to parties who are about to hold or currently hold an asset, since it affects their ability to trade.

Manifestation of _____ is very different from a drop of price to zero.

 a. Credit risk
 b. Currency risk
 c. Tracking error
 d. Liquidity risk

5. _____ is a fee paid on borrowed assets. It is the price paid for the use of borrowed money, or, money earned by deposited funds. Assets that are sometimes lent with _____ include money, shares, consumer goods through hire purchase, major assets such as aircraft, and even entire factories in finance lease arrangements.

 a. Interest
 b. AAB
 c. Insolvency
 d. A Random Walk Down Wall Street

6. An _____ is the price a borrower pays for the use of money they do not own, and the return a lender receives for deferring the use of funds, by lending it to the borrower. _____s are normally expressed as a percentage rate over the period of one year.

_____s targets are also a vital tool of monetary policy and are used to control variables like investment, inflation, and unemployment.

Chapter 11. Liquidity and Reserve Management: Strategies and Policies

    a. ABN Amro   b. Interest rate
    c. A Random Walk Down Wall Street   d. AAB

7. _____ is the risk (variability in value) borne by an interest-bearing asset, such as a loan or a bond, due to variability of interest rates. In general, as rates rise, the price of a fixed rate bond will fall, and vice versa. _____ is commonly measured by the bond's duration.
    a. Official bank rate   b. International Fisher effect
    c. A Random Walk Down Wall Street   d. Interest rate risk

8. In business and accounting, _____s are everything of value that is owned by a person or company. The balance sheet of a firm records the monetary value of the _____s owned by the firm. The two major _____ classes are tangible _____s and intangible _____s.
    a. Accounts payable   b. EBITDA
    c. Income   d. Asset

9. _____ is the term used to describe deposits residing in banks that are located outside the borders of the country that issues the currency the deposit is denominated in. For example a deposit denominated in US dollars residing in a Japanese bank is a _____ deposit, or more specifically a Eurodollar deposit.

Key points are the location of the bank and the denomination of the currency, not the nationality of the bank or the owner of the deposit/loan.

    a. AAB   b. ABN Amro
    c. A Random Walk Down Wall Street   d. Eurocurrency

10. In the United States, _____ are overnight borrowings by banks to maintain their bank reserves at the Federal Reserve. Banks keep reserves at Federal Reserve Banks to meet their reserve requirements and to clear financial transactions. Transactions in the _____ market enable depository institutions with reserve balances in excess of reserve requirements to lend reserves to institutions with reserve deficiencies.
    a. Regulation T   b. Federal funds rate
    c. 4-4-5 Calendar   d. Federal funds

11. In the most general sense, a _____ is anything that is a hindrance, or puts individuals at a disadvantage.

Before we discuss the financial terms, we should note that a _____ can also have a much more important slang meaning.

This is best described in an example.

    a. McFadden Act   b. Limited liability
    c. Liability   d. Covenant

12. In the United States, a _____ is a bond issued by a city or other local government, or their agencies. Potential issuers of these bonds include cities, counties, redevelopment agencies, school districts, publicly owned airports and seaports, and any other governmental entity (or group of governments) below the state level. They may be general obligations of the issuer or secured by specified revenues.

a. Puttable bond
b. Premium bond
c. Senior debt
d. Municipal bond

13. _____ or economic opportunity loss is the value of the next best alternative foregone as the result of making a decision. _____ analysis is an important part of a company's decision-making processes but is not treated as an actual cost in any financial statement. The next best thing that a person can engage in is referred to as the _____ of doing the best thing and ignoring the next best thing to be done.
a. A Random Walk Down Wall Street
b. AAB
c. Opportunity cost
d. ABN Amro

14. A _____ allows a borrower to use a financial security as collateral for a cash loan at a fixed rate of interest. In a repo, the borrower agrees to immediately sell a security to a lender and also agrees to buy the same security from the lender at a fixed price at some later date. A repo is equivalent to a cash transaction combined with a forward contract.
a. Total return swap
b. Volatility arbitrage
c. Contango
d. Repurchase Agreement

15. _____ mature in one year or less. Like zero-coupon bonds, they do not pay interest prior to maturity; instead they are sold at a discount of the par value to create a positive yield to maturity. Many regard _____ as the least risky investment available to U.S. investors.
a. Treasury securities
b. Treasury bills
c. 4-4-5 Calendar
d. Treasury Inflation Protected Securities

16. In finance, a _____ is a debt security, in which the authorized issuer owes the holders a debt and, depending on the terms of the _____, is obliged to pay interest (the coupon) and/or to repay the principal at a later date, termed maturity.

Thus a _____ is a loan: the issuer is the borrower, the _____ holder is the lender, and the coupon is the interest. _____s provide the borrower with external funds to finance long-term investments, or, in the case of government _____s, to finance current expenditure.

a. Convertible bond
b. Puttable bond
c. Catastrophe bonds
d. Bond

17. In economics, business, and accounting, a _____ is the value of money that has been used up to produce something, and hence is not available for use anymore. In business, the _____ may be one of acquisition, in which case the amount of money expended to acquire it is counted as _____. In this case, money is the input that is gone in order to acquire the thing.
a. Sliding scale fees
b. Marginal cost
c. Cost
d. Fixed costs

18. A _____ is a fungible, negotiable instrument representing financial value. They are broadly categorized into debt securities (such as banknotes, bonds and debentures), and equity securities; e.g., common stocks. The company or other entity issuing the _____ is called the issuer.
a. Securities lending
b. Book entry
c. Security
d. Tracking stock

Chapter 11. Liquidity and Reserve Management: Strategies and Policies

19. A '_____' is a 'Charge' that is paid to obtain the right to delay a payment. Essentially, the payer purchases the right to make a given payment in the future instead of in the Present. The '_____', or 'Charge' that must be paid to delay the payment, is simply the difference between what the payment amount would be if it were paid in the present and what the payment amount would be paid if it were paid in the future.
    a. Value at risk
    b. Risk modeling
    c. Risk aversion
    d. Discount

20. The _____ provide stable, on-demand, low-cost funding to American financial institutions for home mortgage loans, small business, rural, agricultural, and economic development lending. With their members, the _____ank System represents the largest collective source of home mortgage and community credit in the United States. The banks do not provide loans directly to individuals, only to other banks.
    a. 529 plan
    b. 7-Eleven
    c. Federal Home Loan Banks
    d. 4-4-5 Calendar

21. The role of the _____ is to issue accounting standards in the United Kingdom. It is recognised for that purpose under the Companies Act 1985. It took over the task of setting accounting standards from the Accounting Standards Committee (ASC) in 1990.
    a. AAB
    b. Accounting Standards Board
    c. A Random Walk Down Wall Street
    d. ABN Amro

22. The _____ is a private, not-for-profit organization whose primary purpose is to develop generally accepted accounting principles (GAAP) within the United States in the public's interest. The Securities and Exchange Commission (SEC) designated the _____ as the organization responsible for setting accounting standards for public companies in the U.S. It was created in 1973, replacing the Accounting Principles Board and the Committee on Accounting Procedure of the American Institute of Certified Public Accountants. The _____'s mission is 'to establish and improve standards of financial accounting and reporting for the guidance and education of the public, including issuers, auditors, and users of financial information.'

    The _____ is not a governmental body.

    a. MRU Holdings
    b. Credit karma
    c. FASB
    d. PlaNet Finance

23. The _____ is a United States government corporation created by the Glass-Steagall Act of 1933. It provides deposit insurance, which guarantees the safety of checking and savings deposits in member banks, currently up to $250,000 per depositor per bank. Insured deposits are backed by the full faith and credit of the United States.
    a. Ford Foundation
    b. Federal Deposit Insurance Corporation
    c. FASB
    d. NYSE Group

24. _____ is the field of accountancy concerned with the preparation of financial statements for decision makers, such as stockholders, suppliers, banks, employees, government agencies, owners, and other stakeholders. The fundamental need for _____ is to reduce principal-agent problem by measuring and monitoring agents' performance and reporting the results to interested users.

    _____ is used to prepare accounting information for people outside the organization or not involved in the day to day running of the company.

Chapter 11. Liquidity and Reserve Management: Strategies and Policies

a. Financial Accounting
c. 7-Eleven

b. 4-4-5 Calendar
d. 529 plan

25. The _____ is a private, not-for-profit organization whose primary purpose is to develop generally accepted accounting principles (GAAP) within the United States in the public's interest. The Securities and Exchange Commission (SEC) designated the _____ as the organization responsible for setting accounting standards for public companies in the U.S. It was created in 1973, replacing the Accounting Principles Board and the Committee on Accounting Procedure of the American Institute of Certified Public Accountants. The _____'s mission is 'to establish and improve standards of financial accounting and reporting for the guidance and education of the public, including issuers, auditors, and users of financial information.'

The _____ is not a governmental body.

a. Federal Deposit Insurance Corporation
c. World Congress of Accountants

b. KPMG
d. Financial Accounting Standards Board

26. A _____ is the price of a single share of a no. of saleable stocks of the company. Once the stock is purchased, the owner becomes a shareholder of the company that issued the share.
a. Whisper numbers
c. Stock split

b. Trading curb
d. Share price

27.

In finance, the _____ can be the expected rate of return above the risk-free interest rate. When measuring risk, a common sense approach is to compare the risk-free return on T-bills and the very risky return on other investments. The difference between these two returns can be interpreted as a measure of the excess return on the average risky asset. This excess return is known as the _____.

a. Risk aversion
c. Risk adjusted return on capital

b. Risk premium
d. Risk modeling

28. In the United States, the _____ is the interest rate at which private depository institutions (mostly banks) lend balances (federal funds) at the Federal Reserve to other depository institutions, usually overnight. Changing the target rate is one form of open market operations that the Chairman of the Federal Reserve uses to regulate the supply of money in the U.S. economy.

U.S. banks and thrift institutions are obligated by law to maintain certain levels of reserves, either as reserves with the Fed or as vault cash.

a. Federal funds rate
c. Regulation T

b. Taylor rule
d. 4-4-5 Calendar

29. _____ is the provision of resources (such as granting a loan) by one party to another party where that second party does not reimburse the first party immediately, thereby generating a debt, and instead arranges either to repay or return those resources (or material(s) of equal value) at a later date. The first party is called a creditor, also known as a lender, while the second party is called a debtor, also known as a borrower.

Movements of financial capital are normally dependent on either _____ or equity transfers.

a. Clearing house
c. Comparable
b. Warrant
d. Credit

30. The _____ is a bank regulation that sets the minimum reserves each bank must hold to customer deposits and notes. These reserves are designed to satisfy withdrawal demands, and would normally be in the form of fiat currency stored in a bank vault (vault cash), or with a central bank.

The reserve ratio is sometimes used as a tool in the monetary policy, influencing the country's economy, borrowing, and interest rates.

a. Variable rate mortgage
c. Wall Street Journal prime rate
b. Reserve requirement
d. Prime rate

31. _____ is the removal or simplification of government rules and regulations that constrain the operation of market forces. _____ does not mean elimination of laws against fraud, but eliminating or reducing government control of how business is done, thereby moving toward a more free market.

The stated rationale for '_____' is often that fewer and simpler regulations will lead to a raised level of competitiveness, therefore higher productivity, more efficiency and lower prices overall.

a. Demand shock
c. Value added
b. Supply shock
d. Deregulation

32. In banking and finance, _____ denotes all activities from the time a commitment is made for a transaction until it is settled. _____ is necessary because the speed of trades is much faster than the cycle time for completing the underlying transaction.

In its widest sense _____ involves the management of post-trading, pre-settlement credit exposures, to ensure that trades are settled in accordance with market rules, even if a buyer or seller should become insolvent prior to settlement.

a. Share
c. Clearing
b. Clearing house
d. Procter ' Gamble

33. _____ is a regulation of the U.S. Securities and Exchange Commission It allows an issuer to sell securities without registering them with the SEC. Rule 501 contains definitions that apply to the rest of _____. Rule 502 contains the general conditions that must be met to take advantage of the exemptions under _____. Generally speaking, these conditions are that all sales within a certain time period that are part of the same Reg D offering must be 'integrated', information and disclosures must be provided, there must be no 'general solicitation', and that the securities being sold contain restrictions on their resale.

a. Regulation D
c. 4-4-5 Calendar
b. 7-Eleven
d. 529 plan

Chapter 11. Liquidity and Reserve Management: Strategies and Policies

34. _____, in bookkeeping, refers to assets, liabilities, income, and expenses recorded on individual pages of the so called book of final entry or ledger. Changes in _____ value are made by chronologically posting debit (DR) and credit (CR) entries to its page. Examples of _____s are cash, _____s receivable, mortgages, loans, land and buildings, common stock, sales, services provided, wages, and payroll overhead.
   a. Alpha
   b. Accretion
   c. Account
   d. Option

35. _____ is a United States government regulation that put a limit on the interest rates that banks could pay, including a rate of zero on demand deposits (checking accounts.) Section 11 of the Banking Act of 1933 (12 U.S.C. 371a) prohibits member banks from paying interest on demand deposits, which is implemented by _____
   a. Truth in Lending Act
   b. Fair Credit Billing Act
   c. Fair Credit Reporting Act
   d. Regulation Q

36. In finance, the _____ of a financial asset measures the sensitivity of the asset's price to interest rate movements, expressed as a number of years. The reason for expressing this sensitivity in years is that the time that will elapse until a cash flow is received allows more interest to accumulate. Therefore the price of an asset with long term cashflows has more interest rate sensitivity than an asset with cashflows in the near future.
   a. 4-4-5 Calendar
   b. Yield to maturity
   c. Duration
   d. Macaulay duration

Chapter 12. Managing and Pricing Deposit Services

1. The _____ is one of several stock market indices, created by nineteenth-century Wall Street Journal editor and Dow Jones ' Company co-founder Charles Dow. Dow compiled the index to gauge the performance of the industrial sector of the American stock market. It is the second-oldest U.S. market index, after the Dow Jones Transportation Average, which Dow also created.
   a. Dow Jones Industrial Average
   b. 529 plan
   c. 4-4-5 Calendar
   d. 7-Eleven

2. _____ is an American publishing and financial information firm.

   The company was founded in 1882 by three reporters: Charles Dow, Edward Jones, and Charles Bergstresser. Like The New York Times and the Washington Post, the company was in recent years publicly traded but privately controlled.

   a. Dow Jones ' Company
   b. The Dun ' Bradstreet Corporation
   c. Federal National Mortgage Association
   d. Holding company

3. _____ is a type of bank account where the money in the account is legally able to be withdrawn immediately upon demand (or 'at call'.) This type of bank account can also be referred to as a 'cheque' or 'checking' or transactional account.

   This type of bank account, allowing immediate conversion of the account balance into cash or withdrawal to another account, can be contrasted with a time deposit (also known as a certificate of deposit or term deposit), where the funds are not legally available for immediate withdrawal by the depositor.

   a. Synthetic lease
   b. 529 plan
   c. 4-4-5 Calendar
   d. Demand deposit

4. _____ is the removal or simplification of government rules and regulations that constrain the operation of market forces. _____ does not mean elimination of laws against fraud, but eliminating or reducing government control of how business is done, thereby moving toward a more free market.

   The stated rationale for '_____' is often that fewer and simpler regulations will lead to a raised level of competitiveness, therefore higher productivity, more efficiency and lower prices overall.

   a. Value added
   b. Supply shock
   c. Demand shock
   d. Deregulation

5. _____, in bookkeeping, refers to assets, liabilities, income, and expenses recorded on individual pages of the so called book of final entry or ledger. Changes in _____ value are made by chronologically posting debit (DR) and credit (CR) entries to its page. Examples of _____s are cash, _____s receivable, mortgages, loans, land and buildings, common stock, sales, services provided, wages, and payroll overhead.
   a. Account
   b. Accretion
   c. Alpha
   d. Option

6. In finance, the _____ is the global financial market for short-term borrowing and lending. It provides short-term liquidity funding for the global financial system. The _____ is where short-term obligations such as Treasury bills, commercial paper and bankers' acceptances are bought and sold.

Chapter 12. Managing and Pricing Deposit Services

a. Debt-for-equity swap
b. Cramdown
c. Consumer debt
d. Money market

7. A _____ is a fungible, negotiable instrument representing financial value. They are broadly categorized into debt securities (such as banknotes, bonds and debentures), and equity securities; e.g., common stocks. The company or other entity issuing the _____ is called the issuer.
   a. Securities lending
   b. Tracking stock
   c. Book entry
   d. Security

8. A _____ is a money deposit at a banking institution that cannot be withdrawn for a certain 'term' or period of time. When the term is over it can be withdrawn or it can be held for another term. Generally speaking, the longer the term the better the yield on the money.
   a. Basel Accord
   b. Time deposit
   c. Private money
   d. Certificate of deposit

9. A _____ is a current account at a banking institution that allows money to be deposited and withdrawn by the account holder, with the transactions and resulting balance being recorded on the bank's books. Some banks charge a fee for this service, while others may pay the customer interest on the funds deposited.

Although restrictions placed on access depend upon the terms and conditions of the account and the provider, the account holder retains rights to have their funds repaid on demand.

   a. Bilateral netting
   b. 4-4-5 Calendar
   c. Contractum trinius
   d. Deposit account

10. A _____ s a time deposit, a financial product commonly offered to consumers by banks, thrift institutions, and credit unions.

They are similar to savings accounts in that they are insured and thus virtually risk-free; they are 'money in the bank'. They are different from savings accounts in that they have a specific, fixed term (often three months, six months, or one to five years), and, usually, a fixed interest rate.

   a. Variable rate mortgage
   b. Reserve requirement
   c. Time deposit
   d. Certificate of deposit

11. An _____ is a retirement plan account that provides some tax advantages for retirement savings in the United States.
   a. ABN Amro
   b. A Random Walk Down Wall Street
   c. AAB
   d. Individual Retirement Arrangement

12. _____ is a fee paid on borrowed assets. It is the price paid for the use of borrowed money , or, money earned by deposited funds . Assets that are sometimes lent with _____ include money, shares, consumer goods through hire purchase, major assets such as aircraft, and even entire factories in finance lease arrangements.
   a. AAB
   b. A Random Walk Down Wall Street
   c. Insolvency
   d. Interest

Chapter 12. Managing and Pricing Deposit Services

13. _____s are full-fledged pension plans for self-employed people in the United States. They are sometimes called HR10 plans and are not Individual Retirement Accounts (IRA.)

Since a _____ is a full-fledged pension, there is a Keogh for every employer-sponsored pension-plan design.

a. 7-Eleven
c. 4-4-5 Calendar
b. 529 plan
d. Keogh plan

14. An _____ is the price a borrower pays for the use of money they do not own, and the return a lender receives for deferring the use of funds, by lending it to the borrower. _____s are normally expressed as a percentage rate over the period of one year.

_____s targets are also a vital tool of monetary policy and are used to control variables like investment, inflation, and unemployment.

a. ABN Amro
c. AAB
b. A Random Walk Down Wall Street
d. Interest rate

15.

A _____ is a type of financial intermediary and a type of bank. Commercial banking is also known as business banking. It is a bank that provides checking accounts, savings accounts, and money market accounts and that accepts time deposits.

a. 529 plan
c. Commercial bank
b. 7-Eleven
d. 4-4-5 Calendar

16. In economics, business, and accounting, a _____ is the value of money that has been used up to produce something, and hence is not available for use anymore. In business, the _____ may be one of acquisition, in which case the amount of money expended to acquire it is counted as _____. In this case, money is the input that is gone in order to acquire the thing.
a. Cost
c. Marginal cost
b. Sliding scale fees
d. Fixed costs

17. The _____ of 1933 established the Federal Deposit Insurance Corporation (FDIC) in the United States and included banking reforms, some of which were designed to control speculation. Some provisions such as Regulation Q, which allowed the Federal Reserve to regulate interest rates in savings accounts, were repealed by the Depository Institutions Deregulation and Monetary Control Act of 1980. Provisions that prohibit a bank holding company from owning other financial companies were repealed on November 12, 1999, by the Gramm-Leach-Bliley Act.
a. 4-4-5 Calendar
c. 529 plan
b. 7-Eleven
d. Glass-Steagall Act

Chapter 12. Managing and Pricing Deposit Services

18. In finance, a _____ is collateral that the holder of a position in securities, options, or futures contracts has to deposit to cover the credit risk of his counterparty (most often his broker.) This risk can arise if the holder has done any of the following:

- borrowed cash from the counterparty to buy securities or options,
- sold securities or options short, or
- entered into a futures contract.

The collateral can be in the form of cash or securities, and it is deposited in a _____ account. On U.S. futures exchanges, '_____' was formally called performance bond.

_____ buying is buying securities with cash borrowed from a broker, using other securities as collateral.

a. Share
b. Margin
c. Procter ' Gamble
d. Credit

19. _____ is the difference between price and the costs of bringing to market whatever it is that is accounted as an enterprise (whether by harvest, extraction, manufacture, or purchase) in terms of the component costs of delivered goods and/or services and any operating or other expenses.

A key difficulty in measuring profit is in defining costs. Pure economic monetary profits can be zero or negative even in competitive equilibrium when accounted monetized costs exceed monetized price.

a. Economic profit
b. Accounting profit
c. A Random Walk Down Wall Street
d. AAB

20. _____, Net Margin, Net _____ or Net Profit Ratio all refer to a measure of profitability. It is calculated using a formula and written as a percentage or a number.

$$\text{Net profit margin} = \frac{\text{Net profit after taxes}}{\text{Net Sales}}$$

The _____ is mostly used for internal comparison.

a. Profit margin
b. Net profit margin
c. 4-4-5 Calendar
d. Profit maximization

21. _____ is a pricing method used by companies. It is used primarily because it is easy to calculate and requires little information. There are several varieties, but the common thread in all of them is that one first calculates the cost of the product, then includes an additional amount to represent profit.

a. Transfer pricing
b. Discounts and allowances
c. Cost-plus pricing
d. Price discrimination

Chapter 12. Managing and Pricing Deposit Services

22. The institution most often referenced by the word '_____' is a public or publicly traded _____, the shares of which are traded on a public stock exchange (e.g., the New York Stock Exchange or Nasdaq in the United States) where shares of stock of _____s are bought and sold by and to the general public. Most of the largest businesses in the world are publicly traded _____s. However, the majority of _____s are said to be closely held, privately held or close _____s, meaning that no ready market exists for the trading of shares.
   a. Depository Trust Company
   b. Protect
   c. Federal Home Loan Mortgage Corporation
   d. Corporation

23. Explicit _____ is a measure implemented in many countries to protect bank depositors, in full or in part, from losses caused by a bank's inability to pay its debts when due. _____ systems are one component of a financial system safety net that promotes financial stability.
   a. Time deposit
   b. Banking panic
   c. Reserve requirement
   d. Deposit Insurance

24. The _____ is a United States government corporation created by the Glass-Steagall Act of 1933. It provides deposit insurance, which guarantees the safety of checking and savings deposits in member banks, currently up to $250,000 per depositor per bank. Insured deposits are backed by the full faith and credit of the United States.
   a. FASB
   b. NYSE Group
   c. Federal Deposit Insurance Corporation
   d. Ford Foundation

25. In economics and finance, _____ is the change in total cost that arises when the quantity produced changes by one unit. It is the cost of producing one more unit of a good. Mathematically, the _____ function is expressed as the first derivative of the total cost (TC) function with respect to quantity (Q). Note that the _____ may change with volume, and so at each level of production, the _____ is the cost of the next unit produced.

   A typical _____ Curve

   a. Sliding scale fees
   b. Marginal cost
   c. Cost accounting
   d. Fixed costs

26. _____ expresses an annual rate of interest taking into account the effect of compounding, usually for deposit or investment products (such as a certificate of deposit.) It is analogous to the Annual percentage rate (APR), which is used for loans. In some jurisdictions, the use and definition of _____ may be regulated by a government agency, in which case it would generally be capitalized.
   a. Annual percentage yield
   b. A Random Walk Down Wall Street
   c. ABN Amro
   d. AAB

27. In finance, the term _____ describes the amount in cash that returns to the owners of a security. Normally it does not include the price variations, at the difference of the total return. _____ applies to various stated rates of return on stocks (common and preferred, and convertible), fixed income instruments (bonds, notes, bills, strips, zero coupon), and some other investment type insurance products (e.g. annuities).

a. Macaulay duration
c. Yield to maturity
b. 4-4-5 Calendar
d. Yield

28. _____ is that which is owed; usually referencing assets owed, but the term can cover other obligations. In the case of assets, _____ is a means of using future purchasing power in the present before a summation has been earned. Some companies and corporations use _____ as a part of their overall corporate finance strategy.

a. Credit cycle
c. Partial Payment
b. Cross-collateralization
d. Debt

Chapter 13. Managing Nondeposit Liabilities and Other Sources of Borrowed Funds

1. _____ is a measure of the ability of a debtor to pay their debts as and when they fall due. It is usually expressed as a ratio or a percentage of current liabilities.

For a corporation with a published balance sheet there are various ratios used to calculate a measure of liquidity.

   a. Operating leverage
   b. Accounting liquidity
   c. Invested capital
   d. Operating profit margin

2. In economics, the concept of the _____ refers to the decision-making time frame of a firm in which at least one factor of production is fixed. Costs which are fixed in the _____ have no impact on a firms decisions. For example a firm can raise output by increasing the amount of labour through overtime.
   a. 529 plan
   b. 4-4-5 Calendar
   c. Long-run
   d. Short-run

3. The _____ provide stable, on-demand, low-cost funding to American financial institutions for home mortgage loans, small business, rural, agricultural, and economic development lending. With their members, the _____ank System represents the largest collective source of home mortgage and community credit in the United States. The banks do not provide loans directly to individuals, only to other banks.
   a. 4-4-5 Calendar
   b. 7-Eleven
   c. 529 plan
   d. Federal Home Loan Banks

4. In the United States, _____ are overnight borrowings by banks to maintain their bank reserves at the Federal Reserve. Banks keep reserves at Federal Reserve Banks to meet their reserve requirements and to clear financial transactions. Transactions in the _____ market enable depository institutions with reserve balances in excess of reserve requirements to lend reserves to institutions with reserve deficiencies.
   a. 4-4-5 Calendar
   b. Regulation T
   c. Federal funds rate
   d. Federal funds

5. In lending agreements, _____ is a borrower's pledge of specific property to a lender, to secure repayment of a loan. The _____ serves as protection for a lender against a borrower's risk of default - that is, a borrower failing to pay the principal and interest under the terms of a loan obligation. If a borrower does default on a loan (due to insolvency or other event), that borrower forfeits (gives up) the property pledged as _____ *ollateral* - and the lender then becomes the owner of the _____.
   a. Future-oriented
   b. Nominal value
   c. Refinancing risk
   d. Collateral

6. The role of the _____ is to issue accounting standards in the United Kingdom. It is recognised for that purpose under the Companies Act 1985. It took over the task of setting accounting standards from the Accounting Standards Committee (ASC) in 1990.
   a. Accounting Standards Board
   b. ABN Amro
   c. A Random Walk Down Wall Street
   d. AAB

Chapter 13. Managing Nondeposit Liabilities and Other Sources of Borrowed Funds

7. The _____ is a private, not-for-profit organization whose primary purpose is to develop generally accepted accounting principles (GAAP) within the United States in the public's interest. The Securities and Exchange Commission (SEC) designated the _____ as the organization responsible for setting accounting standards for public companies in the U.S. It was created in 1973, replacing the Accounting Principles Board and the Committee on Accounting Procedure of the American Institute of Certified Public Accountants. The _____'s mission is 'to establish and improve standards of financial accounting and reporting for the guidance and education of the public, including issuers, auditors, and users of financial information.'

The _____ is not a governmental body.

a. MRU Holdings
b. PlaNet Finance
c. Credit karma
d. FASB

8. The _____ is a United States government corporation created by the Glass-Steagall Act of 1933. It provides deposit insurance, which guarantees the safety of checking and savings deposits in member banks, currently up to $250,000 per depositor per bank. Insured deposits are backed by the full faith and credit of the United States.

a. Ford Foundation
b. FASB
c. NYSE Group
d. Federal Deposit Insurance Corporation

9. _____ is the field of accountancy concerned with the preparation of financial statements for decision makers, such as stockholders, suppliers, banks, employees, government agencies, owners, and other stakeholders. The fundamental need for _____ is to reduce principal-agent problem by measuring and monitoring agents' performance and reporting the results to interested users.

_____ is used to prepare accounting information for people outside the organization or not involved in the day to day running of the company.

a. Financial Accounting
b. 529 plan
c. 4-4-5 Calendar
d. 7-Eleven

10. The _____ is a private, not-for-profit organization whose primary purpose is to develop generally accepted accounting principles (GAAP) within the United States in the public's interest. The Securities and Exchange Commission (SEC) designated the _____ as the organization responsible for setting accounting standards for public companies in the U.S. It was created in 1973, replacing the Accounting Principles Board and the Committee on Accounting Procedure of the American Institute of Certified Public Accountants. The _____'s mission is 'to establish and improve standards of financial accounting and reporting for the guidance and education of the public, including issuers, auditors, and users of financial information.'

The _____ is not a governmental body.

a. World Congress of Accountants
b. KPMG
c. Federal Deposit Insurance Corporation
d. Financial Accounting Standards Board

11. A _____ allows a borrower to use a financial security as collateral for a cash loan at a fixed rate of interest. In a repo, the borrower agrees to immediately sell a security to a lender and also agrees to buy the same security from the lender at a fixed price at some later date. A repo is equivalent to a cash transaction combined with a forward contract.

Chapter 13. Managing Nondeposit Liabilities and Other Sources of Borrowed Funds

a. Total return swap
b. Contango
c. Volatility arbitrage
d. Repurchase Agreement

12. The institution most often referenced by the word '_____' is a public or publicly traded _____, the shares of which are traded on a public stock exchange (e.g., the New York Stock Exchange or Nasdaq in the United States) where shares of stock of _____s are bought and sold by and to the general public. Most of the largest businesses in the world are publicly traded _____s. However, the majority of _____s are said to be closely held, privately held or close _____s, meaning that no ready market exists for the trading of shares.

a. Protect
b. Depository Trust Company
c. Corporation
d. Federal Home Loan Mortgage Corporation

13. A _____ is an exchange of promises between two or more parties to do an act which is enforceable in a court of law. It is where an unqualified offer meets a qualified acceptance and the parties reach Consensus ad Idem. The parties must have the necessary capacity to _____ and the _____ must not be either trifling, indeterminate, impossible or illegal.

a. 4-4-5 Calendar
b. 7-Eleven
c. 529 plan
d. Contract

14. The _____, effective annual interest rate, Annual Equivalent Rate (AER) or simply effective rate is the interest rate on a loan or financial product restated from the nominal interest rate as an interest rate with annual compound interest. It is used to compare the annual interest between loans with different compounding terms (daily, monthly, annually, or other.)

The _____ differs in two important respects from the annual percentage rate (APR):

1. the _____ generally does not incorporate one-time charges such as front-end fees;
2. the _____ is (generally) not defined by legal or regulatory authorities (as APR is in many jurisdictions.)

By contrast, the 'effective APR' is used as a legal term, where front-fees and other costs can be included, as defined by local law.

Annual Percentage Yield or effective annual yield is the analogous concept used for savings or investment products, such as a certificate of deposit.

a. AAB
b. ABN Amro
c. A Random Walk Down Wall Street
d. Effective interest rate

15. _____ is a fee paid on borrowed assets. It is the price paid for the use of borrowed money, or, money earned by deposited funds. Assets that are sometimes lent with _____ include money, shares, consumer goods through hire purchase, major assets such as aircraft, and even entire factories in finance lease arrangements.

a. Interest
b. AAB
c. A Random Walk Down Wall Street
d. Insolvency

16. An _____ is the price a borrower pays for the use of money they do not own, and the return a lender receives for deferring the use of funds, by lending it to the borrower. _____s are normally expressed as a percentage rate over the period of one year.

Chapter 13. Managing Nondeposit Liabilities and Other Sources of Borrowed Funds 111

_____s targets are also a vital tool of monetary policy and are used to control variables like investment, inflation, and unemployment.

a. A Random Walk Down Wall Street
b. ABN Amro
c. AAB
d. Interest rate

17. In banking and finance, _____ denotes all activities from the time a commitment is made for a transaction until it is settled. _____ is necessary because the speed of trades is much faster than the cycle time for completing the underlying transaction.

In its widest sense _____ involves the management of post-trading, pre-settlement credit exposures, to ensure that trades are settled in accordance with market rules, even if a buyer or seller should become insolvent prior to settlement.

a. Clearing
b. Clearing house
c. Share
d. Procter ' Gamble

18. _____ refers to any type of investment that yields a regular (or fixed) return.

For example, if you lend money to a borrower and the borrower has to pay interest once a month, you have been issued a fixed-income security. When a company does this, it is often called a bond or corporate bank debt (although preferred stock is also sometimes considered to be _____).

a. Bond market
b. Fixed Income
c. 4-4-5 Calendar
d. 529 plan

19. _____, refers to consumption opportunity gained by an entity within a specified time frame, which is generally expressed in monetary terms. However, for households and individuals, '_____ is the sum of all the wages, salaries, profits, interests payments, rents and other forms of earnings received... in a given period of time.' For firms, _____ generally refers to net-profit: what remains of revenue after expenses have been subtracted.

a. Accrual
b. Income
c. OIBDA
d. Annual report

20. In economics, business, and accounting, a _____ is the value of money that has been used up to produce something, and hence is not available for use anymore. In business, the _____ may be one of acquisition, in which case the amount of money expended to acquire it is counted as _____. In this case, money is the input that is gone in order to acquire the thing.

a. Fixed costs
b. Sliding scale fees
c. Marginal cost
d. Cost

21. A '_____' is a 'Charge' that is paid to obtain the right to delay a payment. Essentially, the payer purchases the right to make a given payment in the future instead of in the Present. The '_____', or 'Charge' that must be paid to delay the payment, is simply the difference between what the payment amount would be if it were paid in the present and what the payment amount would be paid if it were paid in the future.

Chapter 13. Managing Nondeposit Liabilities and Other Sources of Borrowed Funds

a. Risk aversion
b. Discount
c. Risk modeling
d. Value at risk

22. In financial accounting, the term _____ is most commonly used to describe any part of shareholders' equity, except for basic share capital. Sometimes, the term is used instead of the term provision; such a use, however, is inconsistent with the terminology suggested by International Accounting Standards Board. For more information about provisions, see provision (accounting.)

a. Reserve
b. FIFO and LIFO accounting
c. Closing entries
d. Treasury stock

23. A _____, reserve bank, or monetary authority is the entity responsible for the monetary policy of a country or of a group of member states. It is a bank that can lend money to other banks in times of need. Its primary responsibility is to maintain the stability of the national currency and money supply, but more active duties include controlling subsidized-loan interest rates, and acting as a lender of last resort to the banking sector during times of financial crisis (private banks often being integral to the national financial system.)

a. Central bank
b. 529 plan
c. 7-Eleven
d. 4-4-5 Calendar

24. The _____ is an interest rate a central bank charges depository institutions that borrow reserves from it.

The term _____ has two meanings:

- the same as interest rate; the term 'discount' does not refer to the meaning of the word, but to the purpose of using the quantity, such as computations of present value, e.g. net present value / discounted cash flow

- the annual effective _____, which is the annual interest divided by the capital including that interest; this rate is lower than the interest rate; it corresponds to using the value after a year as the nominal value, and seeing the initial value as the nominal value minus a discount; it is used for Treasury Bills and similar financial instruments

The annual effective _____ is the annual interest divided by the capital including that interest, which is the interest rate divided by 100% plus the interest rate. It is the annual discount factor to be applied to the future cash flow, to find the discount, subtracted from a future value to find the value one year earlier.

For example, suppose there is a government bond that sells for $95 and pays $100 in a year's time.

a. Black-Scholes
b. Stochastic volatility
c. Fisher equation
d. Discount rate

25. _____ is the provision of resources (such as granting a loan) by one party to another party where that second party does not reimburse the first party immediately, thereby generating a debt, and instead arranges either to repay or return those resources (or material(s) of equal value) at a later date. The first party is called a creditor, also known as a lender, while the second party is called a debtor, also known as a borrower.

Movements of financial capital are normally dependent on either _____ or equity transfers.

Chapter 13. Managing Nondeposit Liabilities and Other Sources of Borrowed Funds 113

a. Warrant
c. Credit

b. Comparable
d. Clearing house

26. Explicit _____ is a measure implemented in many countries to protect bank depositors, in full or in part, from losses caused by a bank's inability to pay its debts when due. _____ systems are one component of a financial system safety net that promotes financial stability.

a. Time deposit
c. Deposit Insurance

b. Banking panic
d. Reserve requirement

27. The _____ of 1991, passed during the Savings and loan crisis, strengthened the power of the Federal Deposit Insurance Corporation.

It allowed the FDIC to borrow directly from the Treasury department and mandated that the FDIC resolve failed banks using the least-costly method available. It also ordered the FDIC to assess insurance premiums according to risk and created new capital requirements.

a. National Securities Markets Improvement Act of 1996
c. Covenant

b. Fair Debt Collection Practices Act
d. Federal Deposit Insurance Corporation Improvement Act

28. A _____ s a time deposit, a financial product commonly offered to consumers by banks, thrift institutions, and credit unions.

They are similar to savings accounts in that they are insured and thus virtually risk-free; they are 'money in the bank'. They are different from savings accounts in that they have a specific, fixed term (often three months, six months, or one to five years), and, usually, a fixed interest rate.

a. Time deposit
c. Reserve requirement

b. Certificate of deposit
d. Variable rate mortgage

29. _____, in bookkeeping, refers to assets, liabilities, income, and expenses recorded on individual pages of the so called book of final entry or ledger. Changes in _____ value are made by chronologically posting debit (DR) and credit (CR) entries to its page. Examples of _____s are cash, _____s receivable, mortgages, loans, land and buildings, common stock, sales, services provided, wages, and payroll overhead.

a. Alpha
c. Accretion

b. Account
d. Option

30. _____ is the term used to describe deposits residing in banks that are located outside the borders of the country that issues the currency the deposit is denominated in. For example a deposit denominated in US dollars residing in a Japanese bank is a _____ deposit, or more specifically a Eurodollar deposit.

Key points are the location of the bank and the denomination of the currency, not the nationality of the bank or the owner of the deposit/loan.

a. ABN Amro
b. AAB
c. A Random Walk Down Wall Street
d. Eurocurrency

31. _____s are deposits denominated in United States dollars at banks outside the United States, and thus are not under the jurisdiction of the Federal Reserve. Consequently, such deposits are subject to much less regulation than similar deposits within the United States, allowing for higher margins. There is nothing 'European' about _____ deposits; a US dollar-denominated deposit in Tokyo or Caracas would likewise be deemed _____ deposits.
   a. AAB
   b. A Random Walk Down Wall Street
   c. ABN Amro
   d. Eurodollar

32. A _____ is a money deposit at a banking institution that cannot be withdrawn for a certain 'term' or period of time. When the term is over it can be withdrawn or it can be held for another term. Generally speaking, the longer the term the better the yield on the money.
   a. Private money
   b. Time deposit
   c. Basel Accord
   d. Certificate of deposit

33. In structured finance the _____ is the most junior security issued by a Structured investment vehicle. It is comparable to the Equity Tranche of a CDO. Investors who buy the _____s are the first in line to bear risk if the cash flows from the SIV's assets are insufficient to cover promised payments to all investors.
   a. Debt
   b. Capital note
   c. Loan to value
   d. Participation loan

34. In the global money market, _____ is an unsecured promissory note with a fixed maturity of one to 270 days. _____ is a money-market security issued (sold) by large banks and corporations to get money to meet short term debt obligations (for example, payroll), and is only backed by an issuing bank or corporation's promise to pay the face amount on the maturity date specified on the note. Since it is not backed by collateral, only firms with excellent credit ratings from a recognized rating agency will be able to sell their _____ at a reasonable price.
   a. Book building
   b. Trade-off theory
   c. Commercial paper
   d. Financial distress

35. In economic models, the _____ time frame assumes no fixed factors of production. Firms can enter or leave the marketplace, and the cost (and availability) of land, labor, raw materials, and capital goods can be assumed to vary. In contrast, in the short-run time frame, certain factors are assumed to be fixed, because there is not sufficient time for them to change.
   a. Short-run
   b. 529 plan
   c. Long-run
   d. 4-4-5 Calendar

36. In structured finance, a _____ is one of a number of related securities offered as part of the same transaction. The word _____ is French for slice, section, series, or portion. In the financial sense of the word, each bond is a different slice of the deal's risk.
   a. 4-4-5 Calendar
   b. Tranche
   c. Yield curve spread
   d. Credit enhancement

37. A _____ is defined as a certificate of agreement of loans which is given under the company's stamp and carries an undertaking that the _____ holder will get a fixed return (fixed on the basis of interest rates) and the principal amount whenever the _____ matures.

Chapter 13. Managing Nondeposit Liabilities and Other Sources of Borrowed Funds

In finance, a _____ is a long-term debt instrument used by governments and large companies to obtain funds. It is defined as 'a debt secured only by the debtor's earning power, not by a lien on any specific asset.' It is similar to a bond except the securitization conditions are different.

- a. Collection agency
- b. Collateral Management
- c. Partial Payment
- d. Debenture

38. _____ is the risk (variability in value) borne by an interest-bearing asset, such as a loan or a bond, due to variability of interest rates. In general, as rates rise, the price of a fixed rate bond will fall, and vice versa. _____ is commonly measured by the bond's duration.

- a. Official bank rate
- b. International Fisher effect
- c. Interest rate risk
- d. A Random Walk Down Wall Street

39. A _____ is a variable associated with an increased risk of disease or infection. They are correlational and not necessarily causal, because correlation does not imply causation. For example, being young cannot be said to cause measles, but young people are more at risk as they are less likely to have developed immunity during a previous epidemic.

- a. 529 plan
- b. 7-Eleven
- c. 4-4-5 Calendar
- d. Risk factor

40. _____ is the long dimension of any object. The _____ of a thing is the distance between its ends, its linear extent as measured from end to end. This may be distinguished from height, which is vertical extent, and width or breadth, which are the distance from side to side, measuring across the object at right angles to the _____.

- a. 529 plan
- b. Length
- c. 7-Eleven
- d. 4-4-5 Calendar

41. The _____ is a bank regulation that sets the minimum reserves each bank must hold to customer deposits and notes. These reserves are designed to satisfy withdrawal demands, and would normally be in the form of fiat currency stored in a bank vault (vault cash), or with a central bank.

The reserve ratio is sometimes used as a tool in the monetary policy, influencing the country's economy, borrowing, and interest rates.

- a. Prime rate
- b. Wall Street Journal prime rate
- c. Variable rate mortgage
- d. Reserve requirement

Chapter 14. Investment Banking, Insurance, and Other Sources of Fee Income

1. _____, refers to consumption opportunity gained by an entity within a specified time frame, which is generally expressed in monetary terms. However, for households and individuals, '_____ is the sum of all the wages, salaries, profits, interests payments, rents and other forms of earnings received... in a given period of time.' For firms, _____ generally refers to net-profit: what remains of revenue after expenses have been subtracted.
    a. OIBDA
    b. Income
    c. Annual report
    d. Accrual

2. _____ is the provision of resources (such as granting a loan) by one party to another party where that second party does not reimburse the first party immediately, thereby generating a debt, and instead arranges either to repay or return those resources (or material(s) of equal value) at a later date. The first party is called a creditor, also known as a lender, while the second party is called a debtor, also known as a borrower.

    Movements of financial capital are normally dependent on either _____ or equity transfers.

    a. Warrant
    b. Comparable
    c. Credit
    d. Clearing house

3. The _____ Act is an Act of the 106th United States Congress which repealed part of the Glass-Steagall Act of 1933, opening up competition among banks, securities companies and insurance companies. The Glass-Steagall Act prohibited any one institution from acting as both an investment bank and a commercial bank, or as both a bank and an insurer.

    The _____ Act (GLBA) allowed commercial and investment banks to consolidate.

    a. 529 plan
    b. Gramm-Leach-Bliley
    c. 4-4-5 Calendar
    d. 7-Eleven

4. A _____ is a fungible, negotiable instrument representing financial value. They are broadly categorized into debt securities (such as banknotes, bonds and debentures), and equity securities; e.g., common stocks. The company or other entity issuing the _____ is called the issuer.
    a. Book entry
    b. Tracking stock
    c. Securities lending
    d. Security

5. A _____ is a company that owns other companies' outstanding stock. It usually refers to a company which does not produce goods or services itself, rather its only purpose is owning shares of other companies. They allow the reduction of risk for the owners and can allow the ownership and control of a number of different companies.
    a. Federal National Mortgage Association
    b. Privately held company
    c. MRU Holdings
    d. Holding company

6. The phrase _____ refers to the aspect of corporate strategy, corporate finance and management dealing with the buying, selling and combining of different companies that can aid, finance, or help a growing company in a given industry grow rapidly without having to create another business entity.

    An acquisition, also known as a takeover, is the buying of one company (the 'target') by another. An acquisition may be friendly or hostile.

Chapter 14. Investment Banking, Insurance, and Other Sources of Fee Income 117

a. 7-Eleven
b. 529 plan
c. 4-4-5 Calendar
d. Mergers and acquisitions

7.

A _____ is a type of financial intermediary and a type of bank. Commercial banking is also known as business banking. It is a bank that provides checking accounts, savings accounts, and money market accounts and that accepts time deposits.

a. 7-Eleven
b. 4-4-5 Calendar
c. Commercial bank
d. 529 plan

8. _____, is when a company issues common stock or shares to the public for the first time. They are often issued by smaller, younger companies seeking capital to expand, but can also be done by large privately-owned companies looking to become publicly traded.

In an _____ the issuer may obtain the assistance of an underwriting firm, which helps it determine what type of security to issue (common or preferred), best offering price and time to bring it to market.

a. Asian Financial Crisis
b. Insolvency
c. Interest
d. Initial public offering

9. _____ in finance is a risk management technique, related to hedging, that mixes a wide variety of investments within a portfolio. Because the fluctuations of a single security have less impact on a diverse portfolio, _____ minimizes the risk from any one investment.

A simple example of _____ is the following: On a particular island the entire economy consists of two companies: one that sells umbrellas and another that sells sunscreen.

a. 4-4-5 Calendar
b. 529 plan
c. 7-Eleven
d. Diversification

10. The _____ of 1933 established the Federal Deposit Insurance Corporation (FDIC) in the United States and included banking reforms, some of which were designed to control speculation. Some provisions such as Regulation Q, which allowed the Federal Reserve to regulate interest rates in savings accounts, were repealed by the Depository Institutions Deregulation and Monetary Control Act of 1980. Provisions that prohibit a bank holding company from owning other financial companies were repealed on November 12, 1999, by the Gramm-Leach-Bliley Act.

a. Glass-Steagall Act
b. 4-4-5 Calendar
c. 529 plan
d. 7-Eleven

11. In business, _____ is income that a company receives from its normal business activities, usually from the sale of goods and services to customers. Some companies also receive _____ from interest, dividends or royalties paid to them by other companies. _____ may refer to business income in general, or it may refer to the amount, in a monetary unit, received during a period of time, as in 'Last year, Company X had _____ of $32 million.'

In many countries, including the UK, _____ is referred to as turnover.

Chapter 14. Investment Banking, Insurance, and Other Sources of Fee Income

a. Revenue
b. Bottom line
c. Matching principle
d. Furniture, Fixtures and Equipment

12. The U.S. _____ is an independent agency of the United States government which holds primary responsibility for enforcing the federal securities laws and regulating the securities industry, the nation's stock and options exchanges, and other electronic securities markets. The SEC was created by section 4 of the SEC of 1934 (now codified as 15 U.S.C. Â§ 78d and commonly referred to as the 1934 Act.)
   a. 529 plan
   b. 7-Eleven
   c. 4-4-5 Calendar
   d. Securities and Exchange Commission

13. An _____ is an investment vehicle traded on stock exchanges, much like stocks. An ETF holds assets such as stocks or bonds and trades at approximately the same price as the net asset value of its underlying assets over the course of the trading day. Most ETFs track an index, such as the Dow Jones Industrial Average or the S'P 500.
   a. AAB
   b. ABN Amro
   c. A Random Walk Down Wall Street
   d. Exchange-traded fund

14. In finance, a _____ is a position established in one market in an attempt to offset exposure to the price risk of an equal but opposite obligation or position in another market -- usually, but not always, in the context of one's commercial activity. Hedging is a strategy designed to minimize exposure to such business risks as a sharp contraction in demand for one's inventory, while still allowing the business to profit from producing and maintaining that inventory. A typical hedger might be a farmer with 2000 acres of unharvested wheat in the ground, who would rather tend his crop without the distraction of uncertain prices.
   a. 529 plan
   b. Hedge
   c. 7-Eleven
   d. 4-4-5 Calendar

15. A _____ is a private investment fund open to a limited range of investors that is permitted by regulators to undertake a wider range of activities than other investment funds and also pays a performance fee to its investment manager. Each fund will have its own strategy which determines the type of investments and the methods of investment it undertakes. _____s as a class invest in a broad range of investments extending over shares, debt, commodities and beyond.
   a. 529 plan
   b. 7-Eleven
   c. 4-4-5 Calendar
   d. Hedge fund

16. A _____ is a professionally managed type of collective investment scheme that pools money from many investors and invests it in stocks, bonds, short-term money market instruments, and/or other securities. The _____ will have a fund manager that trades the pooled money on a regular basis. Currently, the worldwide value of all _____s totals more than $26 trillion.

Since 1940, there have been three basic types of investment companies in the United States: open-end funds, also known in the US as _____s; unit investment trusts (UITs); and closed-end funds.

   a. Trust company
   b. Net asset value
   c. Mutual fund
   d. Financial intermediary

17. _____ is a term used to describe the value of an entity's assets less the value of its liabilities. The term is commonly used in relation to collective investment schemes. It may also be used as a synonym for the book value of a firm.

Chapter 14. Investment Banking, Insurance, and Other Sources of Fee Income

a. Retail broker
b. Financial intermediary
c. Passive management
d. Net asset value

18. In business and accounting, _____s are everything of value that is owned by a person or company. The balance sheet of a firm records the monetary value of the _____s owned by the firm. The two major _____ classes are tangible _____s and intangible _____s.
   a. Income
   b. EBITDA
   c. Accounts payable
   d. Asset

19. The institution most often referenced by the word '_____' is a public or publicly traded _____, the shares of which are traded on a public stock exchange (e.g., the New York Stock Exchange or Nasdaq in the United States) where shares of stock of _____s are bought and sold by and to the general public. Most of the largest businesses in the world are publicly traded _____s. However, the majority of _____s are said to be closely held, privately held or close _____s, meaning that no ready market exists for the trading of shares.
   a. Depository Trust Company
   b. Federal Home Loan Mortgage Corporation
   c. Corporation
   d. Protect

20. An _____ can be defined as a contract which provides an income stream in return for an initial payment.

An immediate _____ is an _____ for which the time between the contract date and the date of the first payment is not longer than the time interval between payments. A common use for an immediate _____ is to provide a pension to a retired person or persons.

   a. Intrinsic value
   b. AT'T Inc.
   c. Amortization
   d. Annuity

21. The term _____ is often used to refer to the investment management of collective investments, (not necessarily) whilst the more generic fund management may refer to all forms of institutional investment as well as investment management for private investors. Investment managers who specialize in advisory or discretionary management on behalf of (normally wealthy) private investors may often refer to their services as wealth management or portfolio management often within the context of so-called 'private banking'.

The provision of 'investment management services' includes elements of financial analysis, asset selection, stock selection, plan implementation and ongoing monitoring of investments.

   a. AAB
   b. A Random Walk Down Wall Street
   c. Asset management
   d. ABN Amro

22. _____ is the discipline of identifying, monitoring and limiting risks. In some cases the acceptable risk may be near zero. Risks can come from accidents, natural causes and disasters as well as deliberate attacks from an adversary.
   a. FIFO
   b. Penny stock
   c. 4-4-5 Calendar
   d. Risk management

Chapter 14. Investment Banking, Insurance, and Other Sources of Fee Income

23. In financial accounting, the term _____ is most commonly used to describe any part of shareholders' equity, except for basic share capital. Sometimes, the term is used instead of the term provision; such a use, however, is inconsistent with the terminology suggested by International Accounting Standards Board. For more information about provisions, see provision (accounting.)
    a. Treasury stock
    b. Closing entries
    c. FIFO and LIFO accounting
    d. Reserve

24. The _____ duty is a legal relationship of confidence or trust between two or more parties, most commonly a _____ or trustee and a principal or beneficiary. One party, for example a corporate trust company or the trust department of a bank, holds a _____ relation or acts in a _____ capacity to another, such as one whose funds are entrusted to it for investment. In a _____ relation one person justifiably reposes confidence, good faith, reliance and trust in another whose aid, advice or protection is sought in some matter.
    a. General obligation
    b. Fiduciary
    c. Legal tender
    d. Financial Institutions Reform Recovery and Enforcement Act

25. An _____ is a call option on the common stock of a company, issued as a form of non-cash compensation. Restrictions on the option (such as vesting and limited transferability) attempt to align the holder's interest with those of the business' shareholders. If the company's stock rises, holders of options experience a direct financial benefit.
    a. Operating ratio
    b. Employee stock option
    c. Underwriting contract
    d. Internal financing

26. An _____ is a contract written by a seller that conveys to the buyer the right -- but not the obligation -- to buy (in the case of a call _____) or to sell (in the case of a put _____) a particular asset, such as a piece of property such as, among others, a futures contract. In return for granting the _____, the seller collects a payment (the premium) from the buyer.

    For example, buying a call _____ provides the right to buy a specified quantity of a security at a set strike price at some time on or before expiration, while buying a put _____ provides the right to sell.

    a. Annuity
    b. Amortization
    c. AT'T Mobility LLC
    d. Option

27. Explicit _____ is a measure implemented in many countries to protect bank depositors, in full or in part, from losses caused by a bank's inability to pay its debts when due. _____ systems are one component of a financial system safety net that promotes financial stability.
    a. Deposit Insurance
    b. Banking panic
    c. Time deposit
    d. Reserve requirement

28. The _____ is a United States government corporation created by the Glass-Steagall Act of 1933. It provides deposit insurance, which guarantees the safety of checking and savings deposits in member banks, currently up to $250,000 per depositor per bank. Insured deposits are backed by the full faith and credit of the United States.
    a. Ford Foundation
    b. NYSE Group
    c. FASB
    d. Federal Deposit Insurance Corporation

Chapter 14. Investment Banking, Insurance, and Other Sources of Fee Income

29. The _____, an agency of the United States Department of the Treasury, is the primary regulator of federal savings associations (sometimes referred to as federal thrifts.) Federal savings associations include both federal savings banks and federal savings and loans. The OTS is also responsible for supervising savings and loan holding companies (SLHCs) and some state-chartered institutions.
   a. A Random Walk Down Wall Street
   b. Office of Thrift Supervision
   c. AAB
   d. ABN Amro

30. Unemployment occurs when a person is available to work and currently seeking work, but the person is without work. The prevalence of unemployment is usually measured using the _____, which is defined as the percentage of those in the labor force who are unemployed. The _____ is also used in economic studies and economic indexes such as the United States' Conference Board's Index of Leading Indicators as a measure of the state of the macroeconomics.
   a. A Random Walk Down Wall Street
   b. AAB
   c. ABN Amro
   d. Unemployment rate

31. _____ refer to services provided by the finance industry.

The finance industry encompasses a broad range of organizations that deal with the management of money. Among these organizations are banks, credit card companies, insurance companies, consumer finance companies, stock brokerages, investment funds and some government sponsored enterprises.

   a. Cost of carry
   b. Financial instruments
   c. Delta hedging
   d. Financial services

32. A _____ is an exchange of promises between two or more parties to do an act which is enforceable in a court of law. It is where an unqualified offer meets a qualified acceptance and the parties reach Consensus ad Idem. The parties must have the necessary capacity to _____ and the _____ must not be either trifling, indeterminate, impossible or illegal.
   a. 529 plan
   b. 4-4-5 Calendar
   c. 7-Eleven
   d. Contract

33. _____, in microeconomics, are the cost advantages that a business obtains due to expansion. _____ may be utilized by any size firm expanding its scale of operation.
   a. Articles of incorporation
   b. Economies of scale
   c. Uniform Commercial Code
   d. Employee Retirement Income Security Act

34. A _____, reserve bank, or monetary authority is the entity responsible for the monetary policy of a country or of a group of member states. It is a bank that can lend money to other banks in times of need. Its primary responsibility is to maintain the stability of the national currency and money supply, but more active duties include controlling subsidized-loan interest rates, and acting as a lender of last resort to the banking sector during times of financial crisis (private banks often being integral to the national financial system.)
   a. 4-4-5 Calendar
   b. 7-Eleven
   c. 529 plan
   d. Central bank

Chapter 15. The Management of Capital

1. In accounting, _____ refers to the portion of net income which is retained by the corporation rather than distributed to its owners as dividends. Similarly, if the corporation makes a loss, then that loss is retained and called variously retained losses, accumulated losses or accumulated deficit. _____ and losses are cumulative from year to year with losses offsetting earnings.
   a. Generally Accepted Accounting Principles
   b. Retained earnings
   c. Historical cost
   d. Matching principle

2. A mutual shareholder or _____ is an individual or company (including a corporation) that legally owns one or more shares of stock in a joint stock company. A company's shareholders collectively own that company. Thus, the typical goal of such companies is to enhance shareholder value.
   a. Trading curb
   b. Stockholder
   c. Limit order
   d. Stock market bubble

3. In financial accounting, the term _____ is most commonly used to describe any part of shareholders' equity, except for basic share capital. Sometimes, the term is used instead of the term provision; such a use, however, is inconsistent with the terminology suggested by International Accounting Standards Board. For more information about provisions, see provision (accounting.)
   a. Treasury stock
   b. FIFO and LIFO accounting
   c. Reserve
   d. Closing entries

4. A _____, reserve bank, or monetary authority is the entity responsible for the monetary policy of a country or of a group of member states. It is a bank that can lend money to other banks in times of need. Its primary responsibility is to maintain the stability of the national currency and money supply, but more active duties include controlling subsidized-loan interest rates, and acting as a lender of last resort to the banking sector during times of financial crisis (private banks often being integral to the national financial system.)
   a. 7-Eleven
   b. 529 plan
   c. 4-4-5 Calendar
   d. Central bank

5. _____ is the provision of resources (such as granting a loan) by one party to another party where that second party does not reimburse the first party immediately, thereby generating a debt, and instead arranges either to repay or return those resources (or material(s) of equal value) at a later date. The first party is called a creditor, also known as a lender, while the second party is called a debtor, also known as a borrower.

Movements of financial capital are normally dependent on either _____ or equity transfers.

   a. Clearing house
   b. Comparable
   c. Warrant
   d. Credit

6. _____ is the risk of loss due to a debtor's non-payment of a loan or other line of credit (either the principal or interest (coupon) or both)

Most lenders employ their own models (credit scorecards) to rank potential and existing customers according to risk, and then apply appropriate strategies. With products such as unsecured personal loans or mortgages, lenders charge a higher price for higher risk customers and vice versa. With revolving products such as credit cards and overdrafts, risk is controlled through careful setting of credit limits.

a. Transaction risk
b. Liquidity risk
c. Market risk
d. Credit risk

7. _____ is a measure of the ability of a debtor to pay their debts as and when they fall due. It is usually expressed as a ratio or a percentage of current liabilities.

For a corporation with a published balance sheet there are various ratios used to calculate a measure of liquidity.

a. Operating profit margin
b. Operating leverage
c. Invested capital
d. Accounting liquidity

8. _____ arises from situations in which a party interested in trading an asset cannot do it because nobody in the market wants to trade that asset. _____ becomes particularly important to parties who are about to hold or currently hold an asset, since it affects their ability to trade.

Manifestation of _____ is very different from a drop of price to zero.

a. Credit risk
b. Tracking error
c. Currency risk
d. Liquidity risk

9. An _____ is a risk arising from execution of a company's business functions. As such, it is a very broad concept including e.g. fraud risks, legal risks, physical or environmental risks, etc. The term _____ is most commonly found in risk management programs of financial institutions that must organize their risk management program according to Basel II.

a. ABN Amro
b. AAB
c. A Random Walk Down Wall Street
d. Operational risk

10. _____ in finance is a risk management technique, related to hedging, that mixes a wide variety of investments within a portfolio. Because the fluctuations of a single security have less impact on a diverse portfolio, _____ minimizes the risk from any one investment.

A simple example of _____ is the following: On a particular island the entire economy consists of two companies: one that sells umbrellas and another that sells sunscreen.

a. Diversification
b. 4-4-5 Calendar
c. 7-Eleven
d. 529 plan

11. In finance, the _____ between two currencies specifies how much one currency is worth in terms of the other. For example an _____ of 102 Japanese yen to the United States dollar means that JPY 102 is worth the same as USD 1. The foreign exchange market is one of the largest markets in the world.

a. ABN Amro
b. AAB
c. Exchange rate
d. A Random Walk Down Wall Street

12. _____ is a form of risk that arises from the change in price of one currency against another. Whenever investors or companies have assets or business operations across national borders, they face _____ if their positions are not hedged.

- Transaction risk is the risk that exchange rates will change unfavourably over time. It can be hedged against using forward currency contracts;
- Translation risk is an accounting risk, proportional to the amount of assets held in foreign currencies. Changes in the exchange rate over time will render a report inaccurate, and so assets are usually balanced by borrowings in that currency.

The exchange risk associated with a foreign denominated instrument is a key element in foreign investment. This risk flows from differential monetary policy and growth in real productivity, which results in differential inflation rates.

a. Credit risk
b. Market risk
c. Tracking error
d. Currency risk

13. _____ is a fee paid on borrowed assets. It is the price paid for the use of borrowed money, or, money earned by deposited funds. Assets that are sometimes lent with _____ include money, shares, consumer goods through hire purchase, major assets such as aircraft, and even entire factories in finance lease arrangements.

a. A Random Walk Down Wall Street
b. Interest
c. Insolvency
d. AAB

14. An _____ is the price a borrower pays for the use of money they do not own, and the return a lender receives for deferring the use of funds, by lending it to the borrower. _____s are normally expressed as a percentage rate over the period of one year.

_____s targets are also a vital tool of monetary policy and are used to control variables like investment, inflation, and unemployment.

a. AAB
b. A Random Walk Down Wall Street
c. Interest rate
d. ABN Amro

15. _____ is the risk (variability in value) borne by an interest-bearing asset, such as a loan or a bond, due to variability of interest rates. In general, as rates rise, the price of a fixed rate bond will fall, and vice versa. _____ is commonly measured by the bond's duration.

a. Official bank rate
b. Interest rate risk
c. A Random Walk Down Wall Street
d. International Fisher effect

16. The institution most often referenced by the word '_____' is a public or publicly traded _____, the shares of which are traded on a public stock exchange (e.g., the New York Stock Exchange or Nasdaq in the United States) where shares of stock of _____s are bought and sold by and to the general public. Most of the largest businesses in the world are publicly traded _____s. However, the majority of _____s are said to be closely held, privately held or close _____s, meaning that no ready market exists for the trading of shares.

Chapter 15. The Management of Capital

a. Federal Home Loan Mortgage Corporation
b. Depository Trust Company
c. Protect
d. Corporation

17. Explicit _____ is a measure implemented in many countries to protect bank depositors, in full or in part, from losses caused by a bank's inability to pay its debts when due. _____ systems are one component of a financial system safety net that promotes financial stability.
   a. Reserve requirement
   b. Banking panic
   c. Time deposit
   d. Deposit Insurance

18. The _____ is a United States government corporation created by the Glass-Steagall Act of 1933. It provides deposit insurance, which guarantees the safety of checking and savings deposits in member banks, currently up to $250,000 per depositor per bank. Insured deposits are backed by the full faith and credit of the United States.
   a. Ford Foundation
   b. NYSE Group
   c. Federal Deposit Insurance Corporation
   d. FASB

19. The _____ is the market for securities, where companies and governments can raise longterm funds. The _____ includes the stock market and the bond market. Financial regulators, such as the U.S. Securities and Exchange Commission, oversee the _____ s in their designated countries to ensure that investors are protected against fraud.
   a. Spot rate
   b. Delta neutral
   c. Forward market
   d. Capital market

20. _____ is a form of corporation equity ownership represented in the securities. It is dangerous in comparison to preferred shares and some other investment options, in that in the event of bankruptcy, _____ investors receive their funds after preferred stockholders, bondholders, creditors, etc. On the other hand, common shares on average perform better than preferred shares or bonds over time.
   a. Stop-limit order
   b. Stock market bubble
   c. Common stock
   d. Stock split

21. _____ in business is an accounting concept that refers to ownership of a company (subsidiary) that is less than 50% of outstanding shares. _____ belongs to other investors and is reported on the consolidated balance sheet of the owning company to reflect the claim on assets belonging to other, non-controlling shareholders. Also, _____ is reported on the consolidated income statement as a share of profit belonging to minority shareholders.
   a. Minority interest
   b. Construction in Progress
   c. Credit memo
   d. Fixed asset

22. _____ is typically a higher ranking stock than voting shares, and its terms are negotiated between the corporation and the investor.

_____ usually carry no voting rights, but may carry superior priority over common stock in the payment of dividends and upon liquidation. _____ may carry a dividend that is paid out prior to any dividends to common stock holders.

   a. Trade-off theory
   b. Preferred stock
   c. Second lien loan
   d. Follow-on offering

Chapter 15. The Management of Capital

23. A _____ is defined as a certificate of agreement of loans which is given under the company's stamp and carries an undertaking that the _____ holder will get a fixed return (fixed on the basis of interest rates) and the principal amount whenever the _____ matures.

In finance, a _____ is a long-term debt instrument used by governments and large companies to obtain funds. It is defined as 'a debt secured only by the debtor's earning power, not by a lien on any specific asset.' It is similar to a bond except the securitization conditions are different.

- a. Partial Payment
- b. Debenture
- c. Collection agency
- d. Collateral Management

24. _____ is the difference between price and the costs of bringing to market whatever it is that is accounted as an enterprise (whether by harvest, extraction, manufacture, or purchase) in terms of the component costs of delivered goods and/or services and any operating or other expenses.

A key difficulty in measuring profit is in defining costs. Pure economic monetary profits can be zero or negative even in competitive equilibrium when accounted monetized costs exceed monetized price.

- a. Economic profit
- b. A Random Walk Down Wall Street
- c. AAB
- d. Accounting profit

25. A _____ is a fungible, negotiable instrument representing financial value. They are broadly categorized into debt securities (such as banknotes, bonds and debentures), and equity securities; e.g., common stocks. The company or other entity issuing the _____ is called the issuer.

- a. Securities lending
- b. Book entry
- c. Tracking stock
- d. Security

26. A _____, in business matters, is an entity that is controlled by a bigger and more powerful entity. The controlled entity is called a company, corporation, or limited liability company, and the controlling entity is called its parent (or the parent company.) The reason for this distinction is that a lone company cannot be a _____ of any organization; only an entity representing a legal fiction as a separate entity can be a _____.

- a. 4-4-5 Calendar
- b. Joint stock company
- c. 529 plan
- d. Subsidiary

27.

A _____ is a type of financial intermediary and a type of bank. Commercial banking is also known as business banking. It is a bank that provides checking accounts, savings accounts, and money market accounts and that accepts time deposits.

- a. Commercial bank
- b. 529 plan
- c. 4-4-5 Calendar
- d. 7-Eleven

28. _____, in bookkeeping, refers to assets, liabilities, income, and expenses recorded on individual pages of the so called book of final entry or ledger. Changes in _____ value are made by chronologically posting debit (DR) and credit (CR) entries to its page. Examples of _____s are cash, _____s receivable, mortgages, loans, land and buildings, common stock, sales, services provided, wages, and payroll overhead.
   a. Alpha
   b. Accretion
   c. Account
   d. Option

29. In financial accounting, the _____ is one of the accounts in shareholders' equity. Sole proprietorships have a single _____ in the owner's equity. Partnerships maintain a _____ for each of the partners.
   a. Duty of loyalty
   b. Market maker
   c. Capital account
   d. Bed Bath ' Beyond Inc.

30. A _____ is an exchange of promises between two or more parties to do an act which is enforceable in a court of law. It is where an unqualified offer meets a qualified acceptance and the parties reach Consensus ad Idem. The parties must have the necessary capacity to _____ and the _____ must not be either trifling, indeterminate, impossible or illegal.
   a. 529 plan
   b. 7-Eleven
   c. 4-4-5 Calendar
   d. Contract

31. In business and accounting, _____s are everything of value that is owned by a person or company. The balance sheet of a firm records the monetary value of the _____s owned by the firm. The two major _____ classes are tangible _____s and intangible _____s.
   a. Accounts payable
   b. EBITDA
   c. Income
   d. Asset

32. In finance, a _____ is a derivative whose value derives from the credit risk on an underlying bond, loan or other financial asset. In this way, the credit risk is on an entity other than the counterparties to the transaction itself. This entity is known as the reference entity and may be a corporate, a sovereign or any other form of legal entity which has incurred debt.
   a. Futures contract
   b. Derivatives markets
   c. STIRT
   d. Credit derivative

33. A _____ is a financial contract whose value is derived from the value of something else (known as the underlying.) The underlying on which a _____ is based can be an asset, weather conditions bonds or other forms of credit.
   a. 529 plan
   b. 4-4-5 Calendar
   c. Derivative
   d. 7-Eleven

34. _____ is the risk that the value of an investment will decrease due to moves in market factors. The five standard _____ factors are:

   - Equity risk, the risk that stock prices will change.
   - Interest rate risk, the risk that interest rates will change.
   - Currency risk, the risk that foreign exchange rates will change.
   - Commodity risk, the risk that commodity prices (e.g. grains, metals) will change.

Chapter 15. The Management of Capital

As with other forms of risk, _____ may be measured in a number of ways. Traditionally, this is done using a Value at Risk methodology. Value at risk is well established as a risk management technique, but it contains a number of limiting assumptions that constrain its accuracy.

a. Market risk
c. Tracking error

b. Currency risk
d. Transaction risk

35. In financial mathematics and financial risk management, _____ is a widely used measure of the risk of loss on a specific portfolio of financial assets. For a given portfolio, probability and time horizon, VaR is defined as a threshold value such that the probability that the mark-to-market loss on the portfolio over the given time horizon exceeds this value (assuming normal markets and no trading) is the given probability level.

For example, if a portfolio of stocks has a one-day 5% VaR of $1 million, there is a 5% probability that the portfolio will fall in value by more than $1 million over a one day period, assuming markets are normal and there is no trading.

a. Value at risk
c. Risk aversion

b. Discount factor
d. Risk modeling

36. _____ refers to the use of formal econometric techniques to determine the aggregate risk in a financial portfolio. _____ is one of many subtasks within the broader area of financial modeling.

_____ uses a variety of techniques including market risk, Value-at-Risk (VaR), Historical Simulation (HS), or Extreme Value Theory (EVT) in order to analyze a portfolio and make forecasts of the likely losses that would be incurred for a variety of risks.

a. Risk premium
c. Value at risk

b. Risk adjusted return on capital
d. Risk modeling

37. _____ is a step in a risk management process. _____ is the determination of quantitative or qualitative value of risk related to a concrete situation and a recognized threat (also called hazard.) Quantitative _____ requires calculations of two components of risk: R, the magnitude of the potential loss L, and the probability p that the loss will occur.

a. 529 plan
c. 4-4-5 Calendar

b. Risk assessment
d. 7-Eleven

38. The term _____ or economic cycle refers to the fluctuations of economic activity (business fluctuations) around a long-term growth trend. The cycle involves shifts over time between periods of relatively rapid growth of output (recovery and prosperity), and periods of relative stagnation or decline (contraction or recession.) These fluctuations are often measured using the real gross domestic product.

a. Deflation
c. Fixed exchange rate

b. Business cycle
d. Behavioral finance

39. The _____ of 1991, passed during the Savings and loan crisis, strengthened the power of the Federal Deposit Insurance Corporation.

Chapter 15. The Management of Capital

It allowed the FDIC to borrow directly from the Treasury department and mandated that the FDIC resolve failed banks using the least-costly method available. It also ordered the FDIC to assess insurance premiums according to risk and created new capital requirements.

a. Federal Deposit Insurance Corporation Improvement Act
b. National Securities Markets Improvement Act of 1996
c. Covenant
d. Fair Debt Collection Practices Act

40. _____ measures the rate of return on the ownership interest (shareholders' equity) of the common stock owners. _____ is viewed as one of the most important financial ratios. It measures a firm's efficiency at generating profits from every dollar of shareholders' equity (also known as net assets or assets minus liabilities.)

a. Return on sales
b. Return of capital
c. Diluted Earnings Per Share
d. Return on equity

41. A _____ is a payment made by a corporation to its shareholder members. When a corporation earns a profit or surplus, that money can be put to two uses: it can either be re-invested in the business (called retained earnings), or it can be paid to the shareholders as a _____. Many corporations retain a portion of their earnings and pay the remainder as a _____.

a. Dividend puzzle
b. Dividend
c. Dividend yield
d. Special dividend

42. _____ is the fraction of net income a firm pays to its stockholders in dividends:

The part of the earnings not paid to investors is left for investment to provide for future earnings growth. Investors seeking high current income and limited capital growth prefer companies with high _____. However investors seeking capital growth may prefer lower payout ratio because capital gains are taxed at a lower rate.

a. Dividend payout ratio
b. Dividend yield
c. Dividend imputation
d. Dividend puzzle

43. _____ indicates the percentage of a company's earnings that are not paid out in dividends but credited to retained earnings. It is the opposite of the dividend payout ratio, so that also called the retention rate.

_____ = 1 - Dividend Payout Ratio

a. Dow Jones Indexes
b. Bankassurer
c. Retention ratio
d. Fair market value

44. _____ is that which is owed; usually referencing assets owed, but the term can cover other obligations. In the case of assets, _____ is a means of using future purchasing power in the present before a summation has been earned. Some companies and corporations use _____ as a part of their overall corporate finance strategy.

a. Cross-collateralization
c. Partial Payment
b. Credit cycle
d. Debt

45. _____ is a process by which a firm can obtain the use of a certain fixed assets for which it must pay a series of contractual, periodic, tax deductable payments. The lessee is the receiver of the services or the assets under the lease contract and the lessor is the owner of the assets. The relationship between the tenant and the landlord is called a tenancy, and can be for a fixed or an indefinite period of time (called the term of the lease).
   a. Foreign Corrupt Practices Act
   c. Leasing
   b. Quiet period
   d. Royalties

46. _____ is the capital that a business raises by taking out a loan. It is a loan made to a company that is normally repaid at some future date. _____ differs from equity or share capital because subscribers to _____ do not become part owners of the business, but are merely creditors, and the suppliers of _____ usually receive a contractually fixed annual percentage return on their loan, and this is known as the coupon rate.
   a. Floating charge
   c. Financial assistance
   b. Debt Capital
   d. Risk-return spectrum

Chapter 16. Lending Policies and Procedures

1. _____ is the provision of resources (such as granting a loan) by one party to another party where that second party does not reimburse the first party immediately, thereby generating a debt, and instead arranges either to repay or return those resources (or material(s) of equal value) at a later date. The first party is called a creditor, also known as a lender, while the second party is called a debtor, also known as a borrower.

Movements of financial capital are normally dependent on either _____ or equity transfers.

   a. Comparable
   b. Clearing house
   c. Warrant
   d. Credit

2. _____ is the method by which one calculates the creditworthiness of a business or organization. The audited financial statements of a large company might be analyzed when it issues or has issued bonds. Or, a bank may analyze the financial statements of a small business before making or renewing a commercial loan.
   a. Credit analysis
   b. Credit report monitoring
   c. Capital note
   d. Credit crunch

3. _____ consists of the sale of goods or merchandise from a fixed location, such as a department store, boutique or kiosk in small or individual lots for direct consumption by the purchaser. _____ may include subordinated services, such as delivery. Purchasers may be individuals or businesses.
   a. 529 plan
   b. 7-Eleven
   c. 4-4-5 Calendar
   d. Retailing

4. _____ or financing is to provide capital (funds), which means money for a project, a person, a business or any other private or public institutions.

Those funds can be allocated for either short term or long term purposes. The health fund is a new way of _____ private healthcare centers.

   a. Funding
   b. Proxy fight
   c. Synthetic CDO
   d. Product life cycle

5. The terms _____ , nominal _____ , and effective _____ describe the interest rate for a whole year (annualized), rather than just a monthly fee/rate, as applied on a loan, mortgage, credit card, etc. Those terms have formal, legal definitions in some countries or legal jurisdictions, but in general:

   - The nominal _____ is the simple-interest rate (for a year.)
   - The effective _____ is the fee+compound interest rate (calculated across a year.)

The nominal _____ is calculated as: the rate, for a payment period, multiplied by the number of payment periods in a year. However, the exact legal definition of 'effective _____' can vary greatly in each jurisdiction, depending on the type of fees included, such as participation fees, loan origination fees, monthly service charges, or late fees. The effective _____ has been called the 'mathematically-true' interest rate for each year. The computation for the effective _____, as the fee+compound interest rate, can also vary depending on whether the up-front fees, such as origination or participation fees, are added to the entire amount, or treated as a short-term loan due in the first payment.

Chapter 16. Lending Policies and Procedures

a. ABN Amro
b. AAB
c. Annual percentage rate
d. A Random Walk Down Wall Street

6. The _____ is a United States law (codified at 15 U.S.C. Â§ 1691 et seq.), enacted in 1974, that makes it unlawful for any creditor to discriminate against any applicant, with respect to any aspect of a credit transaction, on the basis of race, color, religion, national origin, sex, marital status, or age (provided the applicant has the capacity to contract); to the fact that all or part of the applicant's income derives from a public assistance program; or to the fact that the applicant has in good faith exercised any right under the Consumer Credit Protection Act. The law applies to any person who, in the ordinary course of business, regularly participates in a credit decision, including banks, retailers, bankcard companies, finance companies, and credit unions.

a. ABN Amro
b. A Random Walk Down Wall Street
c. AAB
d. Equal Credit Opportunity Act

7. A _____ occurs when a financial sponsor acquires a controlling interest in a company's equity and where a significant percentage of the purchase price is financed through leverage (borrowing.) The assets of the acquired company are used as collateral for the borrowed capital, sometimes with assets of the acquiring company. The bonds or other paper issued for _____s are commonly considered not to be investment grade because of the significant risks involved.

a. Leverage
b. Limited partnership
c. Pension fund
d. Leveraged buyout

8. _____ is the discipline of identifying, monitoring and limiting risks. In some cases the acceptable risk may be near zero. Risks can come from accidents, natural causes and disasters as well as deliberate attacks from an adversary.

a. FIFO
b. Penny stock
c. Risk Management
d. 4-4-5 Calendar

9. In lending agreements, _____ is a borrower's pledge of specific property to a lender, to secure repayment of a loan. The _____ serves as protection for a lender against a borrower's risk of default - that is, a borrower failing to pay the principal and interest under the terms of a loan obligation. If a borrower does default on a loan (due to insolvency or other event), that borrower forfeits (gives up) the property pledged as _____ *ollateral* - and the lender then becomes the owner of the _____.

a. Future-oriented
b. Nominal value
c. Refinancing risk
d. Collateral

10. A _____ (U.S.), or credit reference agency (UK) is a company that collects information from various sources and provides consumer credit information on individual consumers for a variety of uses. This helps lenders assess credit worthiness, the ability to pay back a loan, and can affect the interest rate and other terms of a loan. Interest rates are not the same for everyone, but instead can be based on risk-based pricing, a form of price discrimination based on the different expected risks of different borrowers, as set out in their credit rating.

a. Probability of default
b. Wall Street Journal prime rate
c. Reserve requirement
d. Credit bureau

11. A _____ is a contract entered into between which regulates the terms of a loan. they usually relate to loans of cash, but market specific contracts are also used to regulate securities lending.

They are usually in written form, but there is no legal reason why a _____ cannot be a purely oral contract (although in some countries this may be limited by the Statute of frauds or equivalent legislation).

Chapter 16. Lending Policies and Procedures   133

a. Foreclosure
b. Royalties
c. Lien
d. Loan agreement

12. In finance, a _____ is the party in a loan agreement which receives money or other instrument from a lender and promises to repay the lender in a specified time.
   a. Borrower
   b. Line of credit
   c. Cash credit
   d. Debt management plan

13. _____ is the balance of the amounts of cash being received and paid by a business during a defined period of time, sometimes tied to a specific project. Measurement of _____ can be used

- to evaluate the state or performance of a business or project.
- to determine problems with liquidity. Being profitable does not necessarily mean being liquid. A company can fail because of a shortage of cash, even while profitable.
- to generate project rate of returns. The time of _____s into and out of projects are used as inputs to financial models such as internal rate of return, and net present value.
- to examine income or growth of a business when it is believed that accrual accounting concepts do not represent economic realities. Alternately, _____ can be used to 'validate' the net income generated by accrual accounting.

_____ as a generic term may be used differently depending on context, and certain _____ definitions may be adapted by analysts and users for their own uses. Common terms include operating _____ and free _____.

_____s can be classified into:

1. Operational _____s: Cash received or expended as a result of the company's core business activities.
2. Investment _____s: Cash received or expended through capital expenditure, investments or acquisitions.
3. Financing _____s: Cash received or expended as a result of financial activities, such as interests and dividends.

All three together - the net _____ - are necessary to reconcile the beginning cash balance to the ending cash balance. Loan draw downs or equity injections, that is just shifting of capital but no expenditure as such, are not considered in the net _____.

   a. Real option
   b. Corporate finance
   c. Shareholder value
   d. Cash flow

14. In financial accounting, a _____ or statement of cash flows is a financial statement that shows a company's flow of cash. The money coming into the business is called cash inflow, and money going out from the business is called cash outflow. The statement shows how changes in balance sheet and income accounts affect cash and cash equivalents, and breaks the analysis down to operating, investing, and financing activities.
   a. 529 plan
   b. 7-Eleven
   c. Cash flow Statement
   d. 4-4-5 Calendar

15. A _____, in its most general sense, is a solemn promise to engage in or refrain from a specified action.

More specifically, a _____, in contrast to a contract, is a one-way agreement whereby the _____er is the only party bound by the promise. A _____ may have conditions and prerequisites that qualify the undertaking, including the actions of second or third parties, but there is no inherent agreement by such other parties to fulfill those requirements.

a. Clayton Antitrust Act
b. Partnership
c. Federal Trade Commission Act
d. Covenant

16. _____, in bookkeeping, refers to assets, liabilities, income, and expenses recorded on individual pages of the so called book of final entry or ledger. Changes in _____ value are made by chronologically posting debit (DR) and credit (CR) entries to its page. Examples of _____s are cash, _____s receivable, mortgages, loans, land and buildings, common stock, sales, services provided, wages, and payroll overhead.

a. Accretion
b. Option
c. Alpha
d. Account

17. _____ is one of a series of accounting transactions dealing with the billing of customers who owe money to a person, company or organization for goods and services that have been provided to the customer. In most business entities this is typically done by generating an invoice and mailing or electronically delivering it to the customer, who in turn must pay it within an established timeframe called credit or payment terms.

An example of a common payment term is Net 30, meaning payment is due in the amount of the invoice 30 days from the date of invoice.

a. Income
b. Impaired asset
c. Accounts receivable
d. Accounting methods

18. _____ is a financial transaction whereby a business sells its accounts receivable (i.e., invoices) at a discount. _____ differs from a bank loan in three main ways. First, the emphasis is on the value of the receivables (essentially a financial asset), not the firm's credit worthiness.

a. Credit card balance transfer
b. Financial Literacy Month
c. Debt-for-equity swap
d. Factoring

19. _____ is a list for goods and materials held available in stock by a business. It is also used for a list of the contents of a household and for a list for testamentary purposes of the possessions of someone who has died. In accounting _____ is considered an asset.

a. A Random Walk Down Wall Street
b. Inventory
c. ABN Amro
d. AAB

20. In law, a _____ is a form of security interest granted over an item of property to secure the payment of a debt or performance of some other obligation. The owner of the property, who grants the _____, is referred to as the lienor and the person who has the benefit of the _____ is referred to as the _____ee.

The etymological root is: Anglo-French _____, loyen bond, restraint, from Latin ligamen, from ligare to bind.

Chapter 16. Lending Policies and Procedures

a. Family and Medical Leave Act
b. Joint venture
c. Sarbanes-Oxley Act
d. Lien

21. _____ is a type of property. In the common law systems _____ may also be called chattels or personalty. It is distinguished from real property, or real estate.
   a. Beneficial owner
   b. Loan agreement
   c. McFadden Act
   d. Personal property

22. In the common law, _____ refers to one of the three main classes of property, the other two classes being personal property and intellectual property. _____ generally encompasses land, land improvements resulting from human effort including buildings and machinery sited on land, and various property rights over the preceding.

The concept is variously named and defined in other jurisdictions: heritable property in Scotland, immobilier in France, and immovable property in Canada, United States, India, Pakistan, Bangladesh, Malta, Cyprus, and in countries where civil law systems prevail, including most of Europe, Russia, and South America.

   a. Business valuation
   b. Fair debt collection
   c. Real property
   d. Corporate governance

23. The _____ is one of a number of uniform acts that have been promulgated in conjunction with efforts to harmonize the law of sales and other commercial transactions in all 50 states within the United States of America. This objective is deemed important because of the prevalence today of commercial transactions that extend beyond one state (for example, where the goods are manufactured in state A, warehoused in state B, sold from state C and delivered in state D.) The _____ deals primarily with transactions involving personal property (movable property), not real property (immovable property.)
   a. Assumption of risk
   b. External risks
   c. Executory Interest
   d. Uniform Commercial Code

24. In finance, a _____ or accounting ratio is a ratio of two selected numerical values taken from an enterprise's financial statements. There are many standard ratios used to try to evaluate the overall financial condition of a corporation or other organization. They may be used by managers within a firm, by current and potential shareholders (owners) of a firm, and by a firm's creditors. Security analysts use these to compare the strengths and weaknesses in various companies.
   a. Sustainable growth rate
   b. Price/cash flow ratio
   c. Financial Ratio
   d. Return on capital employed

25. A _____ is something for which there is demand, but which is supplied without qualitative differentiation across a market. It is a product that is the same no matter who produces it, such as petroleum, notebook paper, or milk. In other words, copper is copper.
   a. Commodity
   b. 4-4-5 Calendar
   c. 7-Eleven
   d. 529 plan

26. In finance, _____ occurs when a debtor has not met its legal obligations according to the debt contract, e.g. it has not made a scheduled payment, or has violated a loan covenant (condition) of the debt contract. _____ may occur if the debtor is either unwilling or unable to pay their debt. This can occur with all debt obligations including bonds, mortgages, loans, and promissory notes.

a. Debt validation
b. Vendor finance
c. Credit crunch
d. Default

27. In financial accounting, a _____ or statement of financial position is a summary of a person's or organization's balances. Assets, liabilities and ownership equity are listed as of a specific date, such as the end of its financial year. A _____ is often described as a snapshot of a company's financial condition.
   a. Statement of retained earnings
   b. Balance sheet
   c. Financial statements
   d. Statement on Auditing Standards No. 70: Service Organizations

28. In finance, a _____ is a derivative in which two counterparties agree to exchange one stream of cash flows against another stream. These streams are called the legs of the _____.

The cash flows are calculated over a notional principal amount, which is usually not exchanged between counterparties.

   a. Volatility arbitrage
   b. Local volatility
   c. Volatility swap
   d. Swap

29. An _____ is quite usually a standard guarantee from the seller of a product that specifies the extent to which the quality or performance of the product is assured and states the conditions under which the product can be returned, replaced, or repaired. It is often given in the form of a specific, written 'Warranty' document. However, a warranty may also arise by operation of law based upon the seller's description of the goods, and perhaps their source and quality, and any material deviation from that specification would violate the guarantee.
   a. Express warranty
   b. Economies of scale
   c. Assumption of risk
   d. Economic depreciation

Chapter 17. Lending to Business Firms and Pricing Business Loans

1. The institution most often referenced by the word '_____' is a public or publicly traded _____, the shares of which are traded on a public stock exchange (e.g., the New York Stock Exchange or Nasdaq in the United States) where shares of stock of _____s are bought and sold by and to the general public. Most of the largest businesses in the world are publicly traded _____s. However, the majority of _____s are said to be closely held, privately held or close _____s, meaning that no ready market exists for the trading of shares.
   a. Federal Home Loan Mortgage Corporation
   b. Protect
   c. Depository Trust Company
   d. Corporation

2. _____ is the provision of resources (such as granting a loan) by one party to another party where that second party does not reimburse the first party immediately, thereby generating a debt, and instead arranges either to repay or return those resources (or material(s) of equal value) at a later date. The first party is called a creditor, also known as a lender, while the second party is called a debtor, also known as a borrower.

   Movements of financial capital are normally dependent on either _____ or equity transfers.

   a. Comparable
   b. Warrant
   c. Clearing house
   d. Credit

3. _____ is a list for goods and materials held available in stock by a business. It is also used for a list of the contents of a household and for a list for testamentary purposes of the possessions of someone who has died. In accounting _____ is considered an asset.
   a. AAB
   b. ABN Amro
   c. A Random Walk Down Wall Street
   d. Inventory

4. In economic models, the _____ time frame assumes no fixed factors of production. Firms can enter or leave the marketplace, and the cost (and availability) of land, labor, raw materials, and capital goods can be assumed to vary. In contrast, in the short-run time frame, certain factors are assumed to be fixed, because there is not sufficient time for them to change.
   a. Long-run
   b. 4-4-5 Calendar
   c. Short-run
   d. 529 plan

5. In economics, the concept of the _____ refers to the decision-making time frame of a firm in which at least one factor of production is fixed. Costs which are fixed in the _____ have no impact on a firms decisions. For example a firm can raise output by increasing the amount of labour through overtime.
   a. 4-4-5 Calendar
   b. 529 plan
   c. Long-run
   d. Short-run

6. In lending agreements, _____ is a borrower's pledge of specific property to a lender, to secure repayment of a loan. The _____ serves as protection for a lender against a borrower's risk of default - that is, a borrower failing to pay the principal and interest under the terms of a loan obligation. If a borrower does default on a loan (due to insolvency or other event), that borrower forfeits (gives up) the property pledged as _____ *ollateral* - and the lender then becomes the owner of the _____.
   a. Nominal value
   b. Future-oriented
   c. Refinancing risk
   d. Collateral

138 *Chapter 17. Lending to Business Firms and Pricing Business Loans*

7. A _____ is the system of organizations, people, technology, activities, information and resources involved in moving a product or service from supplier to customer. _____ activities transform natural resources, raw materials and components into a finished product that is delivered to the end customer. In sophisticated _____ systems, used products may re-enter the _____ at any point where residual value is recyclable.

a. 529 plan
b. 7-Eleven
c. 4-4-5 Calendar
d. Supply chain

8. _____ is a financial metric which represents operating liquidity available to a business. Along with fixed assets such as plant and equipment, _____ is considered a part of operating capital. It is calculated as current assets minus current liabilities.

a. 529 plan
b. 4-4-5 Calendar
c. Working capital management
d. Working capital

9. In the broadest sense of the term, a _____ is any loan where the proceeds are used to finance construction of some kind. In the United States Financial Services industry however, the term is used to describe a genre of loans designed for construction and containing features such as interest reserves, where repayment ability may be based on something that can only occour when the project is built. Thus the defining features of these loans are special monitoring and guidelines above normal loan guidelines to ensure that the project is completed so that repayment can begin to take place.

a. Conforming loan
b. Blanket mortgage
c. Construction loan
d. HELOC

10. _____ or financing is to provide capital (funds), which means money for a project, a person, a business or any other private or public institutions.

Those funds can be allocated for either short term or long term purposes. The health fund is a new way of _____ private healthcare centers.

a. Product life cycle
b. Funding
c. Proxy fight
d. Synthetic CDO

11. In finance, a _____ is collateral that the holder of a position in securities, options, or futures contracts has to deposit to cover the credit risk of his counterparty (most often his broker.) This risk can arise if the holder has done any of the following:

- borrowed cash from the counterparty to buy securities or options,
- sold securities or options short, or
- entered into a futures contract.

The collateral can be in the form of cash or securities, and it is deposited in a _____ account. On U.S. futures exchanges, '_____' was formally called performance bond.

_____ buying is buying securities with cash borrowed from a broker, using other securities as collateral.

a. Share
b. Procter ' Gamble
c. Credit
d. Margin

Chapter 17. Lending to Business Firms and Pricing Business Loans

12. _____ is the discipline of identifying, monitoring and limiting risks. In some cases the acceptable risk may be near zero. Risks can come from accidents, natural causes and disasters as well as deliberate attacks from an adversary.
    a. Penny stock
    b. FIFO
    c. Risk Management
    d. 4-4-5 Calendar

13. A _____ is a fungible, negotiable instrument representing financial value. They are broadly categorized into debt securities (such as banknotes, bonds and debentures), and equity securities; e.g., common stocks. The company or other entity issuing the _____ is called the issuer.
    a. Security
    b. Tracking stock
    c. Book entry
    d. Securities lending

14. An _____ is a loan, often for a short term, secured by a company's assets. Real estate, A/R, inventory, and equipment are typical assets used to back the loan. The loan may be backed by a single category of assets or some combination of assets, for instance, a combination of A/R and equipment.
    a. ASCOT
    b. External financing
    c. Asset-based loan
    d. Amortizing loan

15.

A _____ is a type of financial intermediary and a type of bank. Commercial banking is also known as business banking. It is a bank that provides checking accounts, savings accounts, and money market accounts and that accepts time deposits.

   a. 7-Eleven
   b. 4-4-5 Calendar
   c. 529 plan
   d. Commercial bank

16. _____ is a financial transaction whereby a business sells its accounts receivable (i.e., invoices) at a discount. _____ differs from a bank loan in three main ways. First, the emphasis is on the value of the receivables (essentially a financial asset), not the firm's credit worthiness.
    a. Credit card balance transfer
    b. Financial Literacy Month
    c. Debt-for-equity swap
    d. Factoring

17. A _____ (or 'syndicated bank facility') is a large loan in which a group of banks provide funds for a borrower, usually several but without joint liability. There is usually a lead bank or group of banks (the 'Arranger/s' or 'Agent/s') that takes a percentage of the loan and syndicates or sells the rest to other banks. In contrast, a bilateral loan, only involves one borrower and one lender (often a bank or financial institution.)
    a. Debt buyer
    b. Collection agency
    c. Credit score
    d. Syndicated loan

18. In banking and finance, a _____ is a loan where a payment of the entire principal of the loan, and sometimes the principal and interest, is due at the end of the loan term. Likewise for bullet bond. A _____ can be a mortgage, bond, note or any other type of credit.
    a. Bullet loan
    b. Bear raid
    c. Modern portfolio theory
    d. Bankruptcy remote

Chapter 17. Lending to Business Firms and Pricing Business Loans

19. _____s are deposits denominated in United States dollars at banks outside the United States, and thus are not under the jurisdiction of the Federal Reserve. Consequently, such deposits are subject to much less regulation than similar deposits within the United States, allowing for higher margins. There is nothing 'European' about _____ deposits; a US dollar-denominated deposit in Tokyo or Caracas would likewise be deemed _____ deposits.
   a. ABN Amro
   b. AAB
   c. A Random Walk Down Wall Street
   d. Eurodollar

20. _____ plant, and equipment, is a term used in accountancy for assets and property which cannot easily be converted into cash. This can be compared with current assets such as cash or bank accounts, which are described as liquid assets. In most cases, only tangible assets are referred to as fixed.
   a. Fixed asset
   b. Percentage of Completion
   c. Remittance advice
   d. Petty cash

21. _____ is a type of credit that does not have a fixed number of payments, in contrast to installment credit. Examples of _____s used by consumers include credit cards. Corporate _____ facilities are typically used to provide liquidity for a company's day-to-day operations.
   a. Reverse stock split
   b. Commercial finance
   c. Revolving credit
   d. Package loan

22. In business and accounting, _____s are everything of value that is owned by a person or company. The balance sheet of a firm records the monetary value of the _____s owned by the firm. The two major _____ classes are tangible _____s and intangible _____s.
   a. EBITDA
   b. Asset
   c. Accounts payable
   d. Income

23. A _____ is the maximum amount of credit that a financial institution or other lender will extend to a debtor for a particular line of credit. For example, the maximum that a credit card company will allow a card holder to borrow at any given point on a specific card.

This limit is based on a variety of factors ranging from an individual's ability to make interest payments, an organization's cashflow and/or ability to repay the principal, to the credit standards employed by the lender.

   a. 4-4-5 Calendar
   b. 7-Eleven
   c. 529 plan
   d. Credit limit

24. A _____ occurs when a financial sponsor acquires a controlling interest in a company's equity and where a significant percentage of the purchase price is financed through leverage (borrowing.) The assets of the acquired company are used as collateral for the borrowed capital, sometimes with assets of the acquiring company. The bonds or other paper issued for _____s are commonly considered not to be investment grade because of the significant risks involved.
   a. Leveraged buyout
   b. Pension fund
   c. Limited partnership
   d. Leverage

25. The phrase _____ refers to the aspect of corporate strategy, corporate finance and management dealing with the buying, selling and combining of different companies that can aid, finance, or help a growing company in a given industry grow rapidly without having to create another business entity.

Chapter 17. Lending to Business Firms and Pricing Business Loans 141

An acquisition, also known as a takeover, is the buying of one company (the 'target') by another. An acquisition may be friendly or hostile.

- a. 529 plan
- b. 7-Eleven
- c. Mergers and acquisitions
- d. 4-4-5 Calendar

26. In financial accounting, a _____ or statement of financial position is a summary of a person's or organization's balances. Assets, liabilities and ownership equity are listed as of a specific date, such as the end of its financial year. A _____ is often described as a snapshot of a company's financial condition.

- a. Financial statements
- b. Statement on Auditing Standards No. 70: Service Organizations
- c. Statement of retained earnings
- d. Balance sheet

27. _____, refers to consumption opportunity gained by an entity within a specified time frame, which is generally expressed in monetary terms. However, for households and individuals, '_____ is the sum of all the wages, salaries, profits, interests payments, rents and other forms of earnings received... in a given period of time.' For firms, _____ generally refers to net-profit: what remains of revenue after expenses have been subtracted.

- a. OIBDA
- b. Annual report
- c. Income
- d. Accrual

28. An _____ is a financial statement for companies that indicates how Revenue is transformed into net income The purpose of the _____ is to show managers and investors whether the company made or lost money during the period being reported.

The important thing to remember about an _____ is that it represents a period of time.

- a. ABN Amro
- b. A Random Walk Down Wall Street
- c. AAB
- d. Income statement

29. _____ are formal records of a business' financial activities.

_____ provide an overview of a business' financial condition in both short and long term. There are four basic _____:

1. **Balance sheet**: also referred to as statement of financial position or condition, reports on a company's assets, liabilities, and net equity as of a given point in time.
2. **Income statement**: also referred to as Profit and Loss statement (or a 'P'L'), reports on a company's income, expenses, and profits over a period of time.
3. **Statement of retained earnings**: explains the changes in a company's retained earnings over the reporting period.
4. **Statement of cash flows**: reports on a company's cash flow activities, particularly its operating, investing and financing activities.

Chapter 17. Lending to Business Firms and Pricing Business Loans

a. Notes to the Financial Statements

b. Statement on Auditing Standards No. 70: Service Organizations

c. Statement of retained earnings

d. Financial statements

30. In finance, a _____ or accounting ratio is a ratio of two selected numerical values taken from an enterprise's financial statements. There are many standard ratios used to try to evaluate the overall financial condition of a corporation or other organization. They may be used by managers within a firm, by current and potential shareholders (owners) of a firm, and by a firm's creditors. Security analysts use these to compare the strengths and weaknesses in various companies.

a. Return on capital employed

b. Sustainable growth rate

c. Price/cash flow ratio

d. Financial ratio

31. In accounting, _____ or sales profit is the difference between revenue and the cost of making a product or providing a service, before deducting overhead, payroll, taxation, and interest payments. Note that this is different than operating profit.

Net sales are calculated:

Net sales = Sales - Sales returns and allowances

_____ is found by deducting the cost of goods sold:

_____ = Net sales - Cost of goods sold

_____ should not be confused with net income:

Net income = _____ - Total operating expenses

Cost of goods sold is calculated differently for merchandising business than for a manufacturer.

a. Gross profit

b. Real option

c. Gross income

d. Cash flow

32. _____ is a financial ratio used to assess the profitability of a firm's core activities, excluding fixed costs.

The general calculation is

$$\text{Gross profit margin} = \frac{\text{Revenue} - \text{Cost of Sales}}{\text{Revenue}}$$

The _____ is related to the net profit margin, which assesses the profitability of an organization after including fixed costs.

Indicates the relationship between net sales revenue and the cost of goods sold.

Chapter 17. Lending to Business Firms and Pricing Business Loans

a. Second lien loan
c. Tender offer
b. Gross profit
d. Gross profit margin

33. The _____ is an equation that equals the cost of goods sold divided by the average inventory. Average inventory equals beginning inventory plus ending inventory divided by 2.

The formula for _____:

$$\text{Inventory Turnover} = \frac{\text{Cost of Goods Sold}}{\text{Average Inventory}}$$

The formula for average inventory:

$$\text{Average Inventory} = \frac{\text{Beginning inventory} + \text{Ending inventory}}{2}$$

A low turnover rate may point to overstocking, obsolescence, or deficiencies in the product line or marketing effort.

a. Operating leverage
c. Information ratio
b. Earnings yield
d. Inventory turnover

34. _____ is the difference between price and the costs of bringing to market whatever it is that is accounted as an enterprise (whether by harvest, extraction, manufacture, or purchase) in terms of the component costs of delivered goods and/or services and any operating or other expenses.

A key difficulty in measuring profit is in defining costs. Pure economic monetary profits can be zero or negative even in competitive equilibrium when accounted monetized costs exceed monetized price.

a. Economic profit
c. AAB
b. A Random Walk Down Wall Street
d. Accounting profit

35. _____, Net Margin, Net _____ or Net Profit Ratio all refer to a measure of profitability. It is calculated using a formula and written as a percentage or a number.

$$\text{Net profit margin} = \frac{\text{Net profit after taxes}}{\text{Net Sales}}$$

The _____ is mostly used for internal comparison.

a. Net profit margin
c. 4-4-5 Calendar
b. Profit margin
d. Profit maximization

Chapter 17. Lending to Business Firms and Pricing Business Loans

36. _____ is a fee paid on borrowed assets. It is the price paid for the use of borrowed money, or, money earned by deposited funds. Assets that are sometimes lent with _____ include money, shares, consumer goods through hire purchase, major assets such as aircraft, and even entire factories in finance lease arrangements.

a. Insolvency
b. A Random Walk Down Wall Street
c. AAB
d. Interest

37. Times interest earned (TIE) or _____ is a measure of a company's ability to honor its debt payments. It may be calculated as either EBIT or EBITDA divided by the total interest payable.

$$\text{Times-Interest-Earned} = \frac{\text{EBIT or EBITDA}}{\text{Interest Charges}}$$

- Financial ratio
- Financial leverage
- EBIT
- EBITDA
- Debt service coverage ratio

Interest Charges = Traditionally 'charges' refers to interest expense found on the income statement.

Times Interest Earned or Interest Coverage is a great tool when measuring a company's ability to meet its debt obligations.

a. Information ratio
b. Interest coverage ratio
c. Earnings per share
d. Assets turnover

38. In business and finance accounting, _____ is equal to the gross profit minus overheads minus interest payable plus/minus one off items for a given time period (usually: accounting period.)

A common synonym for '_____' when discussing financial statements (which include a balance sheet and an income statement) is the bottom line. This term results from the traditional appearance of an income statement which shows all allocated revenues and expenses over a specified time period with the resulting summation on the bottom line of the report.

a. Gross sales
b. Net profit
c. Deferred
d. Salvage value

39. Profit margin, net margin, _____ or net profit ratio all refer to a measure of profitability. It is calculated by finding the net profit as a percentage of the revenue.

The profit margin is mostly used for internal comparison.

a. 4-4-5 Calendar
b. Profit margin
c. Profit maximization
d. Net profit margin

40. In finance, the Acid-test or _____ or liquid ratio measures the ability of a company to use its near cash or quick assets to immediately extinguish or retire its current liabilities. Quick assets include those current assets that presumably can be quickly converted to cash at close to their book values.

Generally, the acid test ratio should be 1:1 or better, however this varies widely by industry.

a. Financial ratio
b. Quick ratio
c. P/E ratio
d. Net assets

41. The _____ is a financial ratio that measures whether or not a firm has enough resources to pay its debts over the next 12 months. It compares a firm's current assets to its current liabilities. It is expressed as follows:

$$\text{Current ratio} = \frac{\text{Current Assets}}{\text{Current Liabilities}}$$

For example, if WXY Company's current assets are $50,000,000 and its current liabilities are $40,000,000, then its _____ would be $50,000,000 divided by $40,000,000, which equals 1.25.

a. Current ratio
b. Sustainable growth rate
c. Debt service coverage ratio
d. PEG ratio

42. _____ is a measure of the ability of a debtor to pay their debts as and when they fall due. It is usually expressed as a ratio or a percentage of current liabilities.

For a corporation with a published balance sheet there are various ratios used to calculate a measure of liquidity.

a. Operating profit margin
b. Operating leverage
c. Invested capital
d. Accounting liquidity

43. In finance, _____ refers to the way a corporation finances its assets through some combination of equity, debt, or hybrid securities. A firm's _____ is then the composition or 'structure' of its liabilities. For example, a firm that sells $20 billion in equity and $80 billion in debt is said to be 20% equity-financed and 80% debt-financed.
a. Rights issue
b. Capital structure
c. Market for corporate control
d. Book building

44. In finance, _____ (or gearing) is borrowing money to supplement existing funds for investment in such a way that the potential positive or negative outcome is magnified and/or enhanced. It generally refers to using borrowed funds, or debt, so as to attempt to increase the returns to equity. Deleveraging is the action of reducing borrowings.

a. Financial endowment
b. Pension fund
c. Limited partnership
d. Leverage

45. _____ is the amount by which a reference rate is multiplied to determine the floating interest rate payable by an inverse floater. Some debt instruments leverage the particular effects of interest rate changes, most commonly in inverse floaters.

As an example, an inverse floater with a multiple may pay interest at the rate of 22 percent minus the product of 2 times the 1-month London Interbank Offered Rate (LIBOR.)

a. Trade date
b. Coupon leverage
c. Gross spread
d. Systematic risk

46. The _____ is a United States government system for classifying industries by a four-digit code. Established in 1937, it is being supplanted by the six-digit North American Industry Classification System, which was released in 1997; however certain government departments and agencies, such as the U.S. Securities and Exchange Commission (SEC), still use the _____ codes.

The following table is from the SEC's site, which allows searching for companies by _____ code in its database of filings.

a. 7-Eleven
b. 4-4-5 Calendar
c. Standard Industrial Classification
d. 529 plan

47. _____ is a mathematical science pertaining to the collection, analysis, interpretation or explanation, and presentation of data. It also provides tools for prediction and forecasting based on data. It is applicable to a wide variety of academic disciplines, from the natural and social sciences to the humanities, government and business.

a. Sample size
b. Covariance
c. Mean
d. Statistics

48. _____ are liabilities that may or may not be incurred by an entity depending on the outcome of a future event such as a court case. These liabilities are recorded in a company's accounts and shown in the balance sheet when both probable and reasonably estimable. A footnote to the balance sheet describes the nature and extent of the _____.

a. Due-on-sale clause
b. 529 plan
c. 4-4-5 Calendar
d. Contingent liabilities

49. An _____ is quite usually a standard guarantee from the seller of a product that specifies the extent to which the quality or performance of the product is assured and states the conditions under which the product can be returned, replaced, or repaired. It is often given in the form of a specific, written 'Warranty' document. However, a warranty may also arise by operation of law based upon the seller's description of the goods, and perhaps their source and quality, and any material deviation from that specification would violate the guarantee.

a. Economies of scale
b. Express warranty
c. Assumption of risk
d. Economic depreciation

Chapter 17. Lending to Business Firms and Pricing Business Loans   147

50. Explicit _____ is a measure implemented in many countries to protect bank depositors, in full or in part, from losses caused by a bank's inability to pay its debts when due. _____ systems are one component of a financial system safety net that promotes financial stability.
   a. Deposit Insurance
   b. Reserve requirement
   c. Banking panic
   d. Time deposit

51. The _____ is a United States government corporation created by the Glass-Steagall Act of 1933. It provides deposit insurance, which guarantees the safety of checking and savings deposits in member banks, currently up to $250,000 per depositor per bank. Insured deposits are backed by the full faith and credit of the United States.
   a. FASB
   b. NYSE Group
   c. Federal Deposit Insurance Corporation
   d. Ford Foundation

52. In the most general sense, a _____ is anything that is a hindrance, or puts individuals at a disadvantage.

Before we discuss the financial terms, we should note that a _____ can also have a much more important slang meaning.

This is best described in an example.

   a. McFadden Act
   b. Limited liability
   c. Covenant
   d. Liability

53. A _____ is a property interest created by agreement or by operation of law over assets to secure the performance of an obligation, usually the payment of a debt. It gives the beneficiary of the _____ certain preferential rights in the disposition of secured assets. Such rights vary according to the type of _____, but in most cases, a holder of the _____ is entitled to seize, and usually sell, the property to discharge the debt that the _____ secures.
   a. FIDC
   b. Retention ratio
   c. Security interest
   d. Netting

54. A _____ is a pool of assets forming an independent legal entity that are bought with the contributions to a pension plan for the exclusive purpose of financing pension plan benefits.

_____s are important shareholders of listed and private companies. They are especially important to the stock market where large institutional investors like the Ontario Teachers' Pension Plan dominate.

   a. Limited liability company
   b. Leverage
   c. Leveraged buyout
   d. Pension fund

55. _____ is a step in a risk management process. _____ is the determination of quantitative or qualitative value of risk related to a concrete situation and a recognized threat (also called hazard.) Quantitative _____ requires calculations of two components of risk: R, the magnitude of the potential loss L, and the probability p that the loss will occur.
   a. 7-Eleven
   b. 529 plan
   c. Risk assessment
   d. 4-4-5 Calendar

Chapter 17. Lending to Business Firms and Pricing Business Loans

56. _____ is the balance of the amounts of cash being received and paid by a business during a defined period of time, sometimes tied to a specific project. Measurement of _____ can be used

- to evaluate the state or performance of a business or project.
- to determine problems with liquidity. Being profitable does not necessarily mean being liquid. A company can fail because of a shortage of cash, even while profitable.
- to generate project rate of returns. The time of _____s into and out of projects are used as inputs to financial models such as internal rate of return, and net present value.
- to examine income or growth of a business when it is believed that accrual accounting concepts do not represent economic realities. Alternately, _____ can be used to 'validate' the net income generated by accrual accounting.

_____ as a generic term may be used differently depending on context, and certain _____ definitions may be adapted by analysts and users for their own uses. Common terms include operating _____ and free _____.

_____s can be classified into:

1. Operational _____s: Cash received or expended as a result of the company's core business activities.
2. Investment _____s: Cash received or expended through capital expenditure, investments or acquisitions.
3. Financing _____s: Cash received or expended as a result of financial activities, such as interests and dividends.

All three together - the net _____ - are necessary to reconcile the beginning cash balance to the ending cash balance. Loan draw downs or equity injections, that is just shifting of capital but no expenditure as such, are not considered in the net _____.

a. Real option
b. Cash flow
c. Corporate finance
d. Shareholder value

57. In financial accounting, a _____ or statement of cash flows is a financial statement that shows a company's flow of cash. The money coming into the business is called cash inflow, and money going out from the business is called cash outflow. The statement shows how changes in balance sheet and income accounts affect cash and cash equivalents, and breaks the analysis down to operating, investing, and financing activities.

a. 4-4-5 Calendar
b. 7-Eleven
c. 529 plan
d. Cash flow Statement

58. In financial accounting, _____ , cash flow provided by operations or cash flow from operating activities, refers to the amount of cash a company generates from the revenues it brings in, excluding costs associated with long-term investment on capital items or investment in securities.

_____ = Cash generated from operations less taxation and interest paid, investment income received and less dividends paid gives rise to _____s per International Financial Reporting Standards.

Chapter 17. Lending to Business Firms and Pricing Business Loans 149

To calculate cash generated from operations, one must calculate cash generated from customers and cash paid to suppliers.

a. Other Comprehensive Basis of Accounting
b. Operating cash flow
c. A Random Walk Down Wall Street
d. Appreciation

59. The term _____ is a term applied to practices that are perfunctory, or seek to satisfy the minimum requirements or to conform to a convention or doctrine. It has different meanings in different fields.

In accounting, _____ earnings are those earnings of companies in addition to actual earnings calculated under the Generally Accepted Accounting Principles (GAAP) in their quarterly and yearly financial reports.

a. Deferred income
b. Long-term liabilities
c. Deferred financing costs
d. Pro forma

60. In finance, _____ occurs when a debtor has not met its legal obligations according to the debt contract, e.g. it has not made a scheduled payment, or has violated a loan covenant (condition) of the debt contract. _____ may occur if the debtor is either unwilling or unable to pay their debt. This can occur with all debt obligations including bonds, mortgages, loans, and promissory notes.

a. Credit crunch
b. Vendor finance
c. Debt validation
d. Default

61. _____ is the risk of loss due to a debtor's non-payment of a loan or other line of credit (either the principal or interest (coupon) or both)

Most lenders employ their own models (credit scorecards) to rank potential and existing customers according to risk, and then apply appropriate strategies. With products such as unsecured personal loans or mortgages, lenders charge a higher price for higher risk customers and vice versa. With revolving products such as credit cards and overdrafts, risk is controlled through careful setting of credit limits.

a. Liquidity risk
b. Transaction risk
c. Market risk
d. Credit risk

62. _____ is a term applied in many countries to a reference interest rate used by banks. The term originally indicated the rate of interest at which banks lent to favored customers, i.e., those with high credibility, though this is no longer always the case. Some variable interest rates may be expressed as a percentage above or below _____.

a. Prime rate
b. Reserve requirement
c. Time deposit
d. Credit bureau

63. A _____ is a rate that determines pay-offs in a financial contract and that is outside the control of the parties to the contract. It is often some form of LIBOR rate, but it can take many forms, such as a consumer price index, a house price index or an unemployment rate. Parties to the contract choose a _____ that neither party has power to manipulate.

a. Risk-free interest rate
b. Reference rate
c. TIBOR
d. London Interbank Offered Rate

64. An _____ is the price a borrower pays for the use of money they do not own, and the return a lender receives for deferring the use of funds, by lending it to the borrower. _____s are normally expressed as a percentage rate over the period of one year.

_____s targets are also a vital tool of monetary policy and are used to control variables like investment, inflation, and unemployment.

   a. Interest rate
   c. ABN Amro
   b. A Random Walk Down Wall Street
   d. AAB

65.

In finance, the _____ can be the expected rate of return above the risk-free interest rate. When measuring risk, a common sense approach is to compare the risk-free return on T-bills and the very risky return on other investments. The difference between these two returns can be interpreted as a measure of the excess return on the average risky asset. This excess return is known as the _____.

   a. Risk aversion
   c. Risk adjusted return on capital
   b. Risk premium
   d. Risk modeling

Chapter 18. Consumer Loans, Credit Cards, and Real Estate Lending

1. _____ is the provision of resources (such as granting a loan) by one party to another party where that second party does not reimburse the first party immediately, thereby generating a debt, and instead arranges either to repay or return those resources (or material(s) of equal value) at a later date. The first party is called a creditor, also known as a lender, while the second party is called a debtor, also known as a borrower.

Movements of financial capital are normally dependent on either _____ or equity transfers.

a. Clearing house
b. Credit
c. Comparable
d. Warrant

2. The institution most often referenced by the word '_____' is a public or publicly traded _____, the shares of which are traded on a public stock exchange (e.g., the New York Stock Exchange or Nasdaq in the United States) where shares of stock of _____s are bought and sold by and to the general public. Most of the largest businesses in the world are publicly traded _____s. However, the majority of _____s are said to be closely held, privately held or close _____s, meaning that no ready market exists for the trading of shares.

a. Protect
b. Depository Trust Company
c. Corporation
d. Federal Home Loan Mortgage Corporation

3. A _____ is a cooperative financial institution that is owned and controlled by its members, and operated for the purpose of promoting thrift, providing credit at reasonable rates, and providing other financial services to its members. Many _____s exist to further community development or sustainable international development on a local level. Worldwide, _____ systems vary significantly in terms of total system assets and average institution asset size since _____s exist in a wide range of sizes, ranging from volunteer operations with a handful of members to institutions with several billion dollars in assets and hundreds of thousands of members.

a. Corporate credit union
b. Credit Union Service Organization
c. Fi-linx
d. Credit union

4. _____ is a type of credit that does not have a fixed number of payments, in contrast to installment credit. Examples of _____s used by consumers include credit cards. Corporate _____ facilities are typically used to provide liquidity for a company's day-to-day operations.

a. Commercial finance
b. Revolving credit
c. Reverse stock split
d. Package loan

5. A _____ is any credit facility extended to a business by a bank or financial institution. A _____ may take several forms such as cash credit, overdraft, demand loan, export packing credit, term loan, discounting or purchase of commercial bills etc. It is like an account that can readily be tapped into if the need arises or not touched at all and saved for emergencies.

a. Cash credit
b. Default Notice
c. Debt-snowball method
d. Line of credit

152 Chapter 18. Consumer Loans, Credit Cards, and Real Estate Lending

6. _____ is the process of decreasing an amount over a period of time. The word comes from Middle English amortisen to kill, alienate in mortmain, from Anglo-French amorteser, alteration of amortir, from Vulgar Latin admortire to kill, from Latin ad- + mort-, mors death. Particular instances of the term include:

- _____ (business), the allocation of a lump sum amount to different time periods, particularly for loans and other forms of finance, including related interest or other finance charges.
    - _____ schedule, a table detailing each periodic payment on a loan (typically a mortgage), as generated by an _____ calculator.
    - Negative _____, an _____ schedule where the loan amount actually increases through not paying the full interest
- Amortized analysis, analyzing the execution cost of algorithms over a sequence of operations.
- _____ of capital expenditures of certain assets under accounting rules, particularly intangible assets, in a manner analogous to depreciation.
- _____ (tax law)

_____ is also used in the context of zoning regulations and describes the time in which a property owner has to relocate when the property's use constitutes a preexisting nonconforming use under zoning regulations.

- Depreciation

a. Intrinsic value
b. AT'T Inc.
c. Option
d. Amortization

7. _____ is a fee paid on borrowed assets. It is the price paid for the use of borrowed money , or, money earned by deposited funds . Assets that are sometimes lent with _____ include money, shares, consumer goods through hire purchase, major assets such as aircraft, and even entire factories in finance lease arrangements.
   a. AAB
   b. Interest
   c. Insolvency
   d. A Random Walk Down Wall Street

8. A _____ (U.S.), or credit reference agency (UK) is a company that collects information from various sources and provides consumer credit information on individual consumers for a variety of uses. This helps lenders assess credit worthiness, the ability to pay back a loan, and can affect the interest rate and other terms of a loan. Interest rates are not the same for everyone, but instead can be based on risk-based pricing, a form of price discrimination based on the different expected risks of different borrowers, as set out in their credit rating.
   a. Probability of default
   b. Reserve requirement
   c. Credit bureau
   d. Wall Street Journal prime rate

9. _____, refers to consumption opportunity gained by an entity within a specified time frame, which is generally expressed in monetary terms. However, for households and individuals, '_____ is the sum of all the wages, salaries, profits, interests payments, rents and other forms of earnings received... in a given period of time.' For firms, _____ generally refers to net-profit: what remains of revenue after expenses have been subtracted.
   a. Accrual
   b. OIBDA
   c. Annual report
   d. Income

Chapter 18. Consumer Loans, Credit Cards, and Real Estate Lending

10. _____ is that which is owed; usually referencing assets owed, but the term can cover other obligations. In the case of assets, _____ is a means of using future purchasing power in the present before a summation has been earned. Some companies and corporations use _____ as a part of their overall corporate finance strategy.
    a. Credit cycle
    b. Partial Payment
    c. Cross-collateralization
    d. Debt

11. The _____ is a United States law (codified at 15 U.S.C. § 1691 et seq.), enacted in 1974, that makes it unlawful for any creditor to discriminate against any applicant, with respect to any aspect of a credit transaction, on the basis of race, color, religion, national origin, sex, marital status, or age (provided the applicant has the capacity to contract); to the fact that all or part of the applicant's income derives from a public assistance program; or to the fact that the applicant has in good faith exercised any right under the Consumer Credit Protection Act. The law applies to any person who, in the ordinary course of business, regularly participates in a credit decision, including banks, retailers, bankcard companies, finance companies, and credit unions.
    a. AAB
    b. A Random Walk Down Wall Street
    c. ABN Amro
    d. Equal Credit Opportunity Act

12. The terms _____ , nominal _____ , and effective _____ describe the interest rate for a whole year (annualized), rather than just a monthly fee/rate, as applied on a loan, mortgage, credit card, etc. Those terms have formal, legal definitions in some countries or legal jurisdictions, but in general:

    - The nominal _____ is the simple-interest rate (for a year.)
    - The effective _____ is the fee+compound interest rate (calculated across a year.)

    The nominal _____ is calculated as: the rate, for a payment period, multiplied by the number of payment periods in a year. However, the exact legal definition of 'effective _____' can vary greatly in each jurisdiction, depending on the type of fees included, such as participation fees, loan origination fees, monthly service charges, or late fees. The effective _____ has been called the 'mathematically-true' interest rate for each year. The computation for the effective _____, as the fee+compound interest rate, can also vary depending on whether the up-front fees, such as origination or participation fees, are added to the entire amount, or treated as a short-term loan due in the first payment.

    a. ABN Amro
    b. A Random Walk Down Wall Street
    c. AAB
    d. Annual percentage rate

13. The _____ is a United States federal law enacted as an amendment to the Truth in Lending Act (codified at 15 U.S.C. § 1601 et seq.). Its purpose is to protect consumers from unfair billing practices and to provide a mechanism for addressing billing errors in 'open end' credit accounts, such as credit card or charge card accounts.
    a. Regulation Q
    b. Fair Credit Billing Act
    c. Truth in Lending Act
    d. Fair Credit Reporting Act

14. The _____ is an American federal law (codified at 15 U.S.C. § 1681 et seq.) that regulates the collection, dissemination, and use of consumer credit information.
    a. Fair Credit Billing Act
    b. Fair Credit Reporting Act
    c. Truth in Lending Act
    d. Regulation Q

15. _____ broadly refers to regulation of the debt collection industry at both the U.S. Federal and state levels of government. At the Federal level, it is primarily governed by the _____ Practices Act ('_____PA'.) In addition, many U.S. States also have debt collection laws that regulate the credit and collection industry and give consumer debtors protection from abusive and deceptive practices.
   a. Securities Investor Protection Act
   b. Fair Debt Collection
   c. Bundesrechnungshof
   d. Covenant

16. The _____ is a United States statute added in 1978 as Title VIII of the Consumer Credit Protection Act. Its purposes are to eliminate abusive practices in the collection of consumer debts, to promote fair debt collection and to provide consumers with an avenue for disputing and obtaining validation of debt information in order to ensure the information's accuracy.
   a. Court of Audit of Belgium
   b. Partnership
   c. Law of one price
   d. Fair Debt Collection Practices Act

17. _____ is a financial term that was popularized by the media during the 'credit crunch' of 2007 and involves financial institutions lending in ways which do not meet 'prime' standards to an extent which puts the loans into the riskiest category of consumer loans typically sold in the secondary market. These standards refer to the size of the loan, 'traditional' or 'nontraditional' structure of the loan, borrower credit rating, ratio of borrower debt to income or assets, ratio of loan to value or collateral, documentation provided on those loans which do not meet Fannie Mae or Freddie Mac underwriting guidelines for prime mortgages (are 'non-conforming'.) Although there is no single, standard definition, in the US subprime loans are usually classified as those where the borrower has a FICO score below 640.
   a. Fixed rate mortgage
   b. Cash-out
   c. Negative equity
   d. Subprime lending

18. In business and accounting, _____s are everything of value that is owned by a person or company. The balance sheet of a firm records the monetary value of the _____s owned by the firm. The two major _____ classes are tangible _____s and intangible _____s.
   a. EBITDA
   b. Accounts payable
   c. Income
   d. Asset

19. _____ are defined as identifiable non-monetary assets that cannot be seen, touched or physically measured, which are created through time and/or effort and that are identifiable as a separate asset. There are two primary forms of intangibles - legal intangibles (such as trade secrets (e.g., customer lists), copyrights, patents, trademarks, and goodwill) and competitive intangibles (such as knowledge activities (know-how, knowledge), collaboration activities, leverage activities, and structural activities.) Legal intangibles generate legal property rights defensible in a court of law.
   a. AAB
   b. ABN Amro
   c. Intangible assets
   d. A Random Walk Down Wall Street

20. In the broadest sense of the term, a _____ is any loan where the proceeds are used to finance construction of some kind. In the United States Financial Services industry however, the term is used to describe a genre of loans designed for construction and containing features such as interest reserves, where repayment ability may be based on something that can only occour when the project is built. Thus the defining features of these loans are special monitoring and guidelines above normal loan guidelines to ensure that the project is completed so that repayment can begin to take place.
   a. HELOC
   b. Conforming loan
   c. Construction loan
   d. Blanket mortgage

Chapter 18. Consumer Loans, Credit Cards, and Real Estate Lending 155

21. The _____ (NYSE: FNM), commonly known as Fannie Mae, is a stockholder-owned corporation chartered by Congress in 1968 as a government sponsored enterprise (GSE), but founded in 1938 during the Great Depression. The corporation's purpose is to purchase and securitize mortgages in order to ensure that funds are consistently available to the institutions that lend money to home buyers.

On September 7, 2008, James Lockhart, director of the Federal Housing Finance Agency (FHFA), announced that Fannie Mae and Freddie Mac were being placed into conservatorship of the FHFA.

   a. Federal National Mortgage Association
   b. The Depository Trust ' Clearing Corporation
   c. SPDR
   d. General partnership

22. _____ is the value of a homeowner's unencumbered interest in their property, i.e. the difference between the home's fair market value and the unpaid balance of the mortgage and any outstanding debt over the home. _____ increases as the mortgage is paid or as the property enjoys appreciation. This is sometimes called real property value in economics.
   a. Home equity
   b. Liquidation value
   c. REIT
   d. Real Estate Investment Trust

23. An _____ is a contract written by a seller that conveys to the buyer the right -- but not the obligation -- to buy (in the case of a call _____) or to sell (in the case of a put _____) a particular asset, such as a piece of property such as, among others, a futures contract. In return for granting the _____, the seller collects a payment (the premium) from the buyer.

For example, buying a call _____ provides the right to buy a specified quantity of a security at a set strike price at some time on or before expiration, while buying a put _____ provides the right to sell.

   a. AT'T Mobility LLC
   b. Amortization
   c. Option
   d. Annuity

24. _____ is a legally declared inability or impairment of ability of an individual or organization to pay their creditors. Creditors may file a _____ petition against a debtor ('involuntary _____') in an effort to recoup a portion of what they are owed or initiate a restructuring. In the majority of cases, however, _____ is initiated by the debtor (a 'voluntary _____' that is filed by the bankrupt individual or organization.)
   a. 529 plan
   b. 4-4-5 Calendar
   c. Debt settlement
   d. Bankruptcy

25. The _____, was a law enacting several significant changes to the U.S. Bankruptcy Code. Referred to colloquially as the 'New Bankruptcy Law', the Act of Congress attempts to, among other things, make it more difficult for some consumers to file bankruptcy under Chapter 7; some of these consumers may instead utilize Chapter 13.
   a. Foreclosure
   b. Personal property
   c. Bankruptcy Abuse Prevention and Consumer Protection Act of 2005
   d. Covenant

156 **Chapter 18. Consumer Loans, Credit Cards, and Real Estate Lending**

26. In statistics, _____ has two related meanings:

- the arithmetic _____
- the expected value of a random variable, which is also called the population _____.

It is sometimes stated that the '_____' is average. This is incorrect if '_____' is taken in the specific sense of 'arithmetic _____' as there are different types of averages: the _____, median, and mode. Other simple statistical analyses use measures of spread, such as range, interquartile range, or standard deviation. For a real-valued random variable X, the _____ is the expectation of X. Note that not every probability distribution has a defined _____; see the Cauchy distribution for an example.

a. Sample size
c. Harmonic mean
b. Mean
d. Probability distribution

27. In finance, the term _____ describes the amount in cash that returns to the owners of a security. Normally it does not include the price variations, at the difference of the total return. _____ applies to various stated rates of return on stocks (common and preferred, and convertible), fixed income instruments (bonds, notes, bills, strips, zero coupon), and some other investment type insurance products (e.g. annuities.)

a. Yield to maturity
c. Macaulay duration
b. 4-4-5 Calendar
d. Yield

28. In finance, the _____ is the relation between the interest rate (or cost of borrowing) and the time to maturity of the debt for a given borrower in a given currency. For example, the current U.S. dollar interest rates paid on U.S. Treasury securities for various maturities are closely watched by many traders, and are commonly plotted on a graph such as the one on the right which is informally called 'the _____.' More formal mathematical descriptions of this relation are often called the term structure of interest rates.

The yield of a debt instrument is the annualized percentage increase in the value of the investment.

a. 4-4-5 Calendar
c. Yield curve
b. 7-Eleven
d. 529 plan

29. A '_____' is a 'Charge' that is paid to obtain the right to delay a payment. Essentially, the payer purchases the right to make a given payment in the future instead of in the Present. The '_____', or 'Charge' that must be paid to delay the payment, is simply the difference between what the payment amount would be if it were paid in the present and what the payment amount would be paid if it were paid in the future.

a. Risk modeling
c. Value at risk
b. Discount
d. Risk aversion

30. The _____ is an interest rate a central bank charges depository institutions that borrow reserves from it.

Chapter 18. Consumer Loans, Credit Cards, and Real Estate Lending 157

The term _____ has two meanings:

- the same as interest rate; the term 'discount' does not refer to the meaning of the word, but to the purpose of using the quantity, such as computations of present value, e.g. net present value / discounted cash flow

- the annual effective _____, which is the annual interest divided by the capital including that interest; this rate is lower than the interest rate; it corresponds to using the value after a year as the nominal value, and seeing the initial value as the nominal value minus a discount; it is used for Treasury Bills and similar financial instruments

The annual effective _____ is the annual interest divided by the capital including that interest, which is the interest rate divided by 100% plus the interest rate. It is the annual discount factor to be applied to the future cash flow, to find the discount, subtracted from a future value to find the value one year earlier.

For example, suppose there is a government bond that sells for $95 and pays $100 in a year's time.

a. Stochastic volatility
b. Discount rate
c. Fisher equation
d. Black-Scholes

31. The phrase _____ refers to the aspect of corporate strategy, corporate finance and management dealing with the buying, selling and combining of different companies that can aid, finance, or help a growing company in a given industry grow rapidly without having to create another business entity.

An acquisition, also known as a takeover, is the buying of one company (the 'target') by another. An acquisition may be friendly or hostile.

a. Mergers and acquisitions
b. 4-4-5 Calendar
c. 7-Eleven
d. 529 plan

32. An _____ is a mortgage loan where the interest rate on the note is periodically adjusted based on a variety of indices. Among the most common indices are the rates on 1-year constant-maturity Treasury (CMT) securities, the Cost of Funds Index (COFI), and the London Interbank Offered Rate (LIBOR.) A few lenders use their own cost of funds as an index, rather than using other indices.

a. AAB
b. ABN Amro
c. Adjustable rate mortgage
d. A Random Walk Down Wall Street

33. An _____ is the price a borrower pays for the use of money they do not own, and the return a lender receives for deferring the use of funds, by lending it to the borrower. _____s are normally expressed as a percentage rate over the period of one year.

_____s targets are also a vital tool of monetary policy and are used to control variables like investment, inflation, and unemployment.

a. ABN Amro
b. A Random Walk Down Wall Street
c. AAB
d. Interest rate

34. _____ or amalgamation is the act of merging many things into one. In business, it often refers to the mergers or acquisitions of many smaller companies into much larger ones. The financial accounting term of _____ refers to the aggregated financial statements of a group company as consolidated account.
   a. Write-off
   b. Cost of goods sold
   c. Retained earnings
   d. Consolidation

Chapter 19. Acquisitions and Mergers in Financial- Services Management

1. _____ or amalgamation is the act of merging many things into one. In business, it often refers to the mergers or acquisitions of many smaller companies into much larger ones. The financial accounting term of _____ refers to the aggregated financial statements of a group company as consolidated account.
   - a. Cost of goods sold
   - b. Consolidation
   - c. Write-off
   - d. Retained earnings

2. _____ is the removal or simplification of government rules and regulations that constrain the operation of market forces. _____ does not mean elimination of laws against fraud, but eliminating or reducing government control of how business is done, thereby moving toward a more free market.

   The stated rationale for '_____' is often that fewer and simpler regulations will lead to a raised level of competitiveness, therefore higher productivity, more efficiency and lower prices overall.
   - a. Value added
   - b. Supply shock
   - c. Demand shock
   - d. Deregulation

3. The phrase _____ refers to the aspect of corporate strategy, corporate finance and management dealing with the buying, selling and combining of different companies that can aid, finance, or help a growing company in a given industry grow rapidly without having to create another business entity.

   An acquisition, also known as a takeover, is the buying of one company (the 'target') by another. An acquisition may be friendly or hostile.
   - a. 7-Eleven
   - b. 4-4-5 Calendar
   - c. 529 plan
   - d. Mergers and acquisitions

4. The _____ Act is an Act of the 106th United States Congress which repealed part of the Glass-Steagall Act of 1933, opening up competition among banks, securities companies and insurance companies. The Glass-Steagall Act prohibited any one institution from acting as both an investment bank and a commercial bank, or as both a bank and an insurer.

   The _____ Act (GLBA) allowed commercial and investment banks to consolidate.
   - a. 529 plan
   - b. 7-Eleven
   - c. 4-4-5 Calendar
   - d. Gramm-Leach-Bliley

5. The institution most often referenced by the word '_____' is a public or publicly traded _____, the shares of which are traded on a public stock exchange (e.g., the New York Stock Exchange or Nasdaq in the United States) where shares of stock of _____s are bought and sold by and to the general public. Most of the largest businesses in the world are publicly traded _____s. However, the majority of _____s are said to be closely held, privately held or close _____s, meaning that no ready market exists for the trading of shares.
   - a. Corporation
   - b. Federal Home Loan Mortgage Corporation
   - c. Depository Trust Company
   - d. Protect

6. _____ refer to services provided by the finance industry.

Chapter 19. Acquisitions and Mergers in Financial- Services Management

The finance industry encompasses a broad range of organizations that deal with the management of money. Among these organizations are banks, credit card companies, insurance companies, consumer finance companies, stock brokerages, investment funds and some government sponsored enterprises.

a. Financial instruments
b. Cost of carry
c. Delta hedging
d. Financial services

7. _____ is the difference between price and the costs of bringing to market whatever it is that is accounted as an enterprise (whether by harvest, extraction, manufacture, or purchase) in terms of the component costs of delivered goods and/or services and any operating or other expenses.

A key difficulty in measuring profit is in defining costs. Pure economic monetary profits can be zero or negative even in competitive equilibrium when accounted monetized costs exceed monetized price.

a. AAB
b. Accounting profit
c. Economic profit
d. A Random Walk Down Wall Street

8. _____ is the balance of the amounts of cash being received and paid by a business during a defined period of time, sometimes tied to a specific project. Measurement of _____ can be used

- to evaluate the state or performance of a business or project.
- to determine problems with liquidity. Being profitable does not necessarily mean being liquid. A company can fail because of a shortage of cash, even while profitable.
- to generate project rate of returns. The time of _____s into and out of projects are used as inputs to financial models such as internal rate of return, and net present value.
- to examine income or growth of a business when it is believed that accrual accounting concepts do not represent economic realities. Alternately, _____ can be used to 'validate' the net income generated by accrual accounting.

_____ as a generic term may be used differently depending on context, and certain _____ definitions may be adapted by analysts and users for their own uses. Common terms include operating _____ and free _____.

_____s can be classified into:

1. Operational _____s: Cash received or expended as a result of the company's core business activities.
2. Investment _____s: Cash received or expended through capital expenditure, investments or acquisitions.
3. Financing _____s: Cash received or expended as a result of financial activities, such as interests and dividends.

All three together - the net _____ - are necessary to reconcile the beginning cash balance to the ending cash balance. Loan draw downs or equity injections, that is just shifting of capital but no expenditure as such, are not considered in the net _____.

a. Corporate finance
b. Cash flow
c. Shareholder value
d. Real option

9. In economics, business, and accounting, a _____ is the value of money that has been used up to produce something, and hence is not available for use anymore. In business, the _____ may be one of acquisition, in which case the amount of money expended to acquire it is counted as _____. In this case, money is the input that is gone in order to acquire the thing.
   a. Sliding scale fees
   b. Marginal cost
   c. Fixed costs
   d. Cost

10. In finance, a _____ is a debt security, in which the authorized issuer owes the holders a debt and, depending on the terms of the _____, is obliged to pay interest (the coupon) and/or to repay the principal at a later date, termed maturity.

Thus a _____ is a loan: the issuer is the borrower, the _____ holder is the lender, and the coupon is the interest. _____s provide the borrower with external funds to finance long-term investments, or, in the case of government _____s, to finance current expenditure.

   a. Puttable bond
   b. Convertible bond
   c. Bond
   d. Catastrophe bonds

11. _____ in finance is a risk management technique, related to hedging, that mixes a wide variety of investments within a portfolio. Because the fluctuations of a single security have less impact on a diverse portfolio, _____ minimizes the risk from any one investment.

A simple example of _____ is the following: On a particular island the entire economy consists of two companies: one that sells umbrellas and another that sells sunscreen.

   a. 7-Eleven
   b. 4-4-5 Calendar
   c. 529 plan
   d. Diversification

12. In political science and economics, the _____ or agency dilemma treats the difficulties that arise under conditions of incomplete and asymmetric information when a principal hires an agent. Various mechanisms may be used to try to align the interests of the agent with those of the principal, such as piece rates/commissions, profit sharing, efficiency wages, performance measurement (including financial statements), the agent posting a bond, or fear of firing. The _____ is found in most employer/employee relationships, for example, when stockholders hire top executives of corporations.
   a. 7-Eleven
   b. 529 plan
   c. 4-4-5 Calendar
   d. Principal-agent problem

13. _____ is the price at which an asset would trade in a competitive Walrasian auction setting. _____ is often used interchangeably with open _____, fair value or fair _____, although these terms have distinct definitions in different standards, and may differ in some circumstances.

International Valuation Standards defines _____ as 'the estimated amount for which a property should exchange on the date of valuation between a willing buyer and a willing seller in an arm'e;s-length transaction after proper marketing wherein the parties had each acted knowledgeably, prudently, and without compulsion.'

_____ is a concept distinct from market price, which is 'e;the price at which one can transact'e;, while _____ is 'e;the true underlying value'e; according to theoretical standards.

   a. Wrap account
   b. Market value
   c. T-Model
   d. Debt restructuring

14. _____ are the earnings returned on the initial investment amount.

In the US, the Financial Accounting Standards Board (FASB) requires companies' income statements to report _____ for each of the major categories of the income statement: continuing operations, discontinued operations, extraordinary items, and net income.

The _____ formula does not include preferred dividends for categories outside of continued operations and net income.

   a. Assets turnover
   b. Earnings per share
   c. Inventory turnover
   d. Average accounting return

15. In business and finance, a _____ (also referred to as equity _____) of stock means a _____ of ownership in a corporation (company.) In the plural, stocks is often used as a synonym for _____s especially in the United States, but it is less commonly used that way outside of North America.

In the United Kingdom, South Africa, and Australia, stock can also refer to completely different financial instruments such as government bonds or, less commonly, to all kinds of marketable securities.

   a. Procter ' Gamble
   b. Bucket shop
   c. Margin
   d. Share

16. In political economy and especially Marxian economics, _____ refers to one of four major attributes of a commodity, i.e., an item or service produced for, and sold on the market. The other three aspects are use value, value and price.

Thus, a commodity has:

- a value
- a use-value (or utility)
- an _____
- a price (it could be an actual selling price or an imputed ideal price)

Chapter 19. Acquisitions and Mergers in Financial-Services Management

These four concepts have a very long history in human thought, from Aristotle to David Ricardo, becoming ever more clearly distinguished as the development of commercial trade progressed. This entry focuses on Marx's summation of the results of economic thought about exchange-value.

a. AAB
b. A Random Walk Down Wall Street
c. Exchange value
d. ABN Amro

17. _____ is a fee paid on borrowed assets. It is the price paid for the use of borrowed money, or, money earned by deposited funds. Assets that are sometimes lent with _____ include money, shares, consumer goods through hire purchase, major assets such as aircraft, and even entire factories in finance lease arrangements.

a. A Random Walk Down Wall Street
b. Insolvency
c. AAB
d. Interest

18. _____ is an accounting term used to reflect the portion of the book value of a business entity not directly attributable to its assets and liabilities; it normally arises only in case of an acquisition. It reflects the ability of the entity to make a higher profit than would be derived from selling the tangible assets. _____ is also known as an intangible asset.

a. Net profit
b. Cost of goods sold
c. Goodwill
d. Consolidation

19. _____ are defined as identifiable non-monetary assets that cannot be seen, touched or physically measured, which are created through time and/or effort and that are identifiable as a separate asset. There are two primary forms of intangibles - legal intangibles (such as trade secrets (e.g., customer lists), copyrights, patents, trademarks, and goodwill) and competitive intangibles (such as knowledge activities (know-how, knowledge), collaboration activities, leverage activities, and structural activities.) Legal intangibles generate legal property rights defensible in a court of law.

a. ABN Amro
b. A Random Walk Down Wall Street
c. Intangible assets
d. AAB

20. _____ consists of the sale of goods or merchandise from a fixed location, such as a department store, boutique or kiosk in small or individual lots for direct consumption by the purchaser. _____ may include subordinated services, such as delivery. Purchasers may be individuals or businesses.

a. 7-Eleven
b. 4-4-5 Calendar
c. 529 plan
d. Retailing

21. In business, a _____ is the purchase of one company (the target) by another (the acquirer or bidder). In the UK the term refers to the acquisition of a public company whose shares are listed on a stock exchange, in contrast to the acquisition of a private company.

Before a bidder makes an offer for another company, it usually first informs that company's board of directors.

a. Stock swap
b. 529 plan
c. Takeover
d. 4-4-5 Calendar

22. The _____ was the first United States Federal statute to limit cartels and monopolies. It falls under antitrust law.

The Act provides: 'Every contract, combination in the form of trust or otherwise, or conspiracy, in restraint of trade or commerce among the several States, or with foreign nations, is declared to be illegal'. The Act also provides: 'Every person who shall monopolize, or attempt to monopolize, or combine or conspire with any other person or persons, to monopolize any part of the trade or commerce among the several States, or with foreign nations, shall be deemed guilty of a felony [. . .]'

a. 529 plan
b. 4-4-5 Calendar
c. 7-Eleven
d. Sherman Antitrust Act

23. In economics, _____ is a function of the number of firms and their respective shares of the total production (alternatively, total capacity or total reserves) in a market. Alternative terms are Industry concentration and Seller concentration.

_____ is related to the concept of industrial concentration, which concerns the distribution of production within an industry, as opposed to a market.

a. 7-Eleven
b. 529 plan
c. 4-4-5 Calendar
d. Market concentration

24. In finance and economics, _____ or divestiture is the reduction of some kind of asset for either financial goals or ethical objectives. A _____ is the opposite of an investment.

Often the term is used as a means to grow financially in which a company sells off a business unit in order to focus their resources on a market it judges to be more profitable, or promising.

a. Portfolio investment
b. Certificate in Investment Performance Measurement
c. Divestment
d. Late trading

25. In financial accounting, the term _____ is most commonly used to describe any part of shareholders' equity, except for basic share capital. Sometimes, the term is used instead of the term provision; such a use, however, is inconsistent with the terminology suggested by International Accounting Standards Board. For more information about provisions, see provision (accounting.)

a. Treasury stock
b. Closing entries
c. FIFO and LIFO accounting
d. Reserve

26. A _____, reserve bank, or monetary authority is the entity responsible for the monetary policy of a country or of a group of member states. It is a bank that can lend money to other banks in times of need. Its primary responsibility is to maintain the stability of the national currency and money supply, but more active duties include controlling subsidized-loan interest rates, and acting as a lender of last resort to the banking sector during times of financial crisis (private banks often being integral to the national financial system.)

a. Central bank
b. 7-Eleven
c. 4-4-5 Calendar
d. 529 plan

Chapter 20. International Banking and the Future of Banking and Financial Services   165

1. In financial accounting, a _____ or statement of financial position is a summary of a person's or organization's balances. Assets, liabilities and ownership equity are listed as of a specific date, such as the end of its financial year. A _____ is often described as a snapshot of a company's financial condition.

   a. Balance sheet
   b. Statement on Auditing Standards No. 70: Service Organizations
   c. Financial statements
   d. Statement of retained earnings

2. _____, refers to consumption opportunity gained by an entity within a specified time frame, which is generally expressed in monetary terms. However, for households and individuals, '_____ is the sum of all the wages, salaries, profits, interests payments, rents and other forms of earnings received... in a given period of time.' For firms, _____ generally refers to net-profit: what remains of revenue after expenses have been subtracted.

   a. Annual report
   b. Accrual
   c. Income
   d. OIBDA

3. The _____ is a bank that provides financial and technical assistance to developing countries for development programs (e.g. bridges, roads, schools, etc.) with the stated goal of reducing poverty.

   The _____ differs from the _____ Group, in that the _____ comprises only two institutions:

   - International Bank for Reconstruction and Development (IBRD)
   - International Development Association (IDA)

   Whereas the latter incorporates these two in addition to three more:

   - International Finance Corporation (IFC)
   - Multilateral Investment Guarantee Agency (MIGA)
   - International Centre for Settlement of Investment Disputes (ICSID)

   John Maynard Keynes (right) represented the UK at the conference, and Harry Dexter White represented the US.

   The _____ was created following the ratification of the United Nations Monetary and Financial Conference | Bretton Woods agreement. The concept was originally conceived in July 1944 at the United Nations Monetary and Financial Conference.

   a. 529 plan
   b. World Bank
   c. 7-Eleven
   d. 4-4-5 Calendar

4. The institution most often referenced by the word '_____' is a public or publicly traded _____, the shares of which are traded on a public stock exchange (e.g., the New York Stock Exchange or Nasdaq in the United States) where shares of stock of _____s are bought and sold by and to the general public. Most of the largest businesses in the world are publicly traded _____s. However, the majority of _____s are said to be closely held, privately held or close _____s, meaning that no ready market exists for the trading of shares.

   a. Protect
   b. Depository Trust Company
   c. Corporation
   d. Federal Home Loan Mortgage Corporation

Chapter 20. International Banking and the Future of Banking and Financial Services

5. A _____ is an entity formed between two or more parties to undertake economic activity together. The parties agree to create a new entity by both contributing equity, and they then share in the revenues, expenses, and control of the enterprise. The venture can be for one specific project only, or a continuing business relationship such as the Sony Ericsson _____.

   a. Pre-emption right
   b. Fair Debt Collection Practices Act
   c. Lien
   d. Joint venture

6. A _____, in business matters, is an entity that is controlled by a bigger and more powerful entity. The controlled entity is called a company, corporation, or limited liability company, and the controlling entity is called its parent (or the parent company.) The reason for this distinction is that a lone company cannot be a _____ of any organization; only an entity representing a legal fiction as a separate entity can be a _____.

   a. 4-4-5 Calendar
   b. Joint stock company
   c. 529 plan
   d. Subsidiary

7. _____ is the provision of resources (such as granting a loan) by one party to another party where that second party does not reimburse the first party immediately, thereby generating a debt, and instead arranges either to repay or return those resources (or material(s) of equal value) at a later date. The first party is called a creditor, also known as a lender, while the second party is called a debtor, also known as a borrower.

   Movements of financial capital are normally dependent on either _____ or equity transfers.

   a. Credit
   b. Warrant
   c. Comparable
   d. Clearing house

8. _____ are various forms of controls imposed by a government on the purchase/sale of foreign currencies by residents or on the purchase/sale of local currency by nonresidents.

   Common _____ include:

   - Banning the use of foreign currency within the country
   - Banning locals from possessing foreign currency
   - Restricting currency exchange to government-approved exchangers
   - Fixed exchange rates
   - Restrictions on the amount of currency that may be imported or exported

   Countries with _____ are also known as 'Article 14 countries,' after the provision in the International Monetary Fund agreement allowing exchange controls for transitional economies. Such controls used to be common in most countries, particularly poorer ones, until the 1990s when free trade and globalization started a trend towards economic liberalization. Today, countries which still impose exchange controls are the exception rather than the rule.

   a. Foreign exchange option
   b. Spot market
   c. Foreign exchange controls
   d. Forex scam

9.

Chapter 20. International Banking and the Future of Banking and Financial Services

A _____ is a type of financial intermediary and a type of bank. Commercial banking is also known as business banking. It is a bank that provides checking accounts, savings accounts, and money market accounts and that accepts time deposits.

a. 7-Eleven
b. 529 plan
c. 4-4-5 Calendar
d. Commercial bank

10. _____ is a political organization established in 2002 and dedicated to the protection of children from abuse, exploitation and neglect. It is a nonprofit, 501(c)(4) membership association with members in every U.S. state and 10 nations. _____ achieved great success in its first three years, winning legislative victories in eight state legislatures.

a. Ford Foundation
b. The Depository Trust ' Clearing Corporation
c. Protect
d. First Prudential Markets

11. A _____ or bank is a financial institution whose primary activity is to act as a payment agent for customers and to borrow and lend money.

The first modern bank was founded in Italy in Genoa in 1406, its name was Banco di San Giorgio (Bank of St. George.)

Many other financial activities were added over time.

a. Banker
b. Black Sea Trade and Development Bank
c. 4-4-5 Calendar
d. Bought deal

12. A _____, reserve bank, or monetary authority is the entity responsible for the monetary policy of a country or of a group of member states. It is a bank that can lend money to other banks in times of need. Its primary responsibility is to maintain the stability of the national currency and money supply, but more active duties include controlling subsidized-loan interest rates, and acting as a lender of last resort to the banking sector during times of financial crisis (private banks often being integral to the national financial system.)

a. 529 plan
b. Central Bank
c. 7-Eleven
d. 4-4-5 Calendar

13. _____ is a form of risk that arises from the change in price of one currency against another. Whenever investors or companies have assets or business operations across national borders, they face _____ if their positions are not hedged.

- Transaction risk is the risk that exchange rates will change unfavourably over time. It can be hedged against using forward currency contracts;
- Translation risk is an accounting risk, proportional to the amount of assets held in foreign currencies. Changes in the exchange rate over time will render a report inaccurate, and so assets are usually balanced by borrowings in that currency.

The exchange risk associated with a foreign denominated instrument is a key element in foreign investment. This risk flows from differential monetary policy and growth in real productivity, which results in differential inflation rates.

168   Chapter 20. International Banking and the Future of Banking and Financial Services

a. Market risk
b. Credit risk
c. Tracking error
d. Currency risk

14. In finance, the _____ between two currencies specifies how much one currency is worth in terms of the other. For example an _____ of 102 Japanese yen to the United States dollar means that JPY 102 is worth the same as USD 1. The foreign exchange market is one of the largest markets in the world.

a. A Random Walk Down Wall Street
b. AAB
c. ABN Amro
d. Exchange rate

15. In finance, the _____ is the system that allows the transfer of money between savers and borrowers.

Put another way: the _____ is a set of complex and closely interconnected financial institutions, markets, instruments, services, practices, and transactions.

a. 4-4-5 Calendar
b. Passive income
c. Financial system
d. Horizontal merger

16. A _____, also FX future or foreign exchange future, is a futures contract to exchange one currency for another at a specified date in the future at a price (exchange rate) that is fixed on the purchase date. Typically, one of the currencies is the US dollar. The price of a future is then in terms of US dollars per unit of other currency.

a. Non-deliverable forward
b. Currency future
c. Currency swap
d. Foreign exchange controls

17. A _____ is an agreement between two parties to buy or sell an asset at a specified point of time in the future. The price of the underlying instrument, in whatever form, is paid before control of the instrument changes. This is one of the many forms of buy/sell orders where the time of trade is not the time where the securities themselves are exchanged.

a. Loan Credit Default Swap Index
b. Derivatives markets
c. Constant maturity credit default swap
d. Forward contract

18. A _____ is an exchange of promises between two or more parties to do an act which is enforceable in a court of law. It is where an unqualified offer meets a qualified acceptance and the parties reach Consensus ad Idem. The parties must have the necessary capacity to _____ and the _____ must not be either trifling, indeterminate, impossible or illegal.

a. 529 plan
b. Contract
c. 4-4-5 Calendar
d. 7-Eleven

19. In finance, a _____ is a standardized contract, to buy or sell a specified commodity of standardized quality at a certain date in the future, at a market determined price (the futures price.)

The price is determined by the instantaneous equilibrium between the forces of supply and demand among competing buy and sell orders on the exchange at the time of the purchase or sale of the contract.

In many cases, the items may be such non-traditional 'commodities' as foreign currencies, commercial or government paper [e.g., bonds], or 'baskets' of corporate equity ['stock indices'] or other financial instruments.

Chapter 20. International Banking and the Future of Banking and Financial Services

a. Heston model
c. Financial future
b. Futures contract
d. Repurchase agreement

20. In finance, a _____ is a position established in one market in an attempt to offset exposure to the price risk of an equal but opposite obligation or position in another market -- usually, but not always, in the context of one's commercial activity. Hedging is a strategy designed to minimize exposure to such business risks as a sharp contraction in demand for one's inventory, while still allowing the business to profit from producing and maintaining that inventory. A typical hedger might be a farmer with 2000 acres of unharvested wheat in the ground, who would rather tend his crop without the distraction of uncertain prices.
   a. 529 plan
   c. Hedge
   b. 4-4-5 Calendar
   d. 7-Eleven

21. A _____ is a foreign exchange agreement between two parties to exchange principal and fixed rate interest payments on a loan in one currency for principal and fixed rate interest payments on an equal (regarding net present value) loan in another currency. They are motivated by comparative advantage.
   a. Currency swap
   c. Currency pair
   b. Forex swap
   d. Foreign exchange market

22. An _____ is a contract written by a seller that conveys to the buyer the right -- but not the obligation -- to buy (in the case of a call _____) or to sell (in the case of a put _____) a particular asset, such as a piece of property such as, among others, a futures contract. In return for granting the _____, the seller collects a payment (the premium) from the buyer.

For example, buying a call _____ provides the right to buy a specified quantity of a security at a set strike price at some time on or before expiration, while buying a put _____ provides the right to sell.

   a. Amortization
   c. Annuity
   b. AT'T Mobility LLC
   d. Option

23. In finance, a _____ is a derivative in which two counterparties agree to exchange one stream of cash flows against another stream. These streams are called the legs of the _____.

The cash flows are calculated over a notional principal amount, which is usually not exchanged between counterparties.

   a. Local volatility
   c. Swap
   b. Volatility arbitrage
   d. Volatility swap

24. In economic models, the _____ time frame assumes no fixed factors of production. Firms can enter or leave the marketplace, and the cost (and availability) of land, labor, raw materials, and capital goods can be assumed to vary. In contrast, in the short-run time frame, certain factors are assumed to be fixed, because there is not sufficient time for them to change.
   a. Short-run
   c. Long-run
   b. 4-4-5 Calendar
   d. 529 plan

Chapter 20. International Banking and the Future of Banking and Financial Services

25. In economics, the concept of the _____ refers to the decision-making time frame of a firm in which at least one factor of production is fixed. Costs which are fixed in the _____ have no impact on a firms decisions. For example a firm can raise output by increasing the amount of labour through overtime.
    a. Long-run
    b. 529 plan
    c. Short-run
    d. 4-4-5 Calendar

26. An _____ represents the ownership in the shares of a foreign company trading on US financial markets. The stock of many non-US companies trades on US exchanges through the use of _____s. _____s enable US investors to buy shares in foreign companies without undertaking cross-border transactions.
    a. AAB
    b. ABN Amro
    c. A Random Walk Down Wall Street
    d. American depository receipt

27. A standard, commercial _____ is a document issued mostly by a financial institution, used primarily in trade finance, which usually provides an irrevocable payment undertaking.

    The _____ can also be the source of payment for a transaction, meaning that redeeming the _____ will pay an exporter. Letters of credit are used primarily in international trade transactions of significant value, for deals between a supplier in one country and a customer in another.

    a. Duty of loyalty
    b. Bond indenture
    c. Letter of credit
    d. McFadden Act

28. A _____ can require immediate payment by the second party to the third upon presentation of the _____. This is called a sight _____. A Cheques is a sight _____. An importer might write a _____ promising payment to an exporter for delivery of goods with payment to occur 60 days after the goods are delivered. Such a _____ is called a time _____.
    a. Draft
    b. Gross profit margin
    c. Cashflow matching
    d. Second lien loan

29. _____ in finance is a risk management technique, related to hedging, that mixes a wide variety of investments within a portfolio. Because the fluctuations of a single security have less impact on a diverse portfolio, _____ minimizes the risk from any one investment.

    A simple example of _____ is the following: On a particular island the entire economy consists of two companies: one that sells umbrellas and another that sells sunscreen.

    a. Diversification
    b. 529 plan
    c. 7-Eleven
    d. 4-4-5 Calendar

30. A _____ is an international bond that is denominated in a currency not native to the country where it is issued. It can be categorised according to the currency in which it is issued. London is one of the centers of the _____ market, but _____s may be traded throughout the world - for example in Singapore or Tokyo.
    a. Interest rate option
    b. Eurobond
    c. Education production function
    d. Economic entity

31. The _____ was a basket of the currencies of the European Community member states, used as the unit of account of the European Community before being replaced by the euro on January 1, 1999, at parity. The _____ itself replaced the European Unit of Account, also at parity, on March 13, 1979. The European Exchange Rate Mechanism attempted to minimize fluctuations between member state currencies and the _____.
   a. Outsourcing
   b. Electronic communication network
   c. OTC Bulletin Board
   d. European currency unit

32. In structured finance, a _____ is one of a number of related securities offered as part of the same transaction. The word _____ is French for slice, section, series, or portion. In the financial sense of the word, each bond is a different slice of the deal's risk.
   a. 4-4-5 Calendar
   b. Credit enhancement
   c. Yield curve spread
   d. Tranche

33. _____ refer to services provided by the finance industry.

The finance industry encompasses a broad range of organizations that deal with the management of money. Among these organizations are banks, credit card companies, insurance companies, consumer finance companies, stock brokerages, investment funds and some government sponsored enterprises.

   a. Delta hedging
   b. Financial services
   c. Cost of carry
   d. Financial instruments

34. _____ is a fee paid on borrowed assets. It is the price paid for the use of borrowed money , or, money earned by deposited funds . Assets that are sometimes lent with _____ include money, shares, consumer goods through hire purchase, major assets such as aircraft, and even entire factories in finance lease arrangements.
   a. A Random Walk Down Wall Street
   b. Insolvency
   c. AAB
   d. Interest

35. An _____ is the price a borrower pays for the use of money they do not own, and the return a lender receives for deferring the use of funds, by lending it to the borrower. _____s are normally expressed as a percentage rate over the period of one year.

_____s targets are also a vital tool of monetary policy and are used to control variables like investment, inflation, and unemployment.

   a. Interest rate
   b. A Random Walk Down Wall Street
   c. AAB
   d. ABN Amro

36. _____ is the risk (variability in value) borne by an interest-bearing asset, such as a loan or a bond, due to variability of interest rates. In general, as rates rise, the price of a fixed rate bond will fall, and vice versa. _____ is commonly measured by the bond's duration.
   a. Interest rate risk
   b. Official bank rate
   c. A Random Walk Down Wall Street
   d. International Fisher effect

37. A _____ is a futures contract on a short term interest rate (STIR.) Contracts vary, but are often defined on an interest rate index such as 3-month sterling or US dollar LIBOR.

172 *Chapter 20. International Banking and the Future of Banking and Financial Services*

They are traded across a wide range of currencies, including the G12 country currencies and many others.

a. Real estate derivatives
b. Notional amount
c. Dual currency deposit
d. Financial future

38. _____ refers to the likelihood that changes in the business environment adversely affect operating profits or the value of assets in a specific country. For example, financial factors such as currency controls, devaluation or regulatory changes, or stability factors such as mass riots, civil war and other potential events contribute to companies' operational risks. This term is also sometimes referred to as political risk, however _____ is a more general term, which generally only refers to risks affecting all companies operating within a particular country.

a. Single-index model
b. Capital asset
c. Solvency
d. Country risk

39. A _____ is a fungible, negotiable instrument representing financial value. They are broadly categorized into debt securities (such as banknotes, bonds and debentures), and equity securities; e.g., common stocks. The company or other entity issuing the _____ is called the issuer.

a. Securities lending
b. Book entry
c. Tracking stock
d. Security

40. _____ is the method by which one calculates the creditworthiness of a business or organization. The audited financial statements of a large company might be analyzed when it issues or has issued bonds. Or, a bank may analyze the financial statements of a small business before making or renewing a commercial loan.

a. Capital note
b. Credit analysis
c. Credit report monitoring
d. Credit crunch

41. In finance, a _____ is a debt security, in which the authorized issuer owes the holders a debt and, depending on the terms of the _____, is obliged to pay interest (the coupon) and/or to repay the principal at a later date, termed maturity.

Thus a _____ is a loan: the issuer is the borrower, the _____ holder is the lender, and the coupon is the interest. _____s provide the borrower with external funds to finance long-term investments, or, in the case of government _____s, to finance current expenditure.

a. Catastrophe bonds
b. Puttable bond
c. Convertible bond
d. Bond

42. In economics, business, and accounting, a _____ is the value of money that has been used up to produce something, and hence is not available for use anymore. In business, the _____ may be one of acquisition, in which case the amount of money expended to acquire it is counted as _____. In this case, money is the input that is gone in order to acquire the thing.

a. Marginal cost
b. Sliding scale fees
c. Fixed costs
d. Cost

Chapter 20. International Banking and the Future of Banking and Financial Services 173

43. _____ are a type of structured asset-backed security (ABS) whose value and payments are derived from a portfolio of fixed-income underlying assets. _____s are assigned different risk classes, or tranches, whereby 'senior' tranches are considered the safest securities. Interest and principal payments are made in order of seniority, so that junior tranches offer higher coupon payments (and interest rates) or lower prices to compensate for additional default risk.
- a. Senior debt
- b. Collateralized debt obligations
- c. Municipal bond
- d. Zero coupon bond

44. _____ is the removal or simplification of government rules and regulations that constrain the operation of market forces. _____ does not mean elimination of laws against fraud, but eliminating or reducing government control of how business is done, thereby moving toward a more free market.

The stated rationale for '_____' is often that fewer and simpler regulations will lead to a raised level of competitiveness, therefore higher productivity, more efficiency and lower prices overall.

- a. Value added
- b. Demand shock
- c. Deregulation
- d. Supply shock

45. _____ is a type of trade policy that allows traders to act and transact without interference from government. Thus, the policy permits trading partners mutual gains from trade, with goods and services produced according to the theory of comparative advantage.

Under a _____ policy, prices are a reflection of true supply and demand, and are the sole determinant of resource allocation.

- a. Seasoned equity offering
- b. Free Trade
- c. Yield spread
- d. Monte Carlo methods

46. _____ refers to a system of banking or banking activity that is consistent with the principles of Islamic law (Sharia) and its practical application through the development of Islamic economics. Sharia prohibits the payment of fees for the renting of money (Riba, usury) for specific terms, as well as investing in businesses that provide goods or services considered contrary to its principles (Haraam, forbidden.) While these principles were used as the basis for a flourishing economy in earlier times, it is only in the late 20th century that a number of Islamic banks were formed to apply these principles to private or semi-private commercial institutions within the Muslim community.
- a. A Random Walk Down Wall Street
- b. AAB
- c. ABN Amro
- d. Islamic banking

47. The _____ is a trilateral trade bloc in North America created by the governments of the United States, Canada, and Mexico. The agreement creating the trade bloc came into force on January 1, 1994. It superseded the Canada-United States Free Trade Agreement between the U.S. and Canada.
- a. 7-Eleven
- b. 529 plan
- c. 4-4-5 Calendar
- d. North American Free Trade Agreement

48. A _____ is a company that owns other companies' outstanding stock. It usually refers to a company which does not produce goods or services itself, rather its only purpose is owning shares of other companies. They allow the reduction of risk for the owners and can allow the ownership and control of a number of different companies.

Chapter 20. International Banking and the Future of Banking and Financial Services

a. Federal National Mortgage Association
b. Privately held company
c. MRU Holdings
d. Holding company

49. The _____ is an important selective, mainly private, international organization designed by its founders to supervise and liberalize international trade. The organization officially commenced on 1 January 1995, under the Marrakesh Agreement, succeeding the 1947 General Agreement on Tariffs and Trade (GATT.)

The _____ deals with regulation of trade between participating countries; it provides a framework for negotiating and formalising trade agreements, and a dispute resolution process aimed at enforcing participants' adherence to _____ agreements which are signed by representatives of member governments and ratified by their parliaments.

a. Financial Crimes Enforcement Network
b. Gamelan Council
c. Public Company Accounting Oversight Board
d. World Trade Organization

50. _____ or amalgamation is the act of merging many things into one. In business, it often refers to the mergers or acquisitions of many smaller companies into much larger ones. The financial accounting term of _____ refers to the aggregated financial statements of a group company as consolidated account.

a. Consolidation
b. Write-off
c. Cost of goods sold
d. Retained earnings

51. _____ consists of the sale of goods or merchandise from a fixed location, such as a department store, boutique or kiosk in small or individual lots for direct consumption by the purchaser. _____ may include subordinated services, such as delivery. Purchasers may be individuals or businesses.

a. 529 plan
b. 4-4-5 Calendar
c. 7-Eleven
d. Retailing

ANSWER KEY

Chapter 1
1. d	2. d	3. d	4. d	5. d	6. c	7. d	8. c	9. a	10. d
11. b	12. b	13. b	14. d	15. a	16. c	17. d	18. c	19. d	20. b
21. d	22. d	23. c	24. d	25. b	26. a	27. c	28. b	29. d	30. d
31. a	32. d	33. b	34. d	35. c	36. a	37. d	38. d	39. d	40. a

Chapter 2
1. c	2. a	3. b	4. d	5. d	6. a	7. a	8. d	9. d	10. c
11. d	12. d	13. a	14. b	15. c	16. d	17. d	18. d	19. d	20. d
21. d	22. d	23. d	24. d	25. d	26. d	27. d	28. d	29. d	30. d
31. d	32. d	33. d	34. c	35. c	36. a	37. c	38. d	39. d	40. c
41. a	42. a	43. d	44. c	45. d	46. d	47. d	48. d	49. d	50. d
51. d	52. c	53. c	54. a	55. c	56. a				

Chapter 3
1. a	2. d	3. d	4. d	5. b	6. d	7. c	8. d	9. c	10. d
11. a	12. a	13. d	14. d	15. c	16. d	17. d	18. c	19. d	20. d
21. a	22. d	23. b	24. a	25. d	26. d	27. d	28. d	29. c	30. d
31. d									

Chapter 4
1. c	2. b	3. a	4. d	5. d	6. d	7. d	8. d	9. d	10. b
11. c	12. d	13. c	14. a						

Chapter 5
1. d	2. b	3. d	4. c	5. c	6. a	7. d	8. d	9. d	10. a
11. c	12. d	13. c	14. d	15. b	16. b	17. d	18. d	19. a	20. d
21. d	22. a	23. d	24. d	25. c	26. d	27. a	28. d	29. d	30. d
31. d	32. a	33. d	34. d	35. c	36. a	37. a	38. d	39. d	40. d
41. b	42. d	43. d	44. d	45. b	46. d	47. b	48. d	49. b	50. d
51. b	52. b	53. d	54. a	55. c	56. d	57. d	58. a	59. c	60. d
61. c	62. b	63. d	64. c	65. c	66. d	67. a	68. d		

Chapter 6
1. d	2. d	3. d	4. d	5. a	6. b	7. c	8. d	9. d	10. d
11. d	12. a	13. b	14. b	15. d	16. b	17. d	18. c	19. a	20. d
21. d	22. d	23. d	24. d	25. d	26. d	27. d	28. a	29. c	30. a
31. d	32. d	33. d	34. d	35. a	36. d	37. d	38. d	39. b	40. d
41. c	42. c	43. a	44. d	45. d	46. d	47. c	48. c	49. b	

Chapter 7
1. d	2. b	3. a	4. d	5. d	6. c	7. a	8. d	9. a	10. c
11. d	12. a	13. b	14. d	15. c	16. d	17. d	18. d	19. d	20. a
21. a	22. d	23. a	24. d	25. d	26. d	27. b	28. b	29. a	30. c
31. d	32. d	33. d	34. d	35. d	36. c	37. b	38. d	39. d	

Chapter 8

1. a	2. d	3. b	4. c	5. b	6. d	7. a	8. d	9. d	10. a
11. b	12. d	13. d	14. a	15. d	16. d	17. b	18. d	19. d	20. c
21. b	22. c	23. d	24. c	25. c	26. c	27. c	28. a	29. d	30. a
31. c	32. d	33. b	34. a	35. d	36. b	37. d	38. d	39. c	40. a
41. d	42. d	43. a	44. d	45. d	46. d	47. c	48. d	49. a	50. d
51. d									

Chapter 9

1. b	2. c	3. b	4. c	5. d	6. b	7. d	8. d	9. b	10. d
11. c	12. c	13. a	14. a	15. d	16. a	17. c	18. a	19. b	20. d
21. b	22. d	23. a	24. b	25. d	26. d	27. d	28. c	29. a	30. c
31. a	32. d	33. b	34. b	35. b	36. a	37. c	38. d	39. d	40. a
41. d	42. d	43. c	44. d						

Chapter 10

1. d	2. c	3. a	4. d	5. d	6. a	7. d	8. c	9. a	10. d
11. d	12. d	13. b	14. c	15. a	16. a	17. d	18. b	19. c	20. d
21. d	22. d	23. d	24. d	25. b	26. a	27. d	28. d	29. c	30. c
31. d	32. d	33. a	34. c	35. d	36. a	37. d	38. c	39. d	40. a
41. d	42. d	43. d	44. a	45. d	46. b	47. d	48. d	49. d	50. d
51. d	52. d	53. d	54. d	55. a	56. c	57. d	58. d	59. a	60. d
61. d	62. b	63. d	64. d	65. a	66. d	67. d	68. a	69. d	70. d

Chapter 11

1. d	2. d	3. c	4. d	5. a	6. b	7. d	8. d	9. d	10. d
11. c	12. d	13. c	14. d	15. b	16. d	17. c	18. c	19. d	20. c
21. b	22. c	23. b	24. a	25. d	26. d	27. b	28. a	29. d	30. b
31. d	32. c	33. a	34. c	35. d	36. c				

Chapter 12

1. a	2. a	3. d	4. d	5. a	6. d	7. d	8. b	9. d	10. d
11. d	12. d	13. d	14. d	15. c	16. a	17. d	18. b	19. b	20. a
21. c	22. d	23. d	24. c	25. b	26. a	27. d	28. d		

Chapter 13

1. b	2. d	3. d	4. d	5. d	6. a	7. d	8. d	9. a	10. d
11. d	12. c	13. d	14. d	15. a	16. d	17. a	18. b	19. b	20. d
21. b	22. a	23. a	24. d	25. c	26. c	27. d	28. b	29. b	30. d
31. d	32. b	33. b	34. c	35. c	36. b	37. d	38. c	39. d	40. b
41. d									

ANSWER KEY

Chapter 14

1. b	2. c	3. b	4. d	5. d	6. d	7. c	8. d	9. d	10. a
11. a	12. d	13. d	14. b	15. d	16. c	17. d	18. d	19. c	20. d
21. c	22. d	23. d	24. b	25. b	26. d	27. a	28. d	29. b	30. d
31. d	32. d	33. b	34. d						

Chapter 15

1. b	2. b	3. c	4. d	5. d	6. d	7. d	8. d	9. d	10. a
11. c	12. d	13. b	14. c	15. b	16. d	17. d	18. c	19. d	20. c
21. a	22. b	23. b	24. d	25. d	26. d	27. a	28. c	29. c	30. d
31. d	32. d	33. c	34. a	35. a	36. d	37. b	38. b	39. a	40. d
41. b	42. a	43. c	44. d	45. c	46. b				

Chapter 16

1. d	2. a	3. d	4. a	5. c	6. d	7. d	8. c	9. d	10. d
11. d	12. a	13. d	14. c	15. d	16. d	17. c	18. d	19. b	20. d
21. d	22. c	23. d	24. c	25. a	26. d	27. b	28. d	29. a	

Chapter 17

1. d	2. d	3. d	4. a	5. d	6. d	7. d	8. d	9. c	10. b
11. d	12. c	13. a	14. c	15. d	16. d	17. d	18. a	19. d	20. a
21. c	22. b	23. d	24. a	25. c	26. d	27. c	28. d	29. d	30. d
31. a	32. d	33. d	34. d	35. b	36. d	37. b	38. b	39. d	40. b
41. a	42. d	43. b	44. d	45. b	46. c	47. d	48. d	49. b	50. a
51. c	52. d	53. c	54. d	55. c	56. b	57. d	58. b	59. d	60. d
61. d	62. a	63. b	64. a	65. b					

Chapter 18

1. b	2. c	3. d	4. b	5. d	6. d	7. b	8. c	9. d	10. d
11. d	12. d	13. b	14. b	15. b	16. d	17. d	18. d	19. c	20. c
21. a	22. a	23. c	24. d	25. c	26. b	27. d	28. c	29. b	30. b
31. a	32. c	33. d	34. d						

Chapter 19

1. b	2. d	3. d	4. d	5. a	6. d	7. b	8. b	9. d	10. c
11. d	12. d	13. b	14. b	15. d	16. c	17. d	18. c	19. c	20. d
21. c	22. d	23. d	24. c	25. d	26. a				

Chapter 20

1. a	2. c	3. b	4. c	5. d	6. d	7. a	8. c	9. d	10. c
11. a	12. b	13. d	14. d	15. c	16. b	17. d	18. b	19. b	20. c
21. a	22. d	23. c	24. c	25. c	26. d	27. c	28. a	29. a	30. b
31. d	32. d	33. b	34. d	35. a	36. a	37. d	38. d	39. d	40. b
41. d	42. d	43. b	44. c	45. b	46. d	47. d	48. d	49. d	50. a
51. d